The Victorian Experience: The Novelists

THE VICTORIAN EXPERIENCE:
The Novelists

Edited by
RICHARD A. LEVINE

OHIO UNIVERSITY PRESS

Contents

The Victorian Experience:
The Novelists

HYPOTHESIS AND PRACTICE:
INTRODUCTORY REMARKS

RICHARD A. LEVINE

I had planned originally to do a book in which I would test a critical hypothesis by examining several nineteenth-century novelists. However, a number of my fellow Victorians around the country suggested that if the theory has validity it should rightly be tested by a number of readers rather than by only one. The suggestion was a good one, contributors were excited at the possibilities of writing such essays, and the Ohio University Press—rapidly becoming a base for Victorian studies—agreed to publish the results.

The theory itself grows out of both a Victorian critic's concerns with the artistic engagement and the sometimes confused, often precarious state of literary studies in our own time. It was Walter Pater who said "Not the fruit of experience, but experience itself, is the end." Pater is talking of the distinction between one's direct engagement with the artistic work (experience) and the intellectual process by which one attempts to recapture and make some rational sense of that engagement (the fruit of experience). If one might quarrel with Pater's sense of the "end," one cannot argue with Pater's chronology here: the experience clearly must precede the fruit of the experience. That some readers, for example, try to interpose the intellectualizing process between themselves and the literary work must be seen as a violation not merely of Pater's notion, but—more importantly—of the vital integrity of the work

3

itself. Upon reflection, most of us would acknowledge that our initial responses to works which moved us or touched us or excited us (and not only in positive or favorable ways) were not, properly speaking, rational. Certainly a portion of that initial response might well be intellectual, but the totality of our response comes much closer to Pater's sense of the fundamentally dynamic and individual quality of perception:

> the whole scope of observation is dwarfed into the narrow chamber of the individual mind. Experience, already reduced to a group of impressions, is ringed round for each one of us by that thick wall of personality through which no real voice has ever pierced on its way to us, or from us to that which we can only conjecture to be without. Every one of those impressions is the impression of the individual in his isolation, each mind keeping as a solitary prisoner its own dream of a world. Analysis goes a step farther still, and assures us that those impressions of the individual mind to which, for each one of us, experience dwindles down, are in perpetual flight; that each of them is limited by time, and that as time is infinitely divisible, each of them is infinitely divisible also; all that is actual in it being a single moment, gone while we try to apprehend it, of which it may ever be more truly said that it has ceased to be than that it is.

And when Pater says that "he who experiences these impressions strongly, and drives directly at the discrimination and analysis of them," he is still articulating the same ordering of critical activity: experience followed by the fruit of experience; experience followed by discrimination and analysis of the experience.

For some teachers of literature, especially in our age of the rhetorician, Pater's priorities can be unnerving, although they should not be. Indeed, Pater might well be offering a necessary corrective to much that has gone wrong in the academy. Too often the intensity of textual analysis—especially when elevated almost to an end in itself—has blunted the reader's sense of experiencing the artistic work rather than complementing and augmenting it. Certainly if we've learned something in the last quarter-century of academic criticism, it is precisely that explication of the text enriches the reader's experience of the work. It is the quality of the engagement of the reader and the literary work which is at the heart of all criticism and scholarship. It is this wedding of experience and the fruit of experience which gives new meaning to Carlyle's statement in *The Hero as Poet*: "We are all poets when we *read* a poem well."

4

The premise of this book is that we can go a step beyond Pater's concept of experience and the fruit of experience by adding as a third possibility a new kind of experience which grows out of the first two. *The Victorian Experience* starts, then, as an experiment in criticism. Unlike most collections of essays on a common topic, this book offers the testing of a theory. Since I asked contributors to give free rein to their imaginations, let me discuss my initial notions about the book. At first I suggested that the book would address the following problem: in an age of increasingly specialized studies, we run the danger of sometimes losing sight of the whole writer and of our chosen mission of teaching. Fundamentally, the book would respond to the question, "Why the Victorians?" as each writer is addressed in terms of contemporary relevance (defined as broadly as possible) as well as in terms of the peculiar relevance of the Victorians. Each critic would discuss a writer from the vantage point of that critic's familiarity with the author's works and age, and in the process respond to a number of very basic questions such as why the critic teaches the writer, his or her involvement with the writer and response to the writer after these years of study. I foresaw the essays as something more than personal testaments and qualitatively very different from critical introductions to major authors. I gave the critics only the most broad and general guidelines and let them carry their essays as their imaginations and interests dictated. I saw the book offering to student and general reader alike a fresh, accessible, and new vantage point.

As I've already implied, the response was enthusiastic, but some expressed caution over the word "relevant." One respondent said, "What may be relevant today may not be relevant five or ten years from now, or even, alas, when the book appears. Similarly what you describe as the 'peculiar relevance' of the Victorians may change very rapidly." This was a germane consideration; the word of caution was well taken. If there is an overused word in the current academic lexicon it is *relevant*. However, I do not use the word in any peculiarly contemporary and modish way nor do I speak of the relevance of the Victorians in terms of the ephemeral fashions of, say, students at this moment in time. On the contrary, when I use the word in both contexts I am talking of something that tran-

5

scends the immediate while at the same time embracing it. The title of the book itself can help make clear what I mean by relevance and what the book will engage. In many ways the word "experience" is crucial as it *means* at several levels. In addition to the experience of Victorian literature itself, we have the critic's experience of having experienced it. I am not playing linguistic games, but rather suggesting one of the unique features of this book's hypothesis: the critic's attempt to isolate and develop his or her experience with a writer. And out of the rendering of that experience must come the relevance of the writer not only in terms of the larger relevance of the nineteenth century to the twentieth but in terms of a number of other "relevances" from esthetic to political and social. Put in another way, we assume that the critic has spent a great deal of time in learning and study, in close analysis, in scholarship and criticism. Now, for a crucially important moment, the "learning" stops and the critic in an imaginative sweep embraces the subject and tries to seize the distillation of all those factors now having been forced to run together.

If we can imagine the contemporary, twentieth-century critic as an experience and the nineteenth century in England as an experience and the particular artist as an experience, then we can sense the possibility of an exciting meeting as these different experiences come together. Not a new kind of criticism, but perhaps one of the logical ends of criticism and scholarship: the results of at least these three sorts of experiences which have been percolating in the same mind and body. This is not intuitive or impressionistic criticism, because the critic's response is predicated on a considerable amount of learning and thought. Even though I think that Pater is right when he talks of the fruit of experience being secondary to the experience itself, I see the essays in this book combining the experience *and* the fruit of experience and in the process producing a different kind of experience. That the particular age in question is the Victorian is simply a bonus for our purposes. Victorian England is that historical period which first faced so many of the problems and changes which in more refined and often more complex terms confront twentieth-century man. For almost any contemporary problem area, we can see its embryonic or infant state in the Victorian age. Further, since we know that the modern era in the life of western man began at the turning of the eighteenth into the nineteenth century, we know that any study of nineteenth-century England must by definition be relevant in terms, once again, which transcend any chronologically local or provincial definition.

William Axton invokes personal, cultural, and literary histories in coming to terms with his experience of Charles Dickens. At the center of Axton's discussion is the question which he believes to be the one "least likely ever to receive a thoroughly satisfactory answer": how can we account for the hold Dickens has on our minds and feelings? In a nicely turned personal account, Axton talks of the failure of his engagement with Dickens in secondary school which was transcended happily by the successful integration of Dickens into his life through the vehicles of mass communication and entertainment. Indeed, Axton suggests that it was through those mass media that Dickens became a "fundamental part of our cultural heritage." I am sure that the reader will find enormously interesting the discussions of popular culture and Dickens' popularity as Axton develops the subject. He indicates further the appropriateness of Dickens' role in twentieth-century technological advances in the areas of popular entertainment, ". . . for it was he who first put into practice Thomas Carlyle's brilliant speculative insight that, in a secularized and egalitarian bourgeois mass-culture based on urbanization and industrialism, the priestly function of maintaining a unifying center of shared traditional values must fall to the man of letters. He alone was capable of speaking authoritatively to a mass audience through the first technological developments of modern mass communications, the machine-driven press, cheap pulp paper, and rapid general distribution of printed matter."

But Axton is clearly aware of the fact that popular culture was but one route toward establishing Dickens' hold on him as a boy and since. And Axton is very good as he tries to sort out the various other factors which went into the shaping of his experience with Dickens, an experience which in so many

7

ways touches upon some of the dominant facets of the twentieth-century western sensibility. Shifts in cultural sensibility,
public mass higher education, the esthetic respectability of the
novel, the sense of man's absurd relationship with his universe,
our seeking after our own identity—all of these and more went
into the "fundamental alteration in sensibility" which "was
required to free Dickens' work." Nor does Axton overlook the
major critical reassessments of Dickens, the new-found influence of Dickens on other major writers, the growth of ex-
pressionism, or the contemporary sense of a discontinuous
universe, all of which in their varying ways underscored the
greatness and the importance of Dickens. To conclude his essay Axton offers a decidedly post-Dickensian, contemporary
defense of Dickens' method. His last sentence captures the
ultimate argument of the entire piece: "Such an alienated, insecure vision of life can hardly be a matter of congratulation,
for either ourselves or Dickens; but it enables us to hear his
voice as one of our own."

"With a mind that lingers over the past, and memories of
roses now withered, his hands caress the vase that once held
them, and that is all he has left to grasp of their fragrance."
Thus Juliet McMaster argues that Thackeray's use of the past
is crucial to one's experience of that author. As she suggests
that "the Thackerayan experience . . . is to be found in his
text," so McMaster develops a strikingly evocative essay
through which the texts resonate and Thackeray's "feeling for
the past combines with his vivid apprehension of immediate
detail to create a world in which time and space intersect, in
which the kind of reality you can lay your hand on in a given
moment is rich with philosophical and temporal implications."

McMaster focuses upon Thackeray the social historian who
constantly probes the past in order to illuminate the present
and whose characters are not only shaped by the past but often
seek to recapture that past. Invoking six major novels, Mc-
Master demonstrates Thackeray's use of emblems as signs of
the past. In the process of illustrating her thesis by reference
to documents, paintings, buttons, diamonds, ribbons, rouge,
wigs, shawls, swords, and catalogues, McMaster is able to con-
jure up the Thackerayan experience. The emblem becomes a

touchstone by which a character, an episode, or an entire novel is re-experienced.

In her concluding remarks McMaster underscores the interplay between past and present which she perceives in Thackeray's novels by elevating her author's technique to a level which transcends any study of a particular writer. "Thackeray, more than the other writers of the period, addresses himself to the very question of the relation of the present to the past. If he knew that experience is burning with a hard and gemlike flame, he also knew that the flame lives off something, and that to deny the past is as absurd as for the flame to reject the candle. Thackeray reminds us that, both personally and culturally, we are what we have been; that the past, though past, is always latent in the present. Thackeray's present has now become our past, and it 'keeps a lingering hold' on us."

Ruth apRoberts looks at Trollope's *He Knew He Was Right* within its social context and concludes that "reading a novel like this of Trollope's is a social act." Precisely because apRoberts knows Trollope and the nineteenth-century social matrix she is able to convince us of the validity of her experience with this novel—and by extension with Trollope and with his age. At one and the same time she is able to balance the eternality of the literary act and the contemporaneity of peculiarly modern questionings of woman's role and of marriage. It is because of her concern with and awareness of the nineteenth century and the twentieth century as historical entities, of social movements of both periods, of the stuff of the British novel in its history and development, and of Trollope's career and canon that apRoberts is in a position to read this single novel as symptomatic of considerably more than itself within each of the areas mentioned before.

Noting that even with considerable change having taken place in the relations between the sexes, apRoberts still argues that "our old literatures of love are not invalidated." From the *Tale of Genji* through Dante, Chaucer, and Shakespeare, and up through the nineteenth century there are familiar processes going on before us. "To discover these familiar processes in their great rich variety of guises is a good part of humane learning. Always these processes are taking place in a cul-

9

tural context, never isolated; and to observe their interplay with the cultural contexts is finally to be more aware of their interplay with our own culture." That seems to be the critical hallmark of apRoberts' approach. Thus she can say of Trollope: "And his treatment of sexual relationships may still be valid to us even if the mores of that hundred years ago are very remote." Even more importantly in terms of the humane learning apRoberts encourages: "We are finding these days, anyhow, that even though the mores have changed, it is enlightening to go back to that time when the necessity for change was being recognized." So it is that one rich vein of Trollope's subject matter remains focused on issues that remain alive within our contemporary field of concerns: in particular, the marriage question.

Ruth apRoberts offers a multi-dimensional frame of reference for her exploration of the marriage question in Trollope. Moving from the large questions of both cultural and literary history to the more discrete area of nineteenth-century urgency regarding the "women's question," she focuses close attention on the novel itself in order to validate her various hypotheses. Here we have a stunning explication in support of the large experience of literary engagement: "Finally we see in this realistic novel of Trollope's a testing of principle and culture by cases, and a great rich variety of ways to find oneself in a social context."

Frederick Karl very neatly places the esthetic, psychological, and ideational world views of the Brontës within larger and contemporary world views. In the process he is able to maintain the often fragile wholeness of the Brontës' nineteenth-century situs (to borrow a term from Rosalie Colie) while at the same time exploring the contemporaneity of their works. One of the central features of Karl's experience with his writers is that in their lives and works "both Victorianism and Modernism collide."

From the opening words of Karl's discussion the reader is made aware of the contemporary frame of reference through which the Brontës are to be viewed. It is not one of the Brontë sisters with whom the essay begins, but rather Doris Lessing. And it is not a conventional nineteenth-century theme which

Karl chooses to write about at the start of his piece, but rather the "literature of enclosure" which he suggests is usually associated with writers as modern as Proust, Kafka, and Beckett. As Karl works out from this theme, he delineates certain fictive concerns of the Brontës which are, strikingly, features of our contemporary sensibility. From "women's rights" to a peculiarly modern sense of man's tragic dilemma to the quest for identity to the *experience* of growth to the cult of self and the "terrible disorder of isolation," Karl explores the experience of viewing the Brontës from a mid-twentieth-century perspective. And the perspective is found to be a congenial one.

Jane Eyre is given special attention because in that work, Karl argues, the reader can engage the basic premises of the seven Brontë novels. He concludes that portion of his essay by saying that "All the great Victorian novelists live for us in varying ways, but the Brontës survive and impinge upon us for their insistence on the intensity of their inner lives and their almost mythical reconstruction of a self. To strike out, however fearfully, was for them virtually an existential act."

Certainly even before the advent of academic feminist criticism, most readers perceived in some nineteenth-century literature a tension between inherited cultural norms and an emerging desire for selfhood for women. Karl focuses on this tension in the Brontës and suggests that "their foreshadowing of several aspects of the current struggle for women's rights was merely one side of their awareness of the individual's rights, or the individual's struggle for identity." And Karl may well be right in labeling as extraordinary a passage from *Shirley* in which that novel's central character announces that "Milton tried to see the first woman, but . . . he saw her not."

Thus Frederick Karl's experience of the Brontës is informed by his contemporary sensibility. Yet in the sometimes singular case of these extraordinary sisters that informing principle is easy and comfortable rather than in any way forced.

Jerome Beaty opens his discussion of George Eliot by reminding us of Lydgate's sudden, youthful realization of his intellectual passion for medical science. Just as the "moment of vocation" had come for Lydgate as he viewed the valves of

11

the heart, so George Eliot's great novel acted upon Beaty: "*Middlemarch* itself performed the function of the dusty old encyclopedia when, twenty-five years ago, I read it for the first time. It immediately and directly planted the seeds of an intellectual passion; it more gradually and indirectly led to a vocation."

The first part of Beaty's essay describes the readying process by which an unconscious predilection for *Middlemarch* is established long before Beaty has read it. His own interest in writing fiction, his assessments of the contemporary novel, and his response to the New Criticism are all factors in the creation of a sensibility waiting to be seized by *Middlemarch*. After Beaty read *Middlemarch* in 1949, he found himself "in the grips of a new literary passion." And further following the Lydgate analogy, Beaty is fascinated by the *valvae* of *Middlemarch*, by "the finely adjusted mechanism of the creative process." Beaty's experience of Eliot had begun and it was extended in the manuscript room of the British Museum. That experience rapidly became his "first Victorian intellectual passion. For the next four years I read through the manuscripts, notebooks, corrected proof, printed books, unpublished and published letters, all sorts of -ana, returning periodically to the text and variants of *Middlemarch*. I was so steeped in George Eliot's life and writings I would sometimes almost infer her thoughts." His experience of Eliot was so intense that Beaty came to offer hunches and make conjectures about the author and her work, speculations which could be articulated only because of his deep involvement with his subject.

The last section of Beaty's essay focuses on the "social or historical texture" of *Middlemarch*. Given Beaty's earlier comments on fiction and criticism, we can here appreciate his enthusiasm for George Eliot's extraordinarily subtle presentation of the historical dimensions of her novel. Beaty is interested in both the craft of that presentation and the relationship between socio-political questions and the individual life which, from Beaty's perspective, is a central concern in George Eliot's fiction. In his development of this major question, Beaty underscores one of the vital thematic centers of his experience of George Eliot. From a Victorian frame of reference—"Social conditions not only have something to do with one's actions but history creates responsibilities, offering perhaps the only definition available in the nineteenth century of 'duty' and 'morality' "—Beaty pursues the question of the "relevance of the larger world" to one's "personal lot" both in fiction and in our own historically real world.

Beaty concludes his discussion by creating an historical dimension within the texture of his own experience of George Eliot. The premise for his development is the following: "*Middlemarch* . . . seems to suggest an efficacy of individual social action, no matter how limited, that goes beyond the implications of the earlier novels." And in the development of that proposition the reader notices that Beaty's intellectual passion remains strong as he eloquently argues on behalf of the efficacy of individual action. "And later-born Dorotheas may be still more effective. We unheroic, insignificant people through words and deeds prepare the social conditions for the heroic, and our effect too can be incalculably diffusive if unhistoric, preparing a medium, a culture for the growth of heroes." Here is an example of a sensitive critic's experience of an author blending with and enriching his experience of our daily lives. A rather wonderful power for a novelist now almost one hundred years dead to exercise.

In one of his last efforts before his death, Lionel Stevenson sums up his long experience with George Meredith in terms of Meredith's technique. It is an effort which we can understand. Throughout his distinguished career in Victorian studies and the history of the English novel, Stevenson insisted on the greatness of Meredith and, particularly, on the inventiveness of his novelistic talents. Certainly Stevenson would invoke Leavis' criterion and place Meredith in the great tradition, because, for Stevenson, Meredith did indeed change the possibilities of fiction for both reader and writer. At the conclusion of the present essay, Stevenson caps his years of reading Meredith by stating the following: "I would be the first to acknowledge the defects in Meredith's novels—extravagance, ostentation, digressiveness, lack of proportion. But, though he often exasperates me, I find him to be, on the whole, the most vital, original, and consistently interesting English novelist of the past hundred years. He was the first to see clearly that a novel can be a work of literary art, meriting all the care for style and all the depth of suggestion that have always been expected of poetry."

Stevenson's experience of Meredith is finally with the technique of his writer and that experience is at least partly defined by Stevenson's desire to justify Meredith in critically sophisticated and modern terms. So it is that Stevenson sets up as a backdrop "what other novelists were doing at the time" against which he is able to discuss the extent of Meredith's innovations. The nineteenth-century reader's normal expectations fell before Meredith's method which is defined in this discussion as the art of implication. In addition to an elucidation of that method, Stevenson focuses upon his reading of Meredith's major thematic concerns and Meredith's own sense of his novelistic motives. For Stevenson, Meredith was "preoccupied with the minute gradations of pretence and self-deception that emerge from the tension between natural impulses and the rigid code of morality and conduct that has developed in a formally structured social system. With this objective, it was essential that he should probe into the inmost depths of mental states; and his purpose could not be achieved through Henry James' technique of limitation to a single recording consciousness. Meredith wanted to demonstrate the relativity of truth by moving from one mind to another, revealing in each a baffling mixture of veracity and falsehood, intelligence and stupidity, perception and prejudice. It was a disquieting experience for a reader to realize that he could not complacently identify himself with the values and judgments of one, particular character."

Stevenson sums up the novelist's own sense of his method by suggesting that "Meredith wanted to convey the relativity of truth, the extent to which every impression is fragmentary and biased." Here, then, in a record of experiencing a writer qualitatively unlike any other in this book, Lionel Stevenson engages Meredith in highly intellectual terms which, by the very art of implication he discusses, can be seen by the reader to be warmly subjective and, indeed, quite personal. One might well choose to call it the personal experience of intellectual preference.

Bernard Paris discusses his experiences with Thomas Hardy in both personal and critical terms. He begins by writing of his early enthusiasm for Hardy's fiction and he places that enthusiasm within the perspective of his own agnostic and iconoclastic years: "I was first attracted to Hardy by his philosophy, which seemed, much of it, to be true. His beliefs and attitudes re-enforced my own; and this is what I was looking for in an author." In his twenties, Paris responded also to what he perceived to be Hardy's "arraignments of God" and "his protests on behalf of man." Further, Paris warmed to the compassion which he saw in Hardy for man, "an innocent, passionate, sensitive creature who is doomed to pain and frustration." Paris summarizes his initial and strong response to Hardy in the following way. "In my own unhappiness, I found Hardy's disenchanted vision consolatory. It assured me that I was discovering the truth about life and that my problems were man's fate rather than something peculiar to myself. They were less humiliating that way. It re-enforced my self-pity, justified my anger, and confirmed my innocence." But this, as we are told, was Paris' initial response.

Later Paris became disenchanted with Hardy. "His philosophy seemed full of contradictions, and his novels seemed crude and incoherent." This new perception was prompted by a rigorous critical examination fostered by the graduate school experience, which turned Paris to a position which argued that the novel should be read much as a poem. In these terms Hardy's fiction failed. It is from this point in his paper that Paris illustrates his developing perceptions of Hardy through a discussion of his views of *Tess of the D'Urbervilles* as they have undergone changes from his undergraduate days forward.

Through his changing perception of the novelistic form and his involvement with psychological analysis of fiction, Paris develops an analysis of Tess which offers some remarkable insights into that character and her relationships with others in the novel. The germ of Paris' new experience of Hardy can be seen in this following statement. "I discovered that certain characters are representatives of people as a result of my ability to analyze them in motivational terms with the help of Horneyan psychology." It is from this psychological vantage

15

point that Paris presents his involvement with Hardy most sharply. Believing that criticism and esthetic responses generally are reflections of the critics—are, in a sense, autobiographical—Paris can conclude the following: "I am not suggesting that we simply ignore or analyze away Hardy's own perspective. We should regard it, rather, as a source of insight into his phenomenology. However confused or defensive his responses may be, Hardy is a sensitive and gifted man who is struggling, like the rest of us, to make sense of reality. It is a rich and powerful experience to enter into his perspective, to see life through the medium of his temperament."

So it is that Bernard Paris can isolate the flaws and blemishes in Hardy's fictive world and can, at the same time, transcend his former critical stance and enter upon a rich literary experience. He captures something exciting in Hardy through a psychological investigation. Reflecting on his method, Paris notes that critics "allow us to see literature through the medium of their highly developed sensibilities and from their particular perspective." And he concludes that "none of them offers more than a partial truth, and none is free from distortion."

Jacob Korg approaches his subject by invoking a larger frame of reference than do most of the book's other contributors. Korg discusses several of George Gissing's major thematic concerns through wide-ranging references to Gissing's life and works. Aware that Gissing is focusing attention on that peculiarly modern literary protagonist—the alienated man— Korg says that wherever Gissing "turned he saw only frustration, ignorance and injustice, and his novels are dominated by such themes as urban poverty, the passion for money, the growing vulgarity of taste, the repressiveness of middle-class life and the deficiencies of the basic institutions of society, such as politics, the economic system, education, religion, and marriage." And Korg strikes a singularly contemporary chord when he says of Gissing: "His purpose was not to call for reforms, for he felt that they were futile, but simply to bear witness to truths he thought others refused to recognize."

One of the fascinating aspects of this analysis of the critic's experience of George Gissing must be Korg's isolation of the sometimes paradoxical combination of beliefs and feelings which existed within Gissing's sensibility. Fascinating because it is that same paradoxical combination of beliefs and feelings which our own twentieth-century educated and "liberal elite" find within themselves, although rarely openly articulated. Irving Howe touched the precisely right critical nerve when he suggested that Gissing was "far from the greatest novelist England has produced, but he was surely one of the most honest." And Jacob Korg's experience of Gissing forces us to re-think and, indeed, re-feel the new energies unleashed by the great age of transition which was nineteenth-century England. As we know more clearly today than ever before, energy is a neutral force which can be channeled for results not necessarily in mankind's best interests. So Gissing saw the new cultural and social explosions of his own lifetime. Whether he deals with that recurrent figure of his novels—the poor, unconnected, educated man who floats without anchor between social classes—or with the "new woman" whose consciousness has been raised beyond her cultural possibilities Gissing treats problems of his and our time. Although his vacillating responses to some of the great questions facing his age may be viewed finally as a basic weakness of perception or even as a weakness of will, I suspect that the reader of our time can undoubtedly come closer to an empathic reading of the novels than could the great majority of Gissing's contemporary audience. Korg writes of his subject: "For him, the best imaginable life was one which offered a refuge from the irremediable woes of society." I suggest that line can be translated into a significant number of contemporary formulations.

In many ways Korg's experience of Gissing is the experience of modern history. Just as it has become a critical commonplace to speak of Dickens' darkening vision as we contrast his earlier and later novels, so it has become clear that western man's vision grows darker as our civilization moves forward from the early years of the nineteenth century. Manful effort and earnest optimism simply were not enough to meet the onrushing problems of modernity. There were no easy solutions to problems which came to be seen as ever more complex. Indeed, there seem to be for some problems no solutions at all.

17

We are not surprised, therefore, to hear Korg say: "In Gissing's novels, urban life is a counterpart of Hardy's nature; both are embodiments of powers indifferent or hostile to human values" or that "the anomalous arrangements of modern society are capable of producing anomalous results by placing people in environments where they do not belong" or that "society, though established by man, is controlled by economic energies which have nothing to do with human needs or desires" or that "mass production must result in mass psychology" or "in an age of trade . . . art must be practiced as a trade" or that mass education "promoted freedom at the expense of allowing the tastes and opinions of the mediocre to prevail."

The number of approaches to this book's hypothesis tells us something about the present vitality of literary studies. They remain alive and well in the 1970's. And the Victorians continue to exert a hold on our intellectual, esthetic and emotional sensibilities. In a word, the Victorian experience remains a considerable shaping force in many twentieth-century lives.

DICKENS NOW

WILLIAM F. AXTON

To describe and assay Charles Dickens' impact on the generation of readers who came to maturity by 1938 and thereafter is a task that comes perilously close to summarizing the cultural history of western civilization over the last four or five decades—the period during which the "twentieth century" came to think of itself as a compact and unified cultural epoch. It is also a task that skirts personal chronicle, insofar as the various intellectual and aesthetic currents abroad during that time impinged on oneself and affected one's awareness of the great novelist's work. For to define Dicken's position as a living writer, more than a hundred years after his death, touches upon a host of central phenomena about ourselves, individually and as a culture, in a multitude of contexts historical, aesthetic, philosophical, and deeply personal. But then, that is the kind of artist Dickens was and, through his works, remains for us at this latter day; and this fact constitutes the main force of his being for me, now, and for those who still respond to his voice.

Of the cultural currents abroad during the "interregnum" between the two world wars which have shaped the sensibility that came to coherence after 1945, perhaps the most notable was the dramatic shift in literary taste ushered in by Yeats, Eliot, and Pound at around the time of the first great war of this century, together with the subsequent development of a critical technology adequate to discuss their writings and those of their kindred. This elaborately systematic technique of ex-

19

plication gradually spilled over from the discussion of poetry to fiction, and resulted in a profound reorientation of critical values to which the works and creative procedures of Dickens were very congenial indeed. At the same time, the growing critical reputation and, through the college classroom, the greatly extended readership of a number of foreign novelists—notably Dostoevski, Tolstoy, and Kafka—all of whom had been influenced in one way or another by Dickens, prepared the post-World-War II audience to receive and appreciate the effects achieved by their Victorian master.

A crucial role in this process was played by the concurrent development in England, Western Europe, and America of public systems of mass higher education, in which the liberal arts curriculum has a central place; for this phenomenon put the explication of literature almost on the basis of an academic industry staffed by ever swelling platoons of researchers and eager students. The consequences have been an overwhelming increase in our knowledge of literature and expertise in dealing with it (or at least in the outflow of information about these matters), together with an enormous increase in the numbers of those who received this information. Of equal importance has been a profound shift of the weight of academic interest away from the study of literary and cultural antiquity—the classical, medieval, and renaissance periods—toward that of more modern and contemporarily relevant times, so that inevitably the literature of the nineteenth century, and of its pre-eminent English novelist, has taken on larger and larger significance. By the same token, the aesthetic respectability of the novel as a literary kind has gradually become established, and hence its worthiness of serious study, with the result that we now approach the novel as readers with greater critical sophistication and a greater willingness to entertain broad differences, even eccentricity, in technique and content than earlier in this century, when fiction had just begun to receive unprejudiced attention. From this, too, so markedly individual a creative genius as Dickens could not fail to profit.

Then again, the last half-century has witnessed an unparalleled development in technologically assisted mass-media systems of communication such as radio, television, motion pictures, recordings, and the like, which has not only significantly heightened the place of popular culture in the total cultural life of our epoch, but which also has profoundly altered the nature of popular culture itself. Indeed, it has effected a revolution in the meaning of the term "culture" through the invention of new aesthetic forms and modes and through a radical reorientation of the relationship between creator, the creative process and its materials, the resulting artifact, and the mode of its apprehension. In a multitude of ways, the works of Charles Dickens have from the outset figured very largely in this radical alteration of our sensibilities, in part as an influence and in part as a product.

Finally, developments in the philosophical history of the twentieth century, together with their aesthetic implications, have provided a congenial environment for the growth of a renewed interest in Dickens' novels. The vision of a world rendered absurd by the theological situation of modern man and by the imponderables of such fundamental matters as that of identity in a relativistic universe, it turned out, was surprisingly congruent with that of the anxiety-ridden protagonists of *Great Expectations*, *Our Mutual Friend*, and *Bleak House*, haunted by other selves, *doppelgangers*, and disturbing counterparts. And the darker passages of *Edwin Drood*, *Hard Times*, *Barnaby Rudge*, *A Tale of Two Cities*, and *David Copperfield*, not to mention the disorienting farce-comedy of *Pickwick Papers*, spoke a familiar tongue to a generation for whom Stalin, Hitler, and nuclear fission had given a renewed appreciation of the pertinence of grotesque subversion of nominal reality.

To some extent, the present high tide of interest in Dickens' novels has resulted from sheer historical accident, the publication in 1937-38 of the deeply flawed but immensely influential *Nonesuch Edition* of Dickens' works and letters in twenty-three volumes, designed by Francis Meynell and edited by Arthur Waugh, Walter Dexter, Thomas Hatton, and Hugh Walpole. The work of loving Dickensians, if inept by modern professional standards (the steel plates and wood engravings of the original illustrations were distributed to the 877 subscribers!), the *Nonesuch Dickens* yet had an impact that far outstripped its limited distribution, for it prompted a new critical interest in the great Victorian novelist which was largely unfettered by received opinion. That opinion had taken a variety of forms, all more or less beside the point nowadays. It had been long held that Dickens was an untutored, indeed unconscious, genius, whose works were mere popular entertainments unsuited for serious intellectual attention, enlivened by a rich vein of comic invention perhaps, but marred by flat characterization, melodramatic and implausible plotting, maudlin sentimentality, and, to a generation raised on Percy Lubbock's *The Craft of Fiction* (1921) and Joseph Warren Beach's *The Method of Henry James* (1928), an unpardonable (because un-Jamesian) tendency toward narrative intrusion by the authorial voice. Another school of readers represented by Lytton Strachey and the young Evelyn Waugh found in Dickens' novels an epitome of complacent, hypocritical Victorian sermonizing and a lack of contemporary frankness about many sensitive subjects, notably sexual ones. Finally, a somewhat mixed bag of critics saw in the novelist's work pioneering documents of social protest which anticipated one or another left-wing political movement of the nineteen-twenties and thirties.

Following the appearance of the *Nonesuch Dickens*, however, George Orwell, Edmund Wilson, and Lionel Trilling, among others, began to look at the novels as if they had been created by as conscious a craftsman as a Donne or a Marvell, one whose world view was as worthy of elucidation as that of Wordsworth or Jonson, and whose technical repertory was at least the equal of Conrad, Hardy, or Melville in the management of symbolism and patterns of imagery. Humphry House's pioneering study of the socio-political background of the novels in *The Dickens World* (1941), followed by F. R. Leavis' appendectomal imprimitur of *Hard Times* in *The Great Tradition* (1948); Edgar Johnson's definitive two-volume critical biography in the early fifties; Kathleen Tillotson's *Novels of the Eighteen-Forties* (1954), and, with John Butt, *Dickens at Work* (1957), which examined Dickens' methods of composition as a serial novelist, combined to complete the process of reassessment and comprehension. Perhaps the process has been too successful, for the last decade has witnessed a veritable deluge of commentary on the novelist and his work. In

1970, the centennial year of Dickens' death witnessed the publication of more than fifty volumes concerned with some aspect of the man or his writings. There are now more than six dozen volumes of Dickens' works available in paperback editions, and three journals devoted exclusively to his study regularly appear in English!

This recapitulation of a recent chapter in the history of literary academe merely chronicles, but does not account for, the phenomenon of Dickens' resurrection and critical apotheosis. What brought this astonishing transmogrification about in the years since 1937-38? Surely not the wartime nostalgia that revived Anthony Trollope, only to wrap him in the winding sheet of the *Trollopian* for decent reinterment, nor yet the enthusiastic hero-worship-cum-yeoman-service performed for decades past by the Dickens Fellowship and its house organ, the *Dickensian*, indispensable as they have been in guarding the flame. The post-war awakening of respectful interest in all things Victorian, but particularly in the graphic and decorative arts and architecture, can hardly be the cause, since the study of Dickens has been the bellwether of this movement and considerably antedates the flurry of monographs during the last decade or so on the Pre-Raphaelites and Art Nouveau. The antiquarian curiosity stirred by House and, a few years later, by R. J. Cruikshank and by John Dodd's volume on 1848, a chance encounter with a piece of Bernard Shaw's shrewd criticism, with Louis Cazamian's 1902 study of the social novel, or with a dusty critique by George Gissing or Oliver Elton, may here or there have fanned a spark of interest. But a fundamental alteration in sensibility was required to free Dickens' work from the yoke of Alexander Woolcott, Stephen Leacock, and G. K. Chesterton, who saw him as the apostle of cheerfulness, the comic genius of bourgeois humor and sentimental farce, and the vigorous critic of safely distant social abuses. "Their" Dickens was the exuberant young journalist-on-the-make, the scourge of particular and localized injustice who retained his faith in the fundamental goodness of people and the gradual betterment of things, and the prototype of "gusto" and creative inventiveness. "Ours" was all of these things, but something more, or at least something else; a *farceur* of the macabre; a comic visionary of disorientation; a realist who saw the underlying irreality of the commonplace and conventional world and was in consequence a fabulist as well; a moralist for whom a particular social problem gave only a "local habitation and a name" to some more universal human dilemma; and, finally, the last artist of stature who, through his own magisterial imaginative power, had found the knack of raising ordinary experience to the level of mythopoeic significance and general appeal to a mass audience.

But all these considerations were decades down the road from us adolescents and young-to-youngish adults of 1937-38, for most of us were struggling in one way or another with the most difficult problem one faces in dealing with any writer —the fact that Dickens' work, and the man himself putatively in the work, have become an institutionalized cultural inheritance for the English-speaking world comparable only to Shakespeare in strength and solidity and general response. On this side of the Atlantic Ocean, Mark Twain alone could make a triad of this coupling. However that may be, Dickens was both a curse and a delight to us, then as now, because of his sheer inescapability in reference, allusion, quotation, syllabus, curriculum, and classroom; because of the embarrassed sanctity that hung about his official status like a blushing halo; and because everyone knew—and told you—what was appropriate to think of him and his works (the two were the same). Looking back on it from this vantage point in time, Dickens' elevation into this select pantheon of the acknowledged "greats" in the popular mind, the secondary school curriculum, and the mass media was an extraordinary achievement in the space of two generations—after all, it took Shakespeare two centuries. But perhaps it is as much a testimony to the power of the urban bourgeoisie over our culture as it is to the imaginative hold the novelist has managed to maintain over a century and a half of readers. Nevertheless, Dickens' status was and remains a special difficulty in any attempt not merely to assess his work but even to understand it without prejudice or preconception, because our contacts with his canon have been so many, so various, so partial, and so irradiated—or obscured—by his place in popular culture.

24

For example, in the secondary school curriculum of the generation 1920-1950, *A Tale of Two Cities*, *Oliver Twist*, and *David Copperfield* were solidly entrenched fixtures, standing in rock-like grandeur alongside of Scott's "The Lady of the Lake" and *Ivanhoe*, George Eliot's *Silas Marner*, *Ethan Frome*, *The House of Seven Gables*, "Julius Caesar," "Macbeth," "Hamlet," "As You Like It," and, mercifully, *Tom Sawyer* and *Huckleberry Finn*. Neither *Hard Times* nor, in my experience, *Great Expectations* was read, much less *Bleak House* or, say, *Our Mutual Friend*; and I think it safe to say that the introduction to literature my classmates and I had then was a thoroughly uncomfortable, not to say distasteful, experience. It was quite impossible to interest us in little Oliver's tribulations, so hideously prolonged were they, and described in a prolix and complex rhetoric that alternately baffled, enraged, or bored us (skipping became a fine art), but never entertained. Indeed, it was not until I picked up House's book in the 'fifties that I learned what it meant when Oliver "asked for more;" and our sympathies were solidly on the side of Fagin, the Artful Dodger, and that crew. Neither *A Tale of Two Cities* nor *Ivanhoe* succeeded in bringing history alive to us—the announced purpose of their inclusion in the curriculum—and I was never able to fathom the pedagogical thinking behind *David Copperfield*. We read *A Christmas Carol* at some point, and thoroughly enjoyed it, for reasons I will develop later. Meanwhile, *Silas Marner* and *Ethan Frome* induced a positively suicidal state of depression and ennui; and only Twain, Hawthorne (curiously, with his ponderous style), and Shakespeare escaped the general tedium. With Shakespeare, the exotic beauty of his language carried the day, and it was a pleasure to memorize the famous speeches and to say them over afterwards.

Needless to say, Dickens' novels were taught under every conceivable disadvantage, in spite of the fact that my teachers were mostly able, informed, and interested men and women whose memory I revere. But the system was wrong: the wrong books were chosen to be presented to us at the wrong time in our development and under the worst possible conditions of critical opinion. Looking back on it now, this latter factor may

25

contain the crux of the difficulty then, for I was, quite independently and without any awareness of its literary merits, reading *Moby Dick* on my own (as a sea story) with great zest—particularly the cetological sections! On one hand, Dickens, Scott, and Eliot were offered to us as acknowledged classics, almost too sacrosanct for criticism, and as vehicles of values and educational ideals that had little meaning for us. At the same time, there was abroad in the classroom and in the great world outside a pejorative term, "mid-Victorian," which was employed by the young-to-early-middle-aged to denote any set of values, habit of mind, or way of life that was bourgeois-puritan conservative in taste, politics, ethics, or manners. Demonstrably, Dickens was mid-Victorian, if a classic; so that there grew up around any discussion of the novels an unreal *ambiance* of reverence and contempt that lay cheek-by-jowl. The greatest praise alternated almost sentence by sentence with the most appalling admission of technical, ethical, or ideological bankruptcy. If one escaped a lifelong aversion to what he had understood to be literature, he might well be left with a settled animus to the Romanticists and Victorians. At the very least, the world of critical discourse read like one of the more grotesque chapters out of *Alice in Wonderland*.

Nor should we congratulate ourselves on having left those bad old days behind, for the complex of incompatible attitudes sketched in the paragraph above has maintained a remarkably persistent half-life down to the present day. Teachers of Victorian literature with whom I have talked unite in lamenting how many shibboleths and chimeras must first be laid to rest before the period can receive an unprejudiced discussion in the classroom; and my own experience confirms this impression. Nor has the recent upswing of interest in sexuality and feminism done much more than to muddy the waters of Victorian studies concerning these sensitive matters. In spite of the valuable work by Stephen Marcus, Duncan Crow, Martha Vicinus, and others in these interrelated subjects, we still know next to nothing about the actual relations between the sexes a century ago—*The French Lieutenant's Woman* to the contrary notwithstanding. Meanwhile, confident assertions about Victorian inhibition, hypocrisy, reticence, and taboos fly about on every hand. The general scorn and ridicule directed toward Dickens' treatment of his female protagonists illustrate very well the way in which unexamined—indeed unsupported—assumptions about Victorian sexual attitudes interfere with clear-sighted reading of the novels. Esther Summerson, for example, is still, I believe, widely regarded as epitomizing Victorian idealization of treacle-clad womankind; whereas there is a wealth of evidence in *Bleak House* and in the critical literature to demonstrate that her characterization is a shrewd if sympathetic study of a neurotically divided personality, one whose very insipidity is a function of her sickness. But this hypothesis is ignored on the grounds of a begged question: as a Victorian, Dickens lacked sophisticated psychological insight about women because his guilty sexuality forced him unconsciously to idealize them!

Curiously, in my generation at least the strongest countervoice to this complex of attitudes was to be heard in the popular culture of the nineteen-twenties and -thirties, and particularly in its burgeoning mass-media modes of communication and entertainment—the Hollywood motion picture, the radio, and the recording industry. There, Dickens and to a lesser extent his fellow writers in the nineteenth century came grandly and pervasively—nay, inescapably—to life for us, became in fact what they now are for most literate moderns, a fundamental part of our cultural heritage.

It is altogether appropriate that Dickens should have shared so largely in this phenomenon of the twentieth-century's technology, for it was he who first put into practice Thomas Carlyle's brilliant speculative insight that, in a secularized and egalitarian bourgeois mass-culture based on urbanization and industrialism, the priestly function of maintaining a unifying center of shared traditional values must fall to the man of letters. He alone was capable of speaking authoritatively to a mass audience through the first technological developments of modern mass communications: the machine-driven press, cheap pulp paper, and rapid general distribution of printed matter. More than any other writer of his time, Dickens assumed this sacerdotal office in print, in part through the enormous popularity of his novels in monthly shilling serial parts, in part

27

through cheap reprints and collected editions, in part through such journalistic enterprises as his two personally edited magazines, "Household Words" and "All the Year 'Round," both of which reached wide readership, and finally through the series of public dramatic readings from his own works that attracted huge audiences on both sides of the Atlantic and the English Channel. In an England whose population in 1850 was approximately 17,000,000, subscriptions to serial parts of Dickens' novels averaged between 30,000 and 50,000 a month. Translated roughly into 1976 terms for the United States, with a population of about 200,000,000, these figures would suggest an equivalent readership now of between 360,000 and 600,000, an extraordinary sale that does not consider the very large number of hard-bound volumes sold after the conclusion of serialization. We do, however, know that, in the twelve years following his death in 1870, Dickens' publishers sold a total of four-and-a-quarter million volumes of his works.

What these figures suggest is that well before his death Dickens had institutionalized himself as a folk-culture figure of such pervasive influence and enduring value as Dick Whittington, Lemuel Gulliver, or George Washington. Sanctified by school curricula and suppliers of fancy library editions for an emergent and culture-hungry middle class, and popularized by theatrical producers and anthologists for generations during his life and after his death, characters of his creation like Pickwick, Sam Weller, Sairy Gamp, Barkis, Oliver, Mr. Podsnap, Pecksniff, and Bumble entered the main stream of the cultural inheritance shared by all who had, or now have, any claims to literacy as a stock of instantly recognizable types suitable for the purposes of commonplace allusion or simile. Even the malady from which the Fat Boy suffered is now a part of the materia medica as the "Pickwickian Syndrome." Thus by the time I was growing up in the nineteen-twenties and -thirties, Dickens' characters had assumed the dignity of archetypes of certain kinds of venial or eccentric behavior, moral states, or conditions of mind.

Dickens' peculiar persistence as a force in folk culture might have remained an essentially abstract one, which lived on in lexicographies and annotations, had it not been for the coincidental development of the recording industry, the motion picture, and radio broadcasting. With its genius for fastening on the absolutely familiar and commonplace as the subject of aesthetic contemplation since at least the time of Moll Flanders and Clarissa Harlowe, the bourgeois sensibility found in Dickens' works an irresistible vehicle for transmission through the new modes of communication and entertainment which arose out of late nineteenth and early twentieth-century technology. Leaving aside the early exploitation of the Dickens canon done by silent film-makers in the years 1910-1930, which was, after all, only an extension of a well-established practice of theatrical entrepreneurs reaching back to the very earliest days of Dickens' popularity—a practice, incidentally, in which the novelist actively participated during his lifetime— the great work of popularization was performed on the radio in the two decades after 1930, when broadcasting matured technologically and as an industry.

It is highly significant that Dickens' *entrée* into broadcast entertainment, and the mass-folk culture it was in part preserving and in part generating through its choice of subject matter, should have been played by Lionel Barrymore, scion of a theatrical family whose roots were in the popular, itinerant world of Victorian thespians with which Dickens, once an aspiring actor himself, was thoroughly familiar, and which he had depicted with superlative comic accuracy in the Crummles family of *Nicholas Nickleby*. As I have suggested before, Dickens was far from averse to exploiting the popular theater as another avenue for reaching the widest possible audience with his works—an audience, as he was aware, at least in part shut out by illiteracy from enjoying his stories in print—and he regularly worked with theatrical managers in bringing his Christmas books to the stage during the holiday season. Indeed, he seems to have shared in the profits of such authorized performances through a licensing arrangement. A case could be made to show that Dickens had at least one eye cocked on possible dramatic adaptation of his Christmas stories during the period of their composition, much in the manner of many modern novelists who seem to have from the start a view of the potential translation of the work to celluloid.

However that may be, Lionel Barrymore's radio production of *A Christmas Carol*, together with its immensely successful recorded version, quickly became the central feature of that annual secular ritual in the United States called the Christmas Season, the present form of which, for good or ill, was definitively established by the mass media of the nineteen-thirties. Millions of American families, mine among them, not dutifully but joyfully sat down before their immense, streamlined, inlaid, cat's-eye Philcos to deplore Scrooge's unbelievably parsimonious hardness-of-heart, to admire Bob Cratchit's no less incredible good spirits and optimism, to be softened into tears by Tiny Tim's cheerful acceptance of his lingering and apparently inevitable fate, and to be delighted at last by the foreknown consummation of the old miser's change of heart into a paragon of Christian charity, fellow-feeling, and social enlightenment. It is hardly an exaggeration to say that, on the night during the Christmas season of the 'thirties when *A Christmas Carol* was broadcast, there was hardly a house in the United States with a dry eye in it.

A number of considerations arise out of this quite extraordinary phenomenon which bear upon the remarkable place in literature and the popular mind now occupied by Dickens. To begin with, we must remember that the institution of Christmas as we know it, in all the manifold secular ritualization distinct from its largely submerged core of religious meaning, had its fundamental characteristics formed during the Victorian era, through a process in which *A Christmas Carol* and Dickens' other Christmas books of the eighteen-forties had at least as large a rôle as Prince Albert's introduction of the Christmas tree, the evolution of St. Nicholas into Santa Claus, the commercialization of Yuletide, and the solidification of the conjugal family unit around its secular festivals. As a ritual atonement of *laissez-faire* individualism, with Scrooge as the Scapegoat, *A Christmas Carol* performs the functions of a mass-in-mufti, a semi-sacred parable in fable form or a morality play laid in a modern metropolis. At least, it provided for the sound-bound audiences of the nineteen-thirties a crucial focus for a competitive, acquisitive society's reaffirmation of some of its most cherished, if often ignored, spiritual values—

solidarity, private humanitarianism, and a temporary abandonment of the work ethic in favor of larger motives.

Furthermore, all this was enacted under the influence of a presiding narrative persona or dramatic voice with whom the reader or listener identified, and which he identified as that of Charles Dickens himself. The upshot is that the storyteller embedded himself in a generation of listeners as the disembodied voice of the principal celebrant of a mass societal ritual observance, the vessel embodying in his person the best values of that society as apprehended and reaffirmed under peculiarly compelling emotional and spiritual circumstances. Dickens was not unaware of, nor was he unwilling to exploit, the almost hypnotic intimacy he was able to establish with his audience under the conditions of serialization (he was, after all, an amateur hypnotist in private life), and at least one important consideration prompting the public readings from his own works was the desire to participate in "a multitude moved by one emotion"—an emotion, be it noted, of his own invention and generation. Intellectuals are reluctant to give over the clear cool exercise of analytical reason to the blandishings of entrancement such as that practiced by Dickens, particularly when that spell is employed to affirm a private humanitarian vision of social virtue, however subversive of certain cherished middle-class laissez-faire attitudes it may be, that was directly at odds with the dialectical habits of mind of the architects of an emergent welfare state and the proponents of modern liberalism. Hence the ridicule that was poured upon the author of A Christmas Carol and his auditors forty-years ago, ridicule that was, I am sure, ignored by the millions of ordinary people who quite unconsciously but happily submitted themselves once a year to a congenial and wholly absorbing hour or two of unconscionable imaginative compulsion, from which they emerged feeling somehow cleansed and ennobled by their participation in the experience.

Others of us, some years later, were to recur to that phenomenal submission of ourselves so wholly and completely to the imaginative sway of Dickens—static, paternal dial-twiddling, and singing commercials notwithstanding—with quite different feelings of curiosity than were aroused when we

31

found ourselves novel in hand, slipping inadvertently into that compact and absolutely compelling universe of Dickens' from which there was no escaping so long as the narrative continued. All other matters laid aside, the question then became one of accounting for this remarkable hold on our minds in terms of technique, artistry, vision; and to this task we set ourselves as scholars and critics. The task remains unaccomplished; indeed, to my mind, it is still the presiding question about Dickens the artist and the one least likely ever to receive a thoroughly satisfying answer. But at the time in the early nineteen-fifties when this sense of participating by virtue of its very urgency in an aesthetic experience which bordered on hallucination—the term is G. H. Lewes' and is more than a century old—my interest in Dickens the novelist may be said to have begun in earnest. From what my colleagues tell me, a not dissimilar experience prompted their own curiosity, sometimes quite without the benefit of Lionel Barrymore.

A second consideration bearing on Dickens' place in our minds today also turns upon the cultural ambience of the 'thirties and 'forties as it finds expression in the remarkable homogeneity of the literary life of that time for the common reader, young or old, in the United States, no matter what was coming out of his cat's-eye Philco. Leaving the sub-pop culture of comic and big-little books, radio serials and soap operas, and all the rest of the nostalgia and trivia games we now play to one side, the 'thirties and early 'forties constituted for the urban middle classes the last time that they could enjoy together with themselves and their children an unselfconsciously shared aesthetic life without either condescension or servility. "The Saturday Evening Post," "Colliers," "Liberty," *Gone With The Wind*, the novels of Nordoff and Hall, Kenneth Roberts, and C. S. Forester, together with many another, provided a common ground upon which precocious adolescents and adults of many different descriptions could meet for lively if unscholarly discussion of Tugboat Annie, the Flying Yorkshireman, Mr. Glencannon, Jeeves and Bertie Wooster, even Faulkner and Fitzgerald—and all in blissful ignorance of informed critical opinion or procedure or even canons of taste.

32

Such things went on, at least in my neighborhood, quietly and continuously and without much self-consciousness or striving after culture; and the ambience generated must have been much like that in which Dickens lived and wrote. Its benefits, to the generation that reached maturity in time to see service in the Second World War or the Korean War, were considerable, and Dickens shared in them richly. If *David Copperfield* or *A Tale of Two Cities* were imposed upon one in the schools amid an odor of aesthetic sanctity, at home these novels, along with *Pickwick Papers* and the Christmas books and possibly—in families more cultivated than those I knew—*Great Expectations*, were simply part of a received cultural stock or tradition quite undiscriminatingly jumbled up with Booth Tarkington, Mark Twain, George Ade, "Crossing the Bar" and "The Light Brigade," speeches from Shakespeare, some Burns and Browning, "Ozymandias," prudential passages from Pope, Robert Service, Will Rogers, and an ill-assorted mountain of other things. Thus, Dickens may have been a classic, but he was one you could deal with in a free and easy way and without the stultifying veneration that accrued to Milton and Tennyson because Dickens was funny, because he could be read aloud in company or dramatized. Then, as he had intended all along, his language came alive, made sense, moved deeply, and entertained hugely, and something of the bardic atmosphere of ancient days remained in force, with all the emotional power generated by the shared experience of a speaking voice. Then too, my parents, neighbors, and their friends harked back to a time when much education had been by rote, and they had poems, orations, and dramatic speeches by heart, and were not shy of a little declamation of a sociable evening over a chaste beverage. They remembered Chautauqua recitations and dramatic productions by touring companies of Shakespeare, sentimental domestic dramas, and novels—notably those of Dickens; and they often re-enacted the more telling moments.

But it remained for Hollywood, and the motion picture industry generally, to secure and transmit Dickens' place in popular culture to my generation. And first place must go to the sumptuously mounted classic productions of *A Tale of Two Cities* and *David Copperfield*, cast, scripted, directed, and pro-

33

moted with all the vulgar genius and tackily reverent inventiveness which made the film form of the thirties so uniquely appropriate—if incomprehensibly so—to be vehicles for Dickens' not altogether dissimilar talents. Base commercial motives and the cultural ambitions and limitations built into the star system, repertory companies, and the motion-picture industry of great studios and distribution networks coincided with the acknowledged indebtedness to Dickens of such profoundly influential artists as Sergei Eisenstein, for whom the novelist's natural mode seemed cinematographic, and with the views of such advanced critics as Edmund Wilson, who regarded Dickens as "the greatest dramatic writer the English had since Shakespeare." Add to this the receptivity of the general public to dramatic representation of the particular works of this culture figure which were known to them, especially under the compelling terms of this new medium, together with the stirrings of serious critical interest in Dickens as a conscious artist. The resulting situation was a rare combination of those aesthetic, social, and economic circumstances which must all be present together for a unifying cultural event to occur such as that which happened at the Globe Theater, London, between 1590 and 1605. For all the differences in scale, quality, form, and society, a roughly comparable phenomenon occurred in the nineteen-thirties with the two films cited above, and, following the interruption of the war, resumed again thereafter in slightly attenuated because more intellectually self-conscious form with Mills' and Guinness' *Great Expectations*, the later *Oliver Twist*, and the rather stiffly mechanical *Pickwick Papers* of the 'forties and 'fifties.

Quite aside from establishing Dickens' superlative pertinence to a new and culturally apposite dramatic art form—not all that new, really, since the modern motion picture and its sound track have simply provided the technological means to make Victorian melodrama an artistically acceptable genre— the film demonstrated to many millions the power and force of the novelist's largely histrionic and theatrical genius. Years later, it also sent many of us as serious students or common readers back to the books with an altered vision, one more prepared on a very fundamental level of aesthetic perception to receive sympathetically what Dickens had to offer us in the way he offered it. Like a playful fly in celluloid amber, the essential qualities of Dickens the writer awaited discovery and life until the motion picture film could show us in what mode he had chosen to speak, all along. This I believe is an important consideration bearing on Dickens' place in the modern sensibility, since his works and genius were among the first to be redefined and more fully comprehended as the result of experiencing them through mass-media exploitation.

I do not mean to suggest that the cinema's *A Tale of Two Cities* and *David Copperfield* are perfect transformations of page to picture, narrative to beheld event. I am not at all sure that Ronald Coleman's genteel organ tones are appropriate to the Sidney Carton I am familiar with; Freddy Bartholomew is a dubious David; and W. C. Fields' Micawber, whatever else it may be, is not Micawber. On the other hand, Edna May Oliver's Aunt Betsy Trotwood is a work of genius to rank with Roland Young's Uriah, the Murdstones are as perfect as the entire Peggotty ménage, and the scenes of genre and the Terror are beautifully managed. But the greatness of these films consists in the fact that they convey the arresting visual impact of their originals, even when they're not being literally faithful to them; and it is this imaginative power to enthrall utterly which constitutes Dickens' characters and makes them memorable. Like the original, Field's impersonation has become a permanent possession of the popular mind, just as Coleman's Carton, last speech and all, has done. To do this is to transmit the essential Dickens, all wrong as the particulars may be; and I believe that that quality communicated itself to us in the great plaster Moorish-baroque motion-picture theatres of the thirties better than it did in my high school classroom. It saved Dickens for me as an interesting creator.

Meanwhile, very much more intellectually reputable forces were at work to create an aesthetic sensibility in the nineteen-forties and -fifties that would find a congenial vision of life in Dickens' novels and that would not accept without cavil a theory of fiction based on Henry James' *The Art of the Novel*, at least as formulated by R. P. Blackmur and Percy Lubbock. A number of complicated movements in literary taste among the *cognoscenti* just prior to World War II and thereafter account for the dawning awareness of Dickens' pertinence to our times if not for his putative modernity. Quite aside from the rather surprising critical reassessments of Wilson, Orwell, Shaw, and Trilling which entered the intellectual literary establishment, a large number of writers were beginning to be read widely and seriously who had been profoundly influenced by Dickens' works and who had tacitly or overtly acknowledged their debt to him.

Dostoevski and Tolstoy had been available for some years in relatively modern translations and by 1939 were being read in the schools; and their melodramatic, sophisticated manipulation of the elements which had been the stock-in-trade of the Victorian novelist, particularly the exploration of symbol and figurative pattern as a principal means of developing a moral fable superimposed on a literal narrative, and their deep interest in states of altered consciousness, grotesque eccentricity, even derangement, must have encouraged readers to remember comparable effects in Dickens' works. Indeed, the very idea of the manner in which states of consciousness may profoundly alter the appearance of the perceived world, even transform it unrecognizably into something rich, strange, or disconcerting, was preparing the ground for a newly serious interest in such conventional—to us now—Dickensian themes as dementia, monomania, fantasy, criminality, schizophrenia and dual personality. Roskolnikof, *The Brothers Karamazov*, *The Idiot*, and *The Possessed*, among others, were discussed in classrooms—often by newly arrived European professors who had fled continental fascism—as acknowledged classics of fiction which very largely existed outside the framework of post-Jamesian critical dialectics. Needless to say, Dickens was ignored, or else denigrated, when compared to these acknowledged masterpieces. But an informed awareness of, and respect for, their themes and techniques inevitably led many of us back to the great Victorian novelists, prepared to recognize in them precursors of these continental writers when we discovered what they were up to as conscious craftsmen. All that remained was the revelation of acknowledged indebtedness owed to Dickens or Thackeray or George Eliot by a Dostoevski or a

36

Tolstoy for the full reassessment of these Victorians to begin on a systematic basis.

At the same time that the great Russian novelists of the later nineteenth century were gradually introduced to a wider circle of general readership in translation, a no less significant re-ordering of literary and general aesthetic sensibility was going on as a result of the spreading influence of the expressionistic movement in art and literature. Together with Surrealism and Dadaism, which were more or less associated with Expression-ism in the general mind, these movements reintroduced into aesthetic respectability the values of the patently fantastic, the grotesque disfunction of the familiar, and the projection of subliminal states of feeling—particularly those profoundly irrational fears and fantasies that belong to neurosis and psychosis. Furthermore, the subversion of conventional no-tions of reality and even of the generally accepted relations between things, as well as the introduction into art and litera-ture of the sinister demonic or demotic forces at work under the smooth surface of routine modern life, constituted a vision of the world far more disturbingly discontinuous and discon-certing than that already vouchsafed by the stream-of-con-sciousness novel as handled at least by Virginia Woolf, James Joyce, and William Faulkner. Kafka's *Metamorphosis, The Trial, The Castle, The Penal Colony*, and many other works, we now know from Professor Spilka's excellent study and other sources, were influenced by Dickens' radically alienated vision of his society in such novels as *Great Expectations, Little Dorrit* (in which the social system and values of England are subsumed under a vast analogue to a prison-house), and *Our Mutual Friend* (where the presiding visionary insight of the bourgeoisie is located in the imagery of offal and in the symbolic action–patterns of transposed identities, often through death-and-rebirth by water).

Equally important in this connection, quite aside from Kafka's shared habit with Dickens of developing some vast and disorienting analogue, symbol, or pattern-of-action as the grotesque *donnée* of the fiction—the man-as-beetle at the heart of *Metamorphosis*, for example—is the fact, taken in conjunc-tion with a growing interest in Russian literature, that readers

turned with increasing respect to other writers, indeed to artists of all sorts, whose vision of the world was profoundly subversive of all our reassuring and conventionally accepted ideas
of reality. We went back to Gogol's "The Nose," for example,
and "The Overcoat," to certain things even of Pushkin's, to
Hesse's *Steppenwolf*. We turned from Dali, Stanley Spencer,
Peter Blume, Duchamp, Magritte, Munche, and a host of other painters, to Bosch, the Breughels, Holbein and Dürer, and
the whole grotesque art of German and Flemish primitivism
like "Melancholia" and "The Dance of Death" cycle. Seen
from a sensibility modified by a sympathetic experience of
these artists and writers, Carlyle's *Sartor Resartus*, and indeed
his whole mode of prophetic argument, settled into place as
part of a long and living grotesque tradition in which Dickens
had an important place along with Ben Jonson's comedies,
Gulliver's Travels, *Tristram Shandy*, the T. S. Eliot of
"Sweeney Among the Nightingales" and "The Wasteland,"
Nathanael West's *The Dreamlife of Balso Snell* and *Miss
Lonelyhearts*, some early works of James Gould Cozzens like
S. S. San Pedro, *The Good Soldier Schweick*, *Wozzeck*, and,
more latterly, such writers as Nabokov, Saul Bellow, John
Barth, and Ralph Ellison.

Other notable forces in the reorientation of sensibility that
transpired between the nineteen-thirties and the sixties included a lively reawakening interest in the arts of the *fin-de-
siècle*, art-nouveau, aestheticism, and decadence, with their
visual distortions and stylization and their eccentric posturing
of self-conscious perversity and esoteric aesthetic experience
like that to be found in the illustrations of Aubrey Beardsley,
and in the writings of Huysmans, Wilde, Swinburne, Thomp-
son, Thomson and Beerbohm. This growing respect for the
pertinence to truth of the simplifications inherent in stylization and the caricatural mode, to a significant degree fostered
by the widening audience for the works of Klee, Miro, Sheeler,
Grant Wood, and other artists of the 'twenties and 'thirties,
led us back with altered vision to the great line of English
caricaturists, illustrators, social satirists and commentators
in graphic form—Hogarth, Rowlandson, Gillray, Cruikshank,
even Hablot Browne ("Phiz") and the Frenchman Daumier.

WILLIAM F. AXTON

They, we discovered, had been a principal force in the development of Dickens' imaginative vision of life, his technical procedures in the handling of scene, characterization, and episode, and his aims as an artist.

What the widely diverse modes outlined here had in common for one who came to the mature reading of Dickens under their impress was their standing indictment of the standards of reality, plausibility, and verisimilitude which had formed the traditional basis for dismissing Dickens as a serious artist. His characterization, for example, had been condemned for its one-dimensionality and "flatness," its caricatural simplification of personality, its melodramatic or sentimental excesses, its tendency to employ antic, gestic eccentricity and to exploit objects or properties as keys to identity, and the practice of drawing unbelievably exaggerated pictures of unalloyed good and evil. Dickens' novels lacked substance because they lacked protagonists with "roundness" (to use E. M. Forster's formulation in *Aspects of the Novel*)—that is, with profound psychological depth and complexity, with the ability to grow, change, develop, or "surprise convincingly," and with the capacity to deal with significant intellectual issues in a sophisticated and integrated manner.

To some extent, these strictures are simply wrong, because the critics did not pay careful attention to what certain characters in the novels actually think and do—notably David Copperfield, Pip, Esther Summerson, Mrs. Dombey, Arthur Clennam, and a host of others—which demonstrates their complexity. Then again, Dickens' conception of the novel denied the aesthetic validity of the explicit discussion of ideas and of formal psychological analysis of character. His radical theory of dramatic objectivity required that intellectual content and even characterization must be embodied in action and dialogue rather than represented at second hand in narrative, résumé, or exposition. Thus Dickens' characters characterize themselves and each other, so to speak, through their dramatic interplay in action and dialogue as well as through their creator's manipulation of the objective motifs of idiosyncratic speech, gesture, dress, or other appurtenance or associated object, which act like synecdoche or metonymy as a kind of vivid shorthand no-

39

tation or ideogram that is capable of extensive variation. The rationale for this distinctive practice, quite aside from the need for economy and instant recognizability imposed by serialization, lies in the fact that Dickens employs his characters for representative purposes, as types or personifications of institutions, classes, moral attitudes, and the like, and that he develops them as ensemble players whose referential dimensions are interlocking and mutually enriching.

Then, too, we are now more tolerant of the levels of reality possible with different methods of characterization, and Dickens' reputation has profited hugely from this greater sophistication. For example, a generation of scholars and critics thought Forster's discrimination between "flat" and "round" characters carried with it a condemnation of "flat" characters as a class, and of Dickens' characterization in particular as a special offender in this regard. In fact, of course, Forster makes no such judgment: indeed, he singles out Dickens' minor personages as cause to question whether there isn't more involved in relatively one-dimensional characters than we usually grant them, and goes on to invite further study of such types, stereotypes, and archetypes—an invitation that has been largely ignored by the academic community.

At the same time, we have come to see more clearly than heretofore the vital distinction between caricature, which exaggerates a single trait or feature for comic purposes, and stylization, which reduces a subject to its definitive and essential form. As George Santayana said some seventy years ago, people who think Dickens exaggerates fail to grasp the reality of things, and have only "notions" of them; for the novelist's characterization cuts away superficial complexities and contradictions to get at the substantial, irreducible essence of his characters. Finally, from Freud, Jung, and anthropologists and social psychologists, we have gained renewed appreciation of the mythic or archetypical modalities of apparently disparate individual personality and behavior, the ways in which different people participate in patterns of behavior and relationships that are primordial and universal. One of the principal appeals of Dickens' characters to a modern sensibility—and, for that matter, of their accompanying scenic backdrop, their groupings and relationships, their patterns of action and plotting—lies precisely in this: that they reach out beyond literal, particularized actuality to a world of timeless, ideal formularies of human type, situation, and activity. In *Bleak House*, Dickens imaginatively conceives of the family, and especially the parent-child relationship, as the reigning paradigm of society, and peoples his story with irresponsible parents, neglected, abandoned, or exploited children (some of whom assume the rôle of surrogate parents), and institutions charged with parental responsibilities in the great family of society, like the aristocracy represented by the various members of the Dedlock *ménage* and the High Court of Chancery, which they knowingly or unwittingly ignore or neglect in pursuit of their private interests or inherited prerogatives.

Dickens' method, then, is that of the visionary, who under the impress of some compelling imaginative insight sees all things participating by analogy in a single, simple relationship, however complex may be its ramifications into individual cases. Such a method, again, requires that realistic depiction of recognizable actualities be adjusted or modulated in the direction of the commanding vision of their participation in a symbolic or metaphoric system in which their meaning inheres. The method further demands that everything—literally everything—in the novel must demonstrate its participation in the governing vision, that everything which exists in the naturalistic materials of event, setting, and personage must reveal its place in the larger ideal framework that informs and gives the novel meaning—indeed, that gives life and the world meaning when seen from the perspective taken toward them in a given work.

Thus even the meteorological conditions of the setting of, say, *Bleak House*—England's usual November rain and fog and accompanying mud—which so brilliantly open the novel, are employed to suggest the cloying evils of a moribund, obsolescent legal institution and of an entire social order bent upon resisting healthy, inevitable change and reform. The same rainy weather threatens to inundate the Dedlock family's country seat, and imagery suggests both the primordial obsolescence of such institutions as court and aristocracy and the

41

threat of divine punishment, like that of the Biblical deluge, which hangs over them. Again, the slang term of the "great world," used to denote the English aristocracy represented by the Dedlocks, coins a host of cosmological images that diminish the importance of high society and suggest its forthcoming doom in the natural order of things—a theme picked up by such an unimportant detail as the coal burning in the Dedlocks' fireplace and consuming fossilized life forms long since extinct because, like the Dedlocks and Chancery, they could not adjust to changed conditions.

The legal entanglements of outmoded Chancery procedures have allowed the property in the Jarndyce case, Tom-all-Alone's, to decay into a slum and to become a breeding place for crime, misery, and disease, waiting to attack the body politic. Esther falls victim to a smallpox contracted from the waif, Joe, the crossing-sweeper; and her illness is symbolic counterpart of the moral infection of an irresponsible society that refuses to change its inherited institutions to deal with new social problems. Krook, the rag-and-bone dealer, is another symbolic counterpart to Chancery; and his death, improbably enough by spontaneous combustion, is explicitly identified as a symbolic prefiguration of the fate in store for all corrupt institutions—a death generated by their inherent corruption. It is this fate which falls upon the Dedlocks, initiated by the desire for power over them of their most trusted functionary, the lawyer Tulkinghorn, in his quest after Lady Dedlock's guilty secret.

Even places carry figurative value in Dickens' novels. Bleak House is not bleak, with Mr. Jarndyce and Esther as its inhabitants; but the comment on social injustice implicit in the name bears tellingly on Tom-all-Alone's, Chancery, and Chesney Wold. Mr. Jarndyce is anything but jaundiced in his view of his fellow men, but only at considerable psychological cost; and Esther's burden of guilt for her illegitimacy carries psychic scars that she thinks are shown in her face. The very concept of inheritance receives its share of exploitation in the novel's literal-figurative play, for Chancery governs issues of legal inheritance, the Dedlocks are ensconced in inherited privileges, Mr. Jarndyce is cursed with a case in Chancery he has inherited, Esther is afflicted with the sense of inherited guilt, and Rick Carstone, the lawyer Vholes, and the legal system located in Chancery are governed by the riches they hope to gain from inheritance. Indeed, the idea of gaining something for nothing from inheritance, without responsible present action of one's own, is the moral pestilence which corrupts the society envisaged in *Bleak House.*

This compact imaginative universe which Dickens created in his fiction does not alone account for the compelling hold he exerts over his readers, as important as the unique integration of naturalistic and figurative materials may be, together with their elaborate ramification around a complex system of interlocking analogues. More to the point, perhaps, is Dickens' profound influence on our perception of what is "real," not only in fiction but also in life, and from that, our understanding of reality. For he teaches us through his way of seeing that what is real need not be proffered by transcription of surface appearances only, but may require a vision which does not look but truly "sees," the informing eyesight of a prophet or seer for whom what is "real" is that which is involved in some unifying, ordering principle that gives meaning and coherence to seemingly unrelated matters. By the same token, such a mode of vision may equally see things in the familiar world in such a way as to profoundly disorient or subvert their conventional acceptation, may find the most generally accepted matters to be incongruous, grotesque, even sinister—certainly at variance with conventional views of them: discontinuous, strange, yet recognizable.

This is precisely Dickens' mode of description, both generally and in detail. His habit of defining his personages in terms of things, objects, animals, their surroundings, has been much remarked, together with his tendency to supply inanimate objects with animation and animals with human motivation. Dorothy Van Ghent has argued that his practice suggests Dickens' alienated sense of the dehumanization modern society imposes on man, that humanity has "leaked out of" people and come to occupy their material appurtenances, while human beings have become things. My own view holds rather that Dickens' vision of the modern world focuses on the vital interchange between man and the world of man-created objects which he occupies, which bear the stamp of his personality, and by means of which in part he projects his identity—or finds it. The world of Dickens' novels is one in which the object-world is suffused by the cultural attitudes of those who have made it and live in it; it is animate because it is an expression of the people who move through it. This formulary can be read the other way around, and by so doing accounts for much in Dickens that is to me otherwise inexplicable. That is, the novelist's habitual exploitation of incongruity between tenor and vehicle in all his descriptions was designed not only, as above, to reaffirm the interpenetration of the living and the object worlds, but also to assert the vitality of things before a modern audience jaded by the familiarity of everyday routine.

Dickens' program, then, continued and expanded the artistic aims of his predecessors, the Romantic poets, and of his contemporaries, George Eliot and W. M. Thackeray: to revive and replenish his readers' vision of the commonplace life around them by insisting upon its vitality, variety, and interest. This was and continues to be an important social function of the artist in a mass society, with its tendency to an enforced lack-lustre anonymity and conventionality of vision, then as now. At the same time, much of Dickens' technique devoted to these ends consists of noting the simple incongruities and discontinuities which inhere in the most commonplace things, people, and events; for to some extent the reconstruction of a lively, fresh perspective on the ordinary world requires the act of disorientation of the conventional relations between things and a studied insistence on "the relations between things not apparent generally"—to use Dickens' phrase. But at the other end of the scale the same techniques of description were also employed for darker purposes—as in the celebrated depiction of Coketown in *Hard Times*, of Tom-all-Alone's and Krook's shop in *Bleak House*, Jacob's Island in *Oliver Twist*, Mrs. Clennam's house and the Marshalsea Prison in *Little Dorrit*, and Miss Havisham's house and Jaggers' office in *Great Expectations*— to project a haunting sense of the sinister or corrupt forces working within the familiar world.

Such a vision as that outlined here is congenial to a

twentieth-century temperament which has endured the disconcerting eruption of savage and demonic forces at the very heart of civilized life—two great wars, fascism and genocide, communist purges, subversion, and brainwashing, Hiroshima, Vietnam, and the like. Somewhat less congenial, however, has been Dickens' mode of telling a story by means of an omniscient, third-person narrator. Critical theory premised on the strictures of Henry James' prefaces held that the presence in a fictional narrative of the voice of the novelist himself—telling the story as a frank storyteller, moving in space and time without restriction, dropping into the consciousness of any character at his convenience, commenting on the personages and events, even addressing the reader directly—violated the tacit compact between writer and reader upon which credibility rests. In this regard Dickens, along with Thackeray, was singled out as a special offender who failed to maintain narrative anonymity, invisibility, and objectivity, and who injected his own personality and reactions into the narration, with results fatal to believability and aesthetic distance. The novelist's management of scenes of death or suffering, particularly by children or girls, such as the death of Little Nell in *The Old Curiosity Shop*, were particularly scored on the ground of his obvious emotional involvement in the event.

Greater understanding of the conditions under which Dickens wrote, published, and was read in his own time has been instrumental in a wholesale re-evaluation of his narrative technique during the last two decades. In particular, weekly or monthly serialization, together with the Victorian custom of reading serial parts aloud to a circle of family or friends, generated an intimacy between writer and audience that has been matched only by the ancient bards and that fundamentally altered the relationship between them by making the experience of the fiction no longer a private, individual one but instead a public, social event in which the speaking voice of the narrator assumes paramount importance. Then, too, the extensive period of time required for serialization—between twelve and nineteen months—made the subscribers to some extent participants in the creative process, speculating about future events, advising the author directly or indirectly concerning the story and characters, and as it were living with the personages almost as actual people for a considerable time. This sort of audience involvement greatly enhanced the reality-status of the fiction at the same time that the presence of narrative voice—whether that of a first-person narrator like David Copperfield, Esther Summerson, or Phillip Pirrip (Pip), or that of the putative author or his persona—which was required to provide some sort of strong tonal unity to a regularly interrupted story, tended in a contrary direction toward an admitted fictionality. This I believe conscious manipulation of narrative surface to generate an ambiguity in the reader's mind about the reality-status of the fiction—whether it is a transcription of real life or an artificial thing made for entertainment with no claims of believability on the reader—reinforces Dickens' continuous play elsewhere between literal and figurative levels of meaning, and between realistic and fantastic handling of description, characterization, and plotting.

With respect to the management of narrative in this regard, Dickens' procedure was more complicated and various than it has generally been credited with being. At times he very boldly experimented with mixed narrative modes, as in the alternate points-of-view of *Bleak House*, in which the burden of narration is divided between an omniscient narrator writing in a progressive present tense about one portion of the story, and Esther Summerson, a first-person narrator, whose autobiographical memoir is related in the past tense from a point in time long after the events she describes have transpired, and which concerns another portion of the story. More important, throughout his *oeuvre* Dickens was constantly shifting the ground upon which he stood as narrator in relation to the persons, things, and events he treats and in relation to his reader. He often, of course, adopted the guise of omniscience, describing or narrating but editorializing all the while in order to control reader response, and maintaining a considerable distance between himself and the matters at hand. At other times, however, his imaginative identification with a character in a particular situation—Carker's flight from Dijon in *Dombey and Son* is a case in point—became so great that the presence of the narrator is extinguished by the dramatized workings of the consciousness of the personage. Or again, the imaginative hold on the narrator of a particular scene may be so strong—the death of Jo in *Bleak House* or of Paul Dombey will serve as illustrations —that all aesthetic distance is obliterated by Dickens' emotional involvement in it; and, like it or not, the scene is communicated to the reader in such compelling terms as to convince the reader of its total actuality in the mind of the author. Sometimes, as in the burial of Nemo in *Bleak House*, the narrator may detach himself from the events recorded and take up the stance of his readers as a witness to occurrences over which he has no control, which are totally outside himself, but which elicit from him at length a powerful emotional and moral reaction. At other times, as in the coroners' inquest over Nemo's death, the narrator's presence disappears entirely behind scenario, and author and reader alike are thrust into the scene as neutral recorders of sense data. Very often in descriptive passages, the narrative voice assumes the stance of an alien consciousness who records without any informing comprehension the details of the most commonplace things, usually employing the techniques we would now associate with a moving camera eye; but no less frequently Dickens will indulge in all the patently artificial contrivances we recognize as belonging to farce comedy, burlesque, or parody. Occasionally he will indulge in a passionate exhortation to the reader, but these must be discriminated from outbursts which are directed to no one and which seem rather to be relief to the author's own feelings generated by the more or less autonomous creations of his own imagination, toward which he and reader alike stand as observers and respondents.

To prosecute such a catalogue further would serve no useful purpose beyond what has already been established: that Dickens' narrative procedure keeps in a continuous state of agitation all relations between reader, narrator, fiction and reality, indeed, that calls into question not only the reality-status of the fiction but the very nature of conventional notions of what is real. In a time like ours when "the new philosophy has cast all in doubt,"—not least those questions of personal identity with which Dickens' protagonists like Pip and Esther are so intimately involved—this novelist speaks with special pertinence and piquancy, and we see in him a precursor of the creators of Lafcadio and *The Stranger*. Such an alienated, insecure vision of life can hardly be a matter of congratulation, for either ourselves or Dickens; but it enables us to hear his voice as one of our own.

THACKERAY'S THINGS:
TIME'S LOCAL HABITATION

JULIET McMASTER

Thackeray was a Victorian who spent his working life defining his period. And he habitually defined it in terms of its relation to the past. The body of his novels is a kind of history of the development of his age—a "history familiar rather than heroic," as Esmond says, but a history nevertheless—and in its way as illuminating as histories more conventional. From *Henry Esmond* to *Philip* we are given little windows on scenes of the past: the Jacobite plottings of 1688, the American Revolution against a background of the Georgian age of scandal, the scramble for victory and status that is behind Waterloo and the Regency, the self-satisfied respectability of the Newcomes, and the dirty electioneering that was the prologue to the 1867 reform bill. They are Victorian windows, to be sure, as Thackeray's spectacles perched on his broken nose were adjusted to his personal vision; and so much the more they tell us about Thackeray's period, which defined itself, as other periods do, by reacting from the previous one.

Thackeray chronicled the Bloodless Revolution, which though bloodless was a momentous and public event; but in 1860 he paused in wonder to consider the "silent revolution" that had occurred much more gradually and unobtrusively. When lecturing on George IV (the Victorians determined to be un-Georgian as the Edwardians determined to be un-Victorian) he exclaims:

He is dead but thirty years, and one asks how a great society could have tolerated him? Would we bear him now? In this quarter of a century, what a silent revolution has been working! how it has separated us from old times and manners! how it has changed men themselves! I can see old gentlemen now among us, of perfect good breeding, of quiet lives, with venerable grey heads, fondling their grandchildren; and look at them, and wonder at what they were once. That gentleman of the grand old school, when he was in the 10th Hussars, and dined at the prince's table, would fall under it night after night. Night after night, that gentleman [I wonder if when he delivered these lectures Thackeray fixed his knowing eye on certain patriarchal members of his audience] sat at Brookes's or Raggett's over the dice. If, in the petulance of play or drink, that gentleman spoke a sharp word to his neighbour, he and the other would infallibly go out and try to shoot each other the next morning. (*The Four Georges*, IV)

The metamorphosis by which a brawling regency buck becomes a venerable Victorian grandfather, and changes in taste and values more subtle, are everywhere chronicled in the novels. Becky is governess in a house where the father would be delighted and the evangelical son deeply shocked to know she is reading Smollett's smutty novels with the young girls of the family. And having lived up to the elder generation's values, she adapts herself to the heir's; and her booth in Vanity Fair, at one time a smart little house in Mayfair patronised by a libertine nobleman, becomes ten years later a stall in a charity bazaar. Mrs. Hobson Newcome reacts to the shocking progress of Popery and the fashion for High Church ritual by flouncing out of her pew when the clergyman dares to appear in his pulpit wearing a surplice. Colonel Newcome, fresh back from India, finds his younger brother's state dinner in Park Lane almost ascetic ("Do you know, I scarcely had enough to eat?"), and himself throws a rather dated party at which "the host was challenging everybody to drink wine, in his honest old-fashioned way," and from which the guests go reeling home, two of them at least contemplating a duel in the morning. *The Virginians*, *Vanity Fair* and *Pendennis* record the gestation and birth of the Victorian period. *The Newcomes* and *Philip*, narrated by that conscious and self-regarding mid-Victorian, Arthur Pendennis, pause and contemplate its coming of age.

"Are our women more virtuous than their grandmothers, or only more squeamish?" Thackeray wonders in *The Virginians*. The answer, he implies, is no, they are not more virtuous, for the basic stuff of human nature remains the same; but yes, they *are* more squeamish, for the surface of manners—the ways in which human nature manifests itself—is constantly wearing off and renewing itself, like the human skin. And such changes are momentous enough to be worth chronicling for a writer who specializes in a close-up view that alternates with a panoramic one. "There may be nothing new under and including the sun," Pendennis admits in *The Newcomes*; "but it looks fresh every morning, and we rise with it to toil, hope, scheme, laugh, struggle, love, suffer, until the night comes and quiet. And then will wake Morrow and the eyes that look on it; and so *da capo*." Vanity Fair is Vanity Fair still, though new and exciting to the different generations that encounter it.

If one reads the body of Thackeray's major works in the order he wrote them, one finds oneself moving to and fro in historical chronology. *Vanity Fair* and *Pendennis* move forward; then we jump back with *Esmond*, forward with *The Newcomes*, back again for *The Virginians*, and again forward for *Philip*. *Denis Duval*, the novel he did not live to complete, would fit historically between *The Virginians* and *Vanity Fair* —still leaving space, as George Saintsbury[1] reflected wistfully, for another novel to fill the gap between 1714, when *Esmond* ends, and 1755, when *The Virginians* begins. The chronological shifting is not unlike the progress within a single novel. At one point in *Vanity Fair* Thackeray explains, "Our history is destined in this chapter to go backwards and forwards in a very irresolute manner seemingly, and having conducted our story to to-morrow presently, we shall immediately again have occasion to step back to yesterday, so that the whole of the tale may get a hearing." "The whole of the tale" involves the reasons for this or that event, or attitude, or decision, and the reasons are to be found in the past. Chapter Fifty-two in *Pendennis* is called "Which accounts perhaps for Chapter Fifty-one," and it predictably reverses the chronology. This is a recurrent strategy. It is Thackeray's habit to be constantly accounting for things, to be finding the seeds of the present in the past. As social historian in the whole body of his novels, he demonstrates how each age grows out of the previous one; and in the personal and private histories within each novel, he explores his characters' relations to their own individual pasts. A man is not himself merely, at a given age; he is his own youth, childhood, infancy, an accumulation of his bygone experience; more— he is his forebears and their values and allegiances, even if only to the extent that he is determined not to be like them.

As Chesterton said, Thackeray is the novelist of memory. All his sensitive characters, and his narrators too, are occupied in summoning up remembrance of things past. I don't know if Proust read Thackeray, but Thackeray certainly didn't need to read Proust to learn to take up the quest for the recapture of the past. Esmond, George Warrington and Denis Duval write their memoirs at a stage when one expects all passion to be spent, but though they recollect their emotion in tranquillity they find that it is emotion still. Esmond's love for Beatrix ended in that moment when the roses shuddered out of her cheeks and he saw her as merely an intriguing prostitute to a prince; but yet "I invoke that beautiful spirit from the shades and love her still; or rather I should say such a past is always present to a man; such a passion once felt forms a part of his whole being, and cannot be separated from it."

Such passages run like a refrain through the novels. Beatrix herself as she reappears in *The Virginians*—an irruption from their grandfather's past into the youth of the Warrington boys —genially recalls her own youth at Castlewood: "I remember in this very room, at this very table—oh, ever so many hundred years ago!—so coaxing my father, and mother, and your grandfather, Harry Warrington: and there were eels for supper, as we have had them to-night, and it was that dish of collared eels which brought the circumstance back to my mind. I had been just as wayward that day, when I was seven years old, as I am to-day, when I am seventy." George Warrington, as he recollects the day when his engagement to Theo was broken, writes from his comfortable middle-aged stance, "I can hear now the sobs of the good Aunt Lambert, and to this day the noise of fire-irons stirring a fire in the room overhead gives me a tremor. I heard such a noise that day."

The sound of fire-irons, the taste of collared eels—passports to the past. We are verily in Proustian territory. And Thackeray expanded that backward-looking stance of his characters and narrators, who are engaged in *la recherche du temps perdu*, to inform the themes and plots of his novels. George and Harry Warrington, the Virginians, are engaged in a quest to recover their past: George consciously conducts himself after the manner of his grandfather, Henry Esmond; and the novel opens with Harry's arrival at Castlewood, the seat of his ancestors, where he goes through the painful experience of having his nostalgia collide with the unpleasant facts of the present. Arthur Pendennis, whose own youth was recorded in *Pendennis*, writes biographies of his younger brethren at Greyfriars, Clive Newcome and Philip Firmin, by which process he can to some extent renew his own early experience.

Pendennis also reflects another of Thackeray's attitudes in being both novelist and historian. Thackeray wrote both history and fiction, but for him they were not so much different disciplines as different genres—and not very different at that. Not only did he fill his novels with historical figures and events, but he saw orthodox histories as fictions, and vice versa. Esmond believes "that Mr. Hogarth and Mr. Fielding will give our children a much better idea of the manners of the present age in England, than the *Court Gazette* and the newspapers which we get thence"; and Pendennis claims that "the speeches attributed to Clive, the colonel, and the rest, are as authentic as the orations in Sallust or Livy." Thackeray laughs in his sleeve at Pitt Crawley for making a distinction in kind between Smollett's "history" and the history of Mr. Humphry Clinker. His view of the interrelation of history and fiction is expressed in the formal structure of *The Newcomes*, where Thackeray the novelist transforms himself into Pendennis the biographer. Pen self-consciously works out the process by which a historian must deduce his history:

> As Professor Owen or Professor Agassiz takes a fragment of a bone, and builds an enormous forgotten monster out of it, wallowing in primaeval quagmires, tearing down leaves and branches of plants that flourished thousands of years ago, and perhaps may be coal by this time—so the novelist puts this and that together: from the footprint finds the foot; from the foot, the brute who trod on it; from the brute, the plant he browsed on, the marsh in which he swam. (*Newcomes*, ch. 47)

Of Thackeray's six full-length novels, four are written as pseudo-histories, in the form of memoirs or biographies in which the ostensible writers draw on records, letters, "the Warrington papers" and so forth, as well as memory, to reconstruct their accounts.

Nevertheless, though Thackeray had a philosopher's interest in time as process, and a historian's interest in the nation's past, there are reasons why he wrote—primarily—novels, and not philosophy or history. At most he was a very social historian, a very personal philosopher. His instinct was always towards the embodying of the past, the incarnation of the idea. Geoffrey Tillotson has spoken of Thackeray's very concrete imagination. He has the novelist's instinct to visualize rather than conceptualize. In his mind an idea is naturally located in an emblem, and the emblem becomes an object; a proposition expresses itself in an attitude, the attitude takes shape in a person. It is the object and the person we meet in the novels, but they remain informed by the idea and the proposition. And it is on the concrete manifestations of Thackeray's philosophical and historical interest in time that I want to focus my attention: on the pokers and collared eels, and the dinosaur's footprint that are present and palpable extensions of a lost past. In these, time has a local habitation.

Thackeray felt vividly that all we can grasp of the past is remnants, fragments, relics—history for him is resident in cigar-butts, laundry bills, proofsheets, the fossilized footprint. That is why the document, the last will and testament of a dead time, figures so largely in his "veracious histories." Unlike the historian he was at liberty to invent his own documents; but it is characteristic of the way his imagination worked that he should so often feel the need to invent the documents before his people and their histories would come alive for him. He begins *The Virginians* with an account of the correspondence of the Warrington brothers,

> whose voices I almost fancy I hear, as I read the yellow pages written scores of years since, blotted with the boyish tears of disappointed passion, dutifully dispatched after famous balls and ceremonies of the grand Old World, scribbled by camp-fires, or out of prison: nay, there is one that has a bullet through it, and of which a greater portion of the text is blotted out with the blood of the bearer. (*Virginians*, ch. 1)

54

The seeds of the total action of the novel are here. "Poring over the documents," the narrator explains, he has "endeavoured to revivify the bygone times and people." It is through documents that the past can come to life again.

Thackeray's plots often turn on the finding or losing of a document. The discovery of a lost will or deed or gift by which the hero's fortunes are reversed is the climactic action of *The Newcomes, The Virginians* and *Philip*. And in *Vanity Fair* Thackeray carefully follows the history of George's letter to Becky: delivered in her bouquet at the Richmond ball before Waterloo; surviving the vicissitudes of Becky's career as she carefully preserves it along with other useful mementos; and finally produced to shatter Amelia's idolatrous conception of her dead husband so that she can at last see Dobbin's real worth.

Memorable scenes in the novels are constructed around documents and letters, and characters define themselves according to who does what with which piece of paper. The wily old Beatrix, determined to save Harry from his engagement to the faded Maria, actually robs her niece of his letter of proposal in Church; but Harry annuls her intriguing, and saves his own honour if not his happiness, by staunchly declaring, "written or said—it does not matter which!" The Little Sister in *Philip* plays Judith to Holofernes when she chloroforms her blackmailer and regains the forged bill. Pendennis's progress from generous youth to cautious worldliness is measured by his early reckless written expressions of love for the Fotheringay —his effusions fill drawers—and his later carefully noncommittal letters to Blanche.

Henry Esmond is the character who most courageously resists the determining power of the document. After the duel, when Mohun has killed Francis, Earl of Castlewood, Henry has in his hand the dying confession that declares he himself is the legitimate heir to the title and the estate. Thackeray makes the moment memorable by his telling use of significant detail:

> Esmond went to the fire, and threw the paper into it. 'Twas a great chimney with glazed Dutch tiles. How we remember such trifles in such awful moments!—the scrap of the book that we have read in a great grief—the taste of that last dish that we have eaten before a duel or some such supreme meeting or parting. On the Dutch tiles at the

> bagnio was a rude picture representing Jacob in hairy gloves, cheating
> Isaac of Esau's birthright. The burning paper lighted it up. (*Esmond*,
> I, ch. 14)

Esmond is not the only Esau in his family. His grandson,
George, also sacrifices his birthright to his mother's favourite,
Harry; and that George's grandson, George Warrington in
Pendennis, again voluntarily surrenders professional distinction and the woman he loves to another man. Esmond's act
reverberates down the generations. By contrast, in another
novel we are shown Pendennis's empty gesture of throwing
the manuscript of his novel into a fire that he knows has gone
out. Pendennis is a humbug, but Esmond is made of sterner
stuff.

The almost sinister determining force of the written document—that force George Eliot referred to when she called the
fifth book of *Middlemarch* "The Dead Hand," in which Casaubon and Featherstone through their wills extend their control
over others beyond the grave—is powerfully suggested in Mr.
Osborne's solemn alteration of the records in his family Bible
(the frontispiece represents Abraham's sacrifice of Isaac) when
he disinherits George: "Taking a pen, he carefully obliterated
George's name from the page; and when the leaf was quite
dry, restored the volume to the place from which he had moved
it." From that moment George is doomed, and his fall at Waterloo seems predetermined.

Imagery of death is often collected around documents: for
if Thackeray recurrently suggests the past is always present,
he as frequently reminds us that it is irrecoverably lost, and
that as we outgrow our youthful passions and allegiances, we
die by inches. That contradiction is voiced by George Warrington in *The Virginians*:

> You may be ever so old now; but you remember. It may be all dead and
> buried; but in a moment, up it springs out of its grave, and looks, and
> smiles, and whispers as of yore when it clung to your arm, and dropped
> fresh tears on your heart. It is here, and alive, did I say? O far, far
> away! O lonely hearth and cold ashes! Here is the vase, but the roses
> are gone. (*Virginians*, ch. 66)

So the Warrington papers may bring George and Harry to life
again, as the vase that remains can recall the roses that are

dead; but letters, recording the aspirations of people no longer alive, or emotions of your own that you no longer feel, are also dismal *mementos mori.* "What a dreary mourning it is to dwell upon those vehement protests of dead affection! What lying epitaphs they make over the corpse of love!" While George is preparing to jilt Amelia (he uses *her* love letters to light his cigars with), Amelia cherishes his past missives and refuses to part with them, "as you have seen a woman nurse a child that is dead." Such melancholy lingering over documents recurs often in the novels. Pendennis disinters the manuscript of his early novel, and smiles at the marks of tears:

> As he mused over certain lines he recollected the place and hour where he wrote them: the ghost of the dead feeling came back as he mused, and he blushed to review the faint image. And what meant those blots on the page? As you come in the desert to a ground where camels' hoofs are marked in the clay, and traces of withered herbage are yet visible, you know that water was there once; so the place in Pen's mind was no longer green, and the *fons lacrymarum* was dried up. (*Pendennis*, ch. 41)

In the same way, Pendennis is to muse over the records of other people's lost feelings when he peruses Clive's and Ethel's youthful letters "in the faded ink, on the yellow paper," and reflects again, "Who has not disinterred mementoes like these —from which the past smiles at you so sadly? . . . You open an old letter-box, . . . and excavate your heart." I have been multiplying quotations here to convey that tone of Thackeray's melancholy, always so resonant where he finds some present reminder to recall the past.

But written documents are of course only one, and the most obvious, of many physical objects in which the past has its ghostly residence. Pictures—which in their way are documents too—have the same force, and Thackeray's novels are filled with pictures. They are the present image of the past, as Thackeray shows most clearly in the chronicle of Isabel, Lady Castlewood, and her portrait as Diana by Lely. She, like Miss Havisham (whom she foreshadows, as she also echoes Dickens's Mrs. Skewton in *Dombey and Son*) refuses to acknowledge the passing of time. She paints her cheeks with the blushes of a girl, and persists in believing herself pregnant long after there is any hope of such a possibility. She keeps the Diana picture by her, and believes it is a mirror rather than the image of lost youth: "As goddesses have youth perpetual, this one believed to the day of her death that she never grew older: and always persisted in supposing the picture was still like her." Thackeray uses the same image to measure the difference as well as the similarity between Isabel and her descendant Beatrix, who had *her* youth recorded by Kneller, but who is keenly aware of the difference between image and faded original: "Look at that picture, though I know 'tis but a bad one, and that stupid vapouring Kneller could not paint my eyes, nor my hair, nor my complexion. What a shape I had then—and look at me now, and this wrinkled old neck!" Isabel was all vanity and delusion. There is the same vanity about Beatrix, but she has a penetrating knowledge of the truth of advancing age and approaching death. Thackeray uses that picture again to evoke time, vanity and mortality at Beatrix's deathbed, "as the clock ticks without, and strikes the fleeting hours; as the sun falls upon the Kneller picture of Beatrix in her beauty, with the blushing cheeks, the smiling lips, the waving auburn tresses, and the eyes which seem to look towards the dim figure moaning in the bed."

The history of certain pictures, which Thackeray traces carefully through his novels, is an index not only of the original's estimate of himself, as with Isabel, but of his or her place in the estimation and affection of others. Ethel's memorable gesture of sticking the green "sold" ticket from the painting exhibition on her own dress, and calling herself a *tableau vivant*, is a marvellous physical image of the marriage market theme in *The Newcomes*. Thackeray tellingly exposes Amelia's deliberate self-delusion by showing the transfer of her worship for George to his portrait: she has discovered the man was no saint, but after his death manages to enshrine him nevertheless in her picture of him, which she interposes between herself and Dobbin. "You were pure—Oh yes, you were pure, my saint in heaven!" she tells her picture.

The other picture with a history in *Vanity Fair* is of course the one of Jos on the elephant, and Jos's value is mercilessly canvassed at the sale of the Sedley effects after the bankruptcy: "The gentleman without the elephant is worth five pound," pleads the auctioneer. But poor Jos is knocked down for half a guinea to Mrs. Rawdon Crawley. Becky keeps her picture—her "cheap souvenir," as Barbara Hardy aptly describes it—in the same little desk where she hoards her "purse" of banknotes. And finally she produces it to conquer its original and make him her victim: "She had cast such an anchor in Jos now as would require a strong storm to shake. That incident of the picture had finished him." Jos, the fat fish who had escaped the toils laid for him in the early chapter called "The Green Silk Purse," has finally been hooked, and lands in Becky's net after all.

The grisly portrait of Dr. Firmin presides over his gloomy dining room, and epitomises his house of death:

> Over the sideboard was the doctor, in a black velvet coat and a fur collar, his hand on a skull, like Hamlet. Skulls of oxen, horned, with wreathes, formed the cheerful ornaments of the cornice. On the side-table glittered a pair of cups, given by grateful patients, looking like receptacles rather for funereal ashes than for festive flowers or wine. Brice, the butler, wore the gravity and costume of an undertaker. (*Philip*, ch. 2)

The skull Dr. Firmin holds is an emblem not just for his profession, but for him. In his last completed novel Thackeray is as obsessed with death as Dickens is in *Our Mutual Friend*, and much of the imagery, including that in the illustrations, concerns corpses and death's-heads. In figures like Quilp and Rigaud, Dickens dared to introduce the devil incarnate, and in Dr. Firmin, or "Dr. Fell," Thackeray has suggested not only the devil, but more specifically Death itself. Tufton Hunt, the parson blackmailer, refers to him as "*pallida mors*." He has literal, as well as figurative, skeletons in his cupboards; his house is accommodated with a side door for "*the bodies*"; he wears a watch by which he numbers the heartbeats of his patients; and he himself looks like a death's-head, with a "bald head that glittered like a billiard-ball," deep-set eyes that in certain lighting are shadowy hollows, and "very white false teeth, which perhaps were a little too large for his mouth, and these grinned in the gas-light very fiercely." However, devil and death's-head though he is, the doctor is also a self-dramatising

59

humbug, who manages his own bankruptcy with such prudence and efficiency that he leaves very little in the way of plunder for the scavenging vultures. One thing he does leave behind is that state portrait of himself; and his status as heroic villain is neatly undercut as his image is evaluated and sold: "I am afraid it went for a few shillings only, and in the midst of a roar of Hebrew laughter."

But a fragment that is tenderly rescued from the wreck of Colonel Newcome's ship is the picture of the colonel by his son, undertaken as the first portrait of Clive's career. J. J. Ridley "buys it in" to give back to the family, so the vultures do not get their beaks into the colonel, and his image is the focus of love and compassion as he is himself.

Pictures of course play a leading role in *The Newcomes*, which is the biography of a painter, as manuscripts do in *Pendennis*, the novel about a writer. The stages of Clive's career are reflected in his work: the portrait of his father is his best work, as his filial love is his most enduring quality; his grandiloquent "Battle of Assaye" records his allegiance to British India, his love for Ethel is expressed in "a whole gallery of Ethels"; when she is engaged to Lord Farintosh his subject is "Sir Brian the Templar Carrying off Rebecca"; after the bankruptcy, he paints "The Stranded Boat"; finally, in the ruin and humiliation of his family, he paints his father again, as Belisarius. Unobtrusive touches, these, in the vast accumulation of detail in *The Newcomes*. But Thackeray made paintings express their painters, as well as their subjects.

Thackeray dwells, as creative artists must, on outward and visible manifestations. With a mind that lingers over the past, and memories of roses now withered, his hands caress the vase that once held them, and that is all he has left to grasp of their fragrance. His novels express a faith that what we touch is real—is at any rate the part of reality that we can retain. The opposition of the abstract to the concrete way of thinking is marvellously realized in the love affair between Pen and the Fotheringay in *Pendennis*. He is all passion and poetry; he sees her in a glow of glamour, and art, and vague but noble abstractions concocted out of his own brain. She, however, has her feet firmly on the ground, as Thackeray shows by con-

stantly associating her with down-to-earth ordinary *things*, often edible ones—brown stout, mutton chop, veal-and-ham pie,
beef-steak pudding. She rubs white satin shoes with bread-
crumb while her father blusters theatrically about vipers and
traitors, and when it is decided the engagement must end, she
comments "them filberts is beautiful." At the last, "she
wrapped up Pen's letters, poems, passions, and fancies, and tied
them with a piece of string neatly, as she would a parcel of
sugar." Though the fact that her mind is arrested on the concrete is a measure of her mental limitation, Emily Costigan,
with her grip on what is solid and palpable, comes best out
of that encounter.

The things with which Thackeray crowds his novels—the letters in faded ink on yellow paper, the paintings by painters no
longer fashionable, the gifts from people no longer loved or now
dead, the swords and pistols that have shed blood and are now
ornaments—these things express much about the people they
surround, and Barbara Hardy has written marvellously on
"The Expressive Things" in Thackeray; but especially and recurrently, in the work of this novelist of memory, they express
the past; and their value is as present and palpable extensions
of the past.

As a Victorian lecturing to a Victorian audience on the
Georgian era, Thackeray chose to summon up a sense of the
past by a series of tactual images. This is how he begins *The
Four Georges*:

> A very few years since, I knew familiarly a lady, who had been asked in
> marriage by Horace Walpole, who had been patted on the head by
> George I. This lady had knocked at Johnson's door; had been intimate
> with Fox, the beautiful Georgina of Devonshire, and that brilliant Whig
> society of the reign of George III. . . . I often thought as I took my kind
> old friend's hand, how with it I held on to the old society of wits and
> men of the world. (*Four Georges*, I)

The old symbol of the laying on of hands acquires a new specificity, from the touch of the monarch on the head of the infant and the rapping of the knocker on Johnson's door, to the
old lady's hand in Thackeray's own that is to be his and his
audience's link with the past.

Hands are always powerful symbols in Thackeray, and they

61

touch many of his central concerns. Hands link, grasp, reject, rejoin, remind, create, perform sleights: so they express his themes of love and lovelessness, acquisitiveness and sacrifice. A study of the handshakes in the novels, in which snobs put their social inferiors in their places by offering three, or two, or one finger to shake instead of the whole hand, is an exploration in social discrimination: Becky resoundingly puts down George by her offer of one finger, and Clive Newcome has all our sympathy in stamping on his cousin's toe when Barnes tries "the finger business" on him. Posturing humbugs like Honeyman and Dr. Firmin cultivate gestures for effect: "No man in London understood the ring business, or the pocket-handkerchief business better, or smothered his emotion more beautifully." And hands with rings are reminders, like so much else in Thackeray's novels, of vanity: the Countess Isabel wears as many rings on her gnarled old fingers as the fine lady of Banbury Cross. Thackeray turns heraldic jokes about the red hand that decorates the arms of a baronet: "That blood-red hand of Sir Pitt Crawley's would be in anybody's pocket except his own."

But a handclasp can express reconciliation and enduring affection too, like that of the Warringtons that Thackeray used as the cover design for *The Virginians*, where the joined hands symbolise the union of the brothers in spite of their opposed temperaments, nations, and political beliefs. And hand-holding in love-making can express attitudes ranging from the starry-eyed to the worldly-wise. Witness Pen's rapture with the Fotheringay: "He seized her hand madly and kissed it a thousand times. She did not withdraw it"—and measure against it the characteristically disillusioned tone of the narrator in *The Virginians*: "What a part they play, or used to play, in love-making, those hands! How quaintly they are squeezed at that period of life! . . . What good can there be in pulling and pressing a thumb and four fingers?"

But predictably a recurring use of hand symbolism involves the recapture of the past. Rachel's hand, which she finally bestows on Esmond, is the link of continuity in a life during which he has regarded her as goddess, guilty widow, mother, and wife. In the first scene of the novel, when she meets him at

Castlewood as a boy, she takes his hand and puts her other hand on his head:

> The boy, who had never looked upon so much beauty before, felt as if the touch of a superior being or angel smote him down to the ground, and kissed the fair protecting hand as he knelt on one knee. To the very last hour of his life, Esmond remembered the lady as she then spoke and looked, the rings on her fair hands, the very scent of her robe, the beam of her eyes lighting up with surprise and kindness, her lips blooming in a smile, the sun making a golden halo round her hair. (*Esmond*, I, ch. 1)

It is a passage that sets the tone of the novel. As Esmond remembers her first blessing, so he remembers her unjustified cruelty when she sublimates her sense of guilt at her husband's death by blaming him: "Long ago he has forgiven and blest the soft hand that wounded him: but the mark is there, and the wound is cicatrized only—no time, tears, caresses, or repentance, can obliterate the scar." And at the reconciliation, when he understands she has been fighting an adulterous love, "she gave him her hand, her little fair hand: there was only her marriage ring on it. The quarrel was all over." And when, towards the end of the novel, they revisit the old scenes of Castlewood "hand-in-hand," Esmond is moved not only to reflect on the past but to get a rare glimpse of the future, even that which lies beyond the grave.

> We forget nothing. The memory sleeps, but awakens again; I often think how it shall be when, after the last sleep of death, the réveille shall arouse us for ever, and the past in one flash of self-consciousness rush back, like the soul, revivified. (*Esmond*, III, ch. 7)

It is characteristic of Thackeray that when his narrator visualizes the resurrection, he should envision the resurrection not just of the body but of the past, and suggest that the life everlasting stretches backwards as well as forwards to eternity.

Another woman's hand is focused on in the same way, but this hand links not just one man and woman through their two long lives, but spans generations and identities. It is Ethel's in *The Newcomes*. The great tragedy of Colonel Newcome's life has been the loss of the girl he loved in his youth because she was forced to marry for interest rather than love. When he returns in middle age from India, he finds in the girl Ethel the reincarnation of his lost Léonore:

> He took a little slim white hand and laid it down on his brown palm, where it looked all the whiter: he cleared the grizzled moustache from his mouth, and stooping down he kissed the little white hand with a great deal of grace and dignity. There was no point of resemblance, and yet a something in the girl's look, voice, and movements, which caused his heart to thrill, and an image out of the past to rise up and salute him. . . . He remembered such a fair bending neck and clustering hair, such a light foot and airy figure, such a slim hand lying in his own—and now parted from it with a gap of ten thousand long days between. It is an old saying, that we forget nothing. . . . No doubt, as the old soldier held the girl's hand in his, the little talisman led him back to Hades, and he saw Leonora. (*Newcomes*, ch. 15)

Léonore and Ethel, the colonel's past and present loves, the love he lost and the love he hopes to win for his son, are more elaborately identified in the course of the novel. Thackeray creates another *tableau vivant* as the old woman and the young kiss in front of the picture of Léonore in her youth; and at the death scene of the colonel, when he makes a backward progress through his army days in India, through his early love, to his boyhood when he has become as a little child and answers "Adsum" to the Master, it is Ethel's hand that he snatches (though Léonore is actually present), as he cries "Toujours, toujours!" Past and present are again made one through the clasp of hands.

But Ethel is different from Léonore, and the conflict in her of her love and worldly allegiance is suggested in her subjection to her other mentor, proud old Lady Kew, who can also find in Ethel her youth, and recall it by the touch of her hand. At her moving appeal to the rebellious Ethel, she pleads, "There—give me the little hand. How hot it is! Mine is as cold as a stone—and shakes, doesn't it?—Eh! it was a pretty hand once!" It is a touch that Saintsbury singled out as one of the great things in Thackeray.

That revivification of the past that is created by Ethel's little hand has its sweetness, but also its pain; for inexorably, and in spite of the colonel's resolution that Clive's life is to be different from his own, and happier, the past repeats itself. Clive cannot win Ethel in the marriage market, and so he marries silly little Rosey on the rebound, and to please his father. That power of the past over the present is captured in the moving scene of reconciliation between Clive and his father, when they recognize and acknowledge their identified destinies: Clive has just met Ethel accidentally at the house of old Sarah Mason, who, bewildered, and mistaking the generations, joins his hand with Ethel's and asks them when they are going to be married—to the accompaniment of bitter laughter from Clive. Haggard and wretched, he comes afterwards to the colonel, telling him how he has seen "the ghost of my youth, father, the ghost of my happiness," and weeps over his father's "trembling old brown hand."

> 'And are—are you fond of her still, Clive?'
> 'Still! Once means always in these things, father, doesn't it? Once means to-day and yesterday, and for ever and ever!'
> 'Nay, my boy, you mustn't talk to me so, or even to yourself so. You have the dearest little wife at home, a dear little wife and child.'
> 'You had a son, and have been kind to him, God knows. *You* had a wife: but that doesn't prevent other—other thoughts. Do you know you never spoke twice in your life about my mother? You didn't care for her.'
> 'I—I did my duty by her; I denied her nothing. I scarcely ever had a word with her, and I did my best to make her happy,' interposed the colonel.
> 'I know, but your heart was with the other. So is mine. It's fatal, it runs in the family, father.' (*Newcomes*, ch. 68)

The Newcomes, like the Esmonds, find themselves enmeshed in their family histories, and two slim white hands, Rachel's and Ethel's, have touched and confirmed those destinies.

From the hands that touch to the things they touch. Many novels are visibly shaped by some set of things, solid objects that are the anchors for the points of the web, the "airy citadel," as Keats called it, that the artist spins "from his own inwards." The conceptual weight of *The Nigger of the Narcissus*, as well as the physical load of the corpse of James Wait, is for a long moment sustained by that little nail on the plank that prevents the consignment of the dead to the sea. *Tristram Shandy* is shaped by a green baize bag of obstetrical instruments, a sash window bereft of its lead weight, a hot chestnut; *Great Expectations* by a savoury pork pie, a file, a mouldy wedding cake; *Middlemarch* by an emerald ring and bracelet, a statue of Ariadne, a row of voluminous notebooks towards a Key to All Mythologies. If you moved those things, you would alter or damage the structure and meaning of those novels, as you would a spider's web if you moved the points at which it was achored. Thackeray's things, as I have been showing, express his preoccupation with time. They are there not only to give a physical texture to the world he creates, nor as symbols for its conceptual import, though they do have both those values too. But they have value as they have accumulated associations, as they collect the past. That is why he gives his things histories: they recur, both within a given novel, and, with different import, as motifs, from one novel to another. Ribbons are flaunted, with varying implications, by Beatrix in the Augustan age, by Horrocks the butler's daughter and would-be baronet's lady in the Regency, by Ethel in the mid-Victorian world of *The Newcomes*; and ribbons also decorate the breast of Lord Steyne, that most prestigious and degenerate of noblemen, and of Altamont, the bigamist, army deserter, and fraud. Swords shed the blood of Lord Castlewood in Leicester Fields, dangle as the threat of hereditary madness over the children of the Gaunt family, decorate the walls of the newly established Clavering residence in Grosvenor Place, and hang by the side of the gentle Colonel Newcome. If we look at Thackeray's recurring things, including their associative and emblematic value, we find they take us a long way into the meaning of his novels. So, in my examination of Thackeray's theme of time, I want to extend my discussion from the more obvious records of the past like documents and paintings to a number of things that, like his characters' hands, express relationships changing, time passing, death encroaching.

The meanest flower that blows had moving import for Wordsworth. Thackeray has the same eye for significant detail, the same attention for what is often below other people's notice. Take buttons, for instance: these are Foker's, when he appears in his gear as a "swell": "He had a bulldog between his legs, and in his scarlet shawl neckcloth was a pin representing another bulldog in gold: he wore . . . a green cut-away coat with basket buttons, and a white upper coat ornamented with cheese-plate buttons, on each of which was engraved some stirring incident of the road or the chase." No wonder that one can't stop at Thackeray's formally painted portraits. His tale-telling pictures not only hang on the wall, but lurk as frontispieces to family bibles, tiles on stoves, engravings on buttons. Foker is not only a picture in himself, he is all over pictures. And his buttons are little index entries on Foker the man. We have the same loving attention to significant detail in the account of Colonel Newcome's Stultz coat with its "yellow buttons, now wearing a tinge of their native copper." The coat was bought in 1821, and the colonel still considers it a distinguished and fashionable garment twelve years later. And indeed at Mrs. Newcome's soirée he is the lion of the evening, for his dress is dated enough to be picturesque, and the company is dazzled by his "flashing buttons." But Thackeray attaches more value yet to this insignificant part of a man's clothing. Remember "a certain trumpery gold sleeve-button of Mr. Esmond's" that he misses in prison immediately after Rachel's cruel and unjust denunciation of him. We meet that button again in the last sentence of the novel, when Esmond tells us, "The only jewel by which my wife sets any store, and from which she hath never parted, is that gold button she took from my arm on the day when she visited me in prison, and which she wore ever after, as she told me, on the tenderest heart in the world." That is the final clinching clue that Esmond and the reader need in order to know that Rachel loved him at the very day of her husband's death, and while she was blaming him for it: that she was disguising a guilty and adulterous love; and that the book has been throughout—what careless readers missed—a record of the love story of Rachel and Henry Esmond.

Gold sleeve-buttons figure elsewhere in the novels as the trustworthy tokens of true love. When Rawdon prepares for a duel with Lord Steyne, he gives his comrade and second certain not very coherent instructions about his son: "I say, Mac, if anything goes wrong—if I drop—I should like you to—to go and see him, you know: and say that I was very fond of him, and that. And—dash it—old chap, give him these gold sleeve-buttons: it's all I've got." Similarly, in the opening paragraph of *Pendennis*, where the major's period and allegiances are defined by his heroes, Brummell, Wellington, and the Duke of York, we can tell where his heart lies when we learn that he wears on his wristbands "handsome gold buttons given to him by his Royal Highness the Duke of York." (The Duke of York —the same of whom it was slanderously chanted in the nursery rhyme that he marched his men to the top of the hill and marched them down again—was a favourite figure of Thackeray's for placing his characters in time. He appears upsidedown on his column in the cover design for *Vanity Fair*; and crusty old Lord Ringwood in *Philip* and Denis Duval were both born in the same year with the Duke, and the period of each novel is fixed by our meeting the one in his old age, the other in his childhood and youth.)

Thackeray generally associates gifts of gold with truth and enduring love. Little Miles Warrington in *The Virginians*, when his parents and all the world turn from George Warrington and Theo in their poverty, brings them his gold moidore, which they carefully preserve for its associative rather than its cash value. Colonel Newcome's gift to his favourite Ethel is a gold watch. On the other hand, diamonds are nearly always associated with vanity and a cold-hearted pursuit of prestige. Dr. Firmin's signal is his flashy diamond ring. Blanche Amory jilts Pen for Foker when Foker has come into his father's fortune and gives her "oh, such a magnificent serpentine bracelet, with such a blazing ruby head and diamond tail!" Vanity Fair fairly glitters with diamonds. When Dobbin lends George the money to buy the love-lorn little Amelia a present, George characteristically spends it on a trinket for himself, a diamond shirt-pin. We all remember the tableau of Lady Bareacres in Brussels on the day of Waterloo, sitting in her horseless carriage, with her diamonds sewn into her stays. Those diamonds have a history too, and Becky manages to score off Lady Bareacres again by mentioning them at the dinner at Gaunt House: ". . . everybody's eyes looked into their neighbours'. The famous diamonds had undergone a famous seizure, it appears, about which Becky, of course, knew nothing." The Bareacres have come down in the world, a fall indicated by the fate of their diamonds, and Becky knows just how to put her finger on the fact.

But Becky herself is a diamond collector. Diamonds in effect are her price. There is a marvellous little scene that calls on all Becky's skill in judicious lying, when she is decked in diamonds for her presentation at court, in the company of her husband and his brother. Now the diamonds have come from two sources, neither of them known to her husband, though one is known to his brother Pitt, who has his panicky little qualms of guilt about his clandestine present to his sister-in-law. So when Rawdon asks, "Where the doose did you get the diamonds, Becky?" Becky has her work cut out to answer to the satisfaction of both brothers.

> Becky looked at her husband, and then at Sir Pitt, with an air of saucy triumph, as much as to say, 'Shall I betray you?'
> 'Guess!' she said to her husband. 'Why, you silly man,' she continued, 'where do you suppose I got them—all except the little clasp, which a dear friend of mine gave me long ago. I hired them, to be sure. I hired them at Mr. Polonius's in Coventry Street.' (*Vanity Fair*, ch. 48)

So Sir Pitt and Rawdon are satisfied—Sir Pitt has not been betrayed, and must be warmed by the appellation of "dear friend"; and neither knows the source of all the other diamonds, which are real enough; "but Lord Steyne," we soon hear, "who was in his place at Court, . . . knew whence the jewels came, and who paid for them."

> As he bowed over her he smiled, and quoted the hackneyed and beautiful lines, from the *Rape of the Lock*, about Belinda's diamonds, 'which Jews might kiss and infidels adore.'
> 'But I hope your lordship is orthodox,' said the little lady, with a toss of her head. (*Vanity Fair*, ch. 48)

And so Becky handles her men. But that air of proprietorship with which Steyne bows over her, and his gloating sexual reference, are signals that Becky is sold and the goods are his. The showdown comes soon afterwards, when Becky is again "in a brilliant full toilette, her arms and all her fingers sparkling with bracelets and rings; and the brilliants on her breast which Steyne had given her." When she implores him to tell Rawdon she is innocent, he retorts, "You innocent! Why, every trinket you have on your body is paid for by me." The body has gone along with the trinkets. Rawdon's instinct for justice (like Thackeray's for the final telling detail in his biggest scene) is absolutely accurate when "he tore the diamond ornament out of her breast, and flung it at Lord Steyne. It cut him on his bald forehead. Steyne wore the scar to his dying day." The scene derives a great deal of its power from that specificity about the diamonds, the "serpents, and rings, and baubles," and our knowledge of their history. And it is marvellously enhanced by that last sentence about Steyne's scar that places it in the larger span of time. Thackeray's scene does not begin and end with itself: it is a culmination of what has passed, and it reverberates into the future.

We are not finished with those diamonds yet. Mademoiselle Fifine, the French maid, prudently collects the scattered trinkets, and quietly absconds with them, and with all the other portables she can lay her hands on. "The game, in her opinion, was over in that little domestic establishment." And she is perfectly right. Becky's world, the brilliant and hollow ménage in Curzon Street, has collapsed. Her diamonds have proved to be vanity and emptiness.

Beatrix's diamonds in *Henry Esmond* also have a history. They belong first to old Isabel, locally known to the no-Popery crowds as Jezebel. She always wears them in public, and is rumoured even to wear them in bed. But part with her diamonds at last she must; and she leaves them, no very propitious legacy, along with her other property to Henry Esmond. The rest of her effects he sells, but the diamonds, "having a special use for them," he keeps. He too has his plans to invest in human flesh, though unlike Lord Steyne he doesn't usually speculate in that property. But the flesh he has a mind to— Beatrix's—is costly. The diamonds alone can be no more than a scant deposit on so desirable a property, and when Esmond loses Beatrix herself to the Duke of Hamilton, who can afford the whole price, he gives her the diamonds as a wedding-present before the marriage. They give him at least some rights of ownership, and his reflections are like Steyne's, Pope reference and all, though he doesn't actually voice them:

> She gave a cry of delight, for the stones were indeed very handsome, and of great value; and the next minute the necklace was where

70

Belinda's cross is in Mr. Pope's admirable poem, and glittering on the whitest and most perfectly-shaped neck in all England. (*Esmond*, III, ch. 4)

Esmond and Lord Steyne, "*noble coeur*" and libertine, are made of the same flesh and blood. The suggestion that the gift of the diamonds confers partial ownership is made clear in the following scene, where the Duke of Hamilton interrupts Beatrix just as she is about to "[pay] her cousin with a price, that he would have liked no doubt to receive from those beautiful rosy lips of hers," and disputes Esmond's right to give diamonds to the future Duchess of Hamilton.

After the Duke's death, Beatrix tries to return the ill-fated wedding-present. But Esmond has meanwhile thought of a way to make up the full price, and he wants her to keep the down payment.

'If I do something you have at heart; something worthy of me and you; something that shall make me a name with which to endow you; will you take it? . . . If I bring back that you long for, that I have a thousand times heard you pray for, will you have no reward for him who has done you that service? Put away those trinkets, keep them: . . . I swear a day shall come when there shall be a feast in your house, and you shall be proud to wear them.' (*Esmond*, III, ch. 7)

Esmond bargains with and for Beatrix—I bid my diamonds and the restoration of the Stuart dynasty for the hand and body of Beatrix Esmond, he says in effect. Beatrix, who is like Becky part agent and part object in the transaction, chaffers with him, and perhaps resolves like Becky to render as little property for the price as she can manage. When the time comes that Esmond has brought the prince back to England they remind each other of the deal: "Esmond looked at Beatrix, blazing with her jewels on her beautiful neck. 'I have kept my word,' says he: 'And I mine,' says Beatrix, looking down on the diamonds." But as Steyne is wounded by his own diamond brooch, so Esmond's diamonds are ironically the means of his losing her to the prince:

A light shone out of her eyes; a gleam bright enough to kindle passion in any breast. There were times when this creature was so handsome, that she seemed, as it were, like Venus revealing herself a goddess in a flash of brightness. She appeared so now; radiant, and with

71

eyes bright with a wonderful lustre. A pang, as of rage and jealousy, shot through Esmond's heart, as he caught the look she gave the prince. (*Esmond*, III, ch. 9)

Instead of receiving his bride for his bride-price, he finds he has merely decked her for another bridegroom. When you trade in the markets of Vanity Fair, you don't always get the goods you bargained for.

A passage like that I just quoted, incidentally, shows that Thackeray is not offering us the cheap moralizing that tells us diamonds are trash. He knows and shows that they are beautiful and desirable, and women like Becky and Beatrix, decked in their jewels, not only look brilliant, but *are* brilliant. The diamonds can indeed confer a magical beauty—they have more than just a cash value on the market. So much the more are they to be feared; so much the greater is the fall when all Becky's splendour is reduced to a heap of baubles that the maid absconds with. Esmond and Rachel can be saved from that fate when "our diamonds are turned into ploughs and axes for our plantations."

Beatrix is also associated with ribbons—ribbons are useful emblems for Thackeray, for they economically link two themes: as decorations both for the beautiful woman and the distinguished man, they represent the two vain quests, for beauty and for worldly success. Beatrix's new scarlet ribbon, which she puts on for Esmond's benefit on his homecoming, sets the tone for that marvellous scene in which he is confronted and mastered by her beauty: "From one of these [doors], a wax candle in her hand, and illuminating her, came Mistress Beatrix—the light falling indeed upon the scarlet ribbon which she wore, and upon the most brilliant white neck in the world." There follows the brilliant description of Beatrix's descent of the stairs, in which everything—the glow and concentration of the light, the angle of vision from the worshipper upwards to the goddess, the manifest consciousness of youth and power before melancholy maturity—visibly presents the kind of relationship that is to exist between these two for some ten years. It is a vivid and memorable moment, but as usual in Thackeray, a moment set in time. The paragraph begins, "Esmond had left a child and found a woman"; and ends "As he thinks of her, he who writes feels young again, and remembers a paragon."

Beatrix's ribbon, her beauty and her pride in it, the bond by which she holds Esmond, is like Becky's green silk purse for Jos. To recall again Thackeray's favourite Pope, they are the "slight lines" by which beauty may draw us "with a single hair." We are not allowed to forget Beatrix and her ribbons. Presently we see her "ordering her ribbons . . . before the glass"—an image that prompts Esmond to moralize, "She never at that time could be brought to think but of the world and her beauty." And when Esmond saves her brother by fighting Mohun himself, and the family presents him in form with a sword "with a blue ribbon for a sword-knot," Beatrix tells him as she playfully dubs him knight, "I give the ribbon." From the red ribbon on the woman's neck, to the blue ribbon on the sword, to the obsession of the nobleman who wastes his life "caballing for a blue ribbon." (Thackeray's Roundabout Paper "On Ribbons" is concerned with awards and decorations, rather than the ornamental ribbons of ladies.) Here Thackeray ties in Beatrix's beauty with that other vain pursuit, the competition for royal recognition. As George Worth points out, Beatrix is connected with all Esmond's false quests—Roman Catholicism, the Stuart cause, advancement by service to faithless princes—and in the culminating scene of the novel we see Esmond withdraw from the secret closet in Castlewood the family documents and titles, the long accumulations of the Esmonds' sacrifices and false expectations from the Stuarts, and burn them before the prince, Beatrix's seducer. They include the marquisate, "that precious title that lies in ashes, and this inestimable yard of blue ribbon. I lay this at your feet and stamp upon it: I draw this sword, and break it and deny you." In stamping on the ribbon Esmond frees himself simultaneously from Beatrix and the false goals that have been involved in his pursuit of her. The history of what Esmond does with diamonds and ribbons is a miniature emblematic history of his own development. By stamping on a ribbon and turning diamonds into ploughshares he redefines himself and his values.

There are other personal adornments that Thackeray uses

recurrently and emblematically through the novels. Rouge is one of his comic motifs—he delighted in contrasting the blush, the "pretty symbol of youth, and modesty, and beauty," with the externally applied pigment that lays false claim to those qualities. It is the old opposition of innocence and experience. *The Virginians*, set in the heyday of "painting," has constant references to blushing and rouging. Harry never doubts that his elderly Maria's cheeks are naturally rosy, but is understandably disturbed in the jolting carriage when the rest of her face turns "jonquil" while her bright red cheeks "continued to blush as it seemed with a strange metallic bloom." The most memorable rouge-pot in the novels is Becky's, prudently stowed in the bed at the Elephant, along with the brandy-bottle and plate of broken meats—other emblems of the advanced stage of Experience she has reached—before the visit of her innocent victim Jos.

When young Harry Esmond first sees the viscountess Isabel, her "face was daubed with white and red up to the eyes, to which the paint gave an unearthly glare: she had a tower of lace on her head, under which was a bush of black curls—borrowed curls." Old Isabel has in a sense subsumed herself in her possessions and her artificial aids to beauty, and there are certain grisly suggestions sometimes that she is little more than a rag-bag of trinkets, wigs, clothing, stuffing, paint and pomatums. She is not the only figure that Thackeray sees as sacrificing humanity to empty pretension. This is his marvellous summary of George IV's identity:

> But this George, what was he? I look through all this life, and recognize but a bow and a grin. I try and take him to pieces, and find silk stockings, padding, stays, a coat with frogs and a fur collar, a star and blue ribbon, a pocket-handkerchief prodigiously scented, one of Truefitt's best nutty brown wigs reeking with oil, a set of teeth and a huge black stock, under-waistcoats, more under-waistcoats, and then nothing. (*The Four Georges*, IV)

And then nothing. Vanity and emptiness. Thackeray's dwelling on the externals of appearance recurrently suggests that the appearance is all there is, or at least that the appearance has so swelled and spread as to engulf and nullify the little stunted vestiges of the real human being. So we have Jos at his first appearance, "a very stout, puffy man, in buckskins and hessian boots" (the "puffy" suggests not substance, but the lack of it), almost swallowed in his own neckcloths; Dr. Firmin with his shirt-frill and flashing ring and glittering dentures; and Major Pendennis with his false teeth and his padding, who talks sentimentally about exchanging locks of hair while passing his fingers through his wig. They belong in the world of Blanche Amory, who is simply an encrustation of one sham pasted on another; or of Rosey Newcome, who annihilates herself, preferring "to have her opinions dealt out to her like her frocks, bonnets, handkerchiefs, her shoes and gloves, and the order thereof." A chapter initial in *The Virginians* shows two wigs making love; and the plot of the first volume of that novel turns on Lady Maria's false teeth. The person is lost in his own appurtenances. So it must be in Vanity Fair, where Becky nets a purse in which to catch her fat fish, and a young lady like Agnes Twysden in *Philip* marries not a man, but "a property."

But not all the clothes and decorations in Thackeray's novels signify vanity and emptiness. There are garments, like Colonel Newcome's Stultz coat, or Dobbin's cloak, which "had been new for the campaign of Waterloo, and had covered George and William after the night of Quatre Bras," that have gathered through time their associations of love and suffering. And these two gentlest of Thackeray's men are both associated also with shawls—Cashmere ones, usually, such gifts as befit Anglo-Indian veterans. Their banner over those they love is a shawl. The Colonel bestows a Cashmere shawl on nearly every woman in his family. Dobbin's behaviour with Amelia's shawl is an index to the progress of their relationship through the years. During the evening at Vauxhall, the night he falls in love with her, the two couples ignore him and simply make use of him: "Honest Dobbin contented himself by giving an arm to the shawls, and by paying at the door for the whole party. . . . Perhaps he felt that he would have liked to have something on his own arm besides a shawl (the people laughed at seeing the gawky young officer carrying this female burden)." To Amelia "old Dobbin" is no more than an ambulatory clothes-horse, a useful piece of furniture. After George's death, Dobbin's status improves, and he is allowed to give the shawls rather than merely to carry them. But Amelia still shamefully abuses him. At their difference over the re-introduction of Becky into the family circle she overrides his objections, and, coming downstairs with her shawl over her arm, she "ordered Dobbin to follow. He went and put her shawl—it was a white Cashmere, consigned to her by the major himself from India—over her shoulders. He saw there was nothing for it but to obey." From clothes-horse, he has become a servant. It is one of the more encouraging signs of the ultimate (though qualified) happiness of their marriage that in their reunion scene it is Amelia who unclasps Dobbin's cloak for him, and that she consigns her shawl to someone else to look after.

And Thackeray had a nostalgic fondness for swords. So far as he offers us romance and heroism in the novels, they are often attached to swords. The aspect of *Henry Esmond* that is historical romance centres on the two swords left by Father Holt in the secret closet at Castlewood, kept there by young Henry as relics of the past, and used again for "satisfaction" from the prince when Esmond has broken his own. The most stirring incident of the military campaigns is that where Webb passes the *Gazette* to Marlborough on the point of his sword. And the conferring of a sword marks Esmond's stature as the "true knight" of his family. Crossed swords are the opening image of *The Virginians*. And Colonel Newcome's two swords, "his old regulation sword" and a presentation sword from his men, are the treasured spars which his friends save for him from the general wreck of his property.

Documents, paintings, buttons, diamonds, ribbons, rouge, wigs, shawls, swords—I seem to be collecting the beginnings of a catalogue of Thackeray's recurring motifs, and I should perhaps have put them in alphabetical order. But instead I shall add to my catalogue another item—catalogues. We hear of Rawdon before his marriage that he sends Becky "shawls, kid gloves, silk stockings, gold French watches, bracelets and perfumery . . . with the profusion of blind love and unbounded credit." And it is with the profusion of a devotion to objects and unbounded imagination that Thackeray packs his novels. But his best kind of catalogue is that which is in effect the summary of a history. There are several of these in *Vanity Fair* alone. On that ominous evening when Mr. Osborne locks himself in his study to disinherit George, he opens "a drawer especially devoted to his son's affairs and papers."

> They were all marked and docketed, and tied with red tape. It was— 'From Georgy, requesting 5s., April 23, 18--; answered April 25,'—or 'Georgy about a pony, October 13,'—and so forth. . . . Here was a whip he had when a boy, and in a paper a locket containing his hair, which his mother used to wear. (*Vanity Fair*, ch. 24)

As he muses over "these memorials," "he had the child before his eyes, on a hundred different days when he remembered George." There smiles the ghost of the past again, insubstantially recreated by the little repository of relics. The list of what the maid steals from Becky's house, including the gilt Louis Quatorze candlesticks and a gold enameled snuff-box which had once belonged to Madame du Barri, is a succinct little history of the nature of Becky's Curzon Street operation, as the rouge-pot and the brandy-bottle are of her later and more disreputable way of life. Before Waterloo, Rawdon makes a "little catalogue of effects" of the items he can leave to Becky, and what they will fetch if he dies. It includes:

> My double-barril by Manton, say 40 guineas; my driving-cloak, lined with sable fur, 50£; my duelling pistols in rosewood case (same which I shot Captain Marker), 20£ . . . and so forth, over all of which articles he made Rebecca the mistress. (*Vanity Fair*, ch. 30)

It is a moving document—ill spelling, shaky grammar and all— because through the accumulated emblems of his life Rawdon is bequeathing Becky not just his property but his past—by implication, himself. And there is a touch of humility in that attaching of prices not found in the usual testator: most people contemplating their possible death dwell mentally on the sentimental value of their bequests, and tacitly assume their beneficiaries will keep them as relics. But Rawdon is content that Becky should turn his remains into ready cash.

The sale of effects after a death or a bankruptcy was a favourite scene for Thackeray. When he attended the sale at Lady Blessington's house, well after he had written of the Sedley sale, he wrote in a letter "Ah it was a strange sad picture of Wanaty Fair. My mind is all boiling up with it." It is a scene in which property, prized possessions and the love and allegiances that they represent, the happiness and the suffering and the long experience of years, all come up for auction and are sold for money to the highest bidder. In Vanity Fair everything (and everyone) is for sale. At the Sedley sale Thackeray suggests a disillusioned vision of the total human endeavour: "Down comes the hammer like fate, and we pass to the next lot." And as the people involved in the buying and selling cling to things or sacrifice them, as the speculators finger the merchandise to assess its quality and cash value, or bid for some object because of its past association or its future utility, they demonstrate themselves and their attitude to property, to experience, to life.

I have been talking about Thackeray's favourite objects, his repeating motifs, as they recur through the novels. But of course he adapts them to the issue at hand in a given novel. It would take long to demonstrate this for every novel, but perhaps I can take one novel as a specimen, and examine the orchestration of motifs in *Pendennis*.

Martin Fido and others have pointed out that *Pendennis* is a novel about art and artifice. The hero falls in love first with an actress and next with a flirt who is sham all through; and he himself aspires to be a writer. From the first paragraph on Major Pendennis, when "by a nearer inspection . . . [we see] the factitious nature of his rich brown hair," we are alerted that we are to be on the lookout for the difference between the natural and the artificial, the true and the false. The objects that appear in *Henry Esmond* with a coloring of romance and which even in *Vanity Fair* have a certain sparkle are shown here to be phonies, mere tinsel and stage props. For Becky's and Beatrix's diamonds we have the mountebank's "sham diamond ring covering the first joint of the finger and twiddling in the faces of the pit. . . . The stage has its traditional jewels as the Crown and all great families have." Jos's treasured hessian boots likewise reappear as part of an actor's costume. Instead of Beatrix's irresistible ribbons and the Castlewoods' hard-won marquisate there are the fake decorations on the breast of the imposter Altamont and the pretentious cook, Mirobolant, so that the patronising Pen comments in amusement, "By Jove, here's some more ribbon!"

The charged motion of hands in the other novels is recalled in the Fotheringay's histrionic talents on the stage:

> It was her hand and arm that this magnificent creature most excelled in, and somehow you could never see her but through them. They surrounded her. When she folded them over her bosom in resignation; when she dropped them in mute agony, or raised them in superb command; when in sportive gaiety her hands fluttered and waved before her, . . . it was with these arms and hands that she beckoned, repelled, entreated, embraced her admirers. (*Pendennis*, ch. 4)

We hear later that this is not even inspired art, for the Fotheringay is little more than an automaton who can mimic exactly and repeat her director's orders. There is the same ironic undercutting of a favourite motif in the talk about Blanche and *her* histrionic manoeuvering with "hand No. 1" and "hand No. 2." The duels that actually happen in *Esmond*, *The Virginians* and *Denis Duval* and are threatened in *Vanity Fair* and *The Newcomes* are in this novel only unseemly brawls; and Esmond's *botte de Jesuite*, by which he is the master of Lord Mohun, is replaced by Pen's transparent subterfuge of taking fencing lessons from the boozy old Costigan because he wants to be near his daughter. It is almost inevitable that at some point we should encounter, as we do, "double-handed swords and battle-axes made of *carton-pierre*."

These swords form part of the décor in the newly-decorated Clavering residence in Grosvenor Square, and Thackeray makes one of his vast lists of the trinkets and *bibelots* in the dining- and drawing-rooms:

> . . . marqueterie-tables covered with marvellous gimcracks, china ornaments of all ages and countries, bronzes, gilt daggers, Books of Beauty, yataghans, Turkish papooshes, and boxes of Parisian bonbons. Wherever you sat down there were Dresden shepherds and shepherdesses convenient at your elbow; there were, moreover, light blue poodles and ducks and cocks and hens in porcelain; there were nymphs by Boucher, and shepherdesses by Greuze, very chaste indeed. . . . (*Pendennis*, ch. 37)

It goes on for pages, and it is devastating. This stuff is not only in bad taste, a hodge-podge of borrowed articles from different cultures, a display of opulence; not only useless ("I don't advise you to try one of them gossamer gilt chairs," Lady Clavering amiably warns her guests, "*I* came down on one the night we gave our second dinner-party")—but it's abominably *new*. The décor is pronounced " 'very chaste,' that being the proper phrase." It is both virginal and sterile: a collection of souvenirs that remind no one of anything. This house is the *Pendennis* contrast to Castlewood, which is still partly a ruin from the cannon shots of the Protectorate. With its family portraits, its secret entrances for Jesuits, its secreted swords and incriminating documents—Castlewood is an accumulation of an ugly past, perhaps, but still it *has* one. And a list like this reminds us of the different quality of Rawdon's catalogue of effects or Osborne's drawerful of relics. For Thackeray the value of a place or an object lies in its freight of association. The Clavering interior has no past, and so in a sense it has no present either.

As paintings have a special function in *The Newcomes*, and cards in *The Virginians*, that novel about play and gambling, this novel about a writer features manuscripts and letters in a special role. Pen is naturally disappointed to find that the love-letters he has been keeping next to his heart were not even written by his Emily's hand, but that his actress love employed an amanuensis. Blanche's manuscript book of poems about her thorny past, *Mes Larmes*, does not bear inspection for genuineness, either: "They were not particularly briny, Miss Blanche's tears, that is the truth." We are given a specimen of "the Muse's" talent, à-propos of her little brother: " 'Oh, let me, let me love you! the world will prove to you As false as 'tis to others, but *I* am ever true.' And behold the muse was boxing the darling brother's ears instead of kneeling at his feet." Pen's own compositions, for all his striving to be honest, recurrently prove him a humbug, as he adapts poems written in passion to one woman for another, and pretends to throw his manuscript in the fire when he knows the fire is out.

And written works—whether letters, manuscripts, or books —often go through a metamorphosis that changes them from mere sequences of words into things concrete, or consumable, or sometimes almost animate. We see Pen's letters and poems to the Fotheringay tied in a parcel like a pound of sugar; the major's letters at his breakfast table are personified into their writers, and become "so many grand folks who attended his levee"; Bludyer the savage reviewer converts the books he reviews into dinner and a pint of brandy; Pen sends Blanche a box of bonbons with each sugarplum wrapped in a tender verse. If words become things, the metamorphosis works in the other direction too, so that Blanche's actual sighs and tears become *Mes Soupirs* (which runs into two editions) and *Mes Larmes*; and the cook Mirobolant makes his elaborate declaration of love to Blanche in the form of a meal composed of white and pink dishes, in honour of her name and colouring. Like Sterne in *Tristram Shandy*, Thackeray in his novel about a novelist reminds us of the interrelation of the word and the flesh, and makes his things dance in tune with his language.

Thackeray's characters are morally grouped according to their attitude to the past. His familiar rough division of humanity into those who answer to the outer directives of the world and those who answer to the inward directives of love is a rough and ready one, but it works. Becky leads the first group, Amelia the second. Thackeray sees clearly enough the disadvantages of both systems, and his most morally aware characters are those like Pendennis, Ethel and Clive Newcome, and George Warrington of *The Virginians*, who find themselves tested between the two extremes.

It is characteristic of those like Becky who are the denizens of Vanity Fair that their commitment to the past is of the slightest. At its most obvious level this independence of the past takes the form of not honouring one's debts—like Becky and Rawdon, who make a system out of living on nothing a year, or Sir Francis Clavering, who "would sign almost anything for to-morrow, provided to-day could be left unmolested." But those who haunt Vanity Fair take a more elaborate and comprehensive advantage of conveniently short memories. At one point, when the narrator has been brooding over the melancholy satire of old love letters, he lays it down as a maxim: "There ought to be a law in Vanity Fair ordering the destruction of every written document (except receipted tradesmen's bills) after a certain brief and proper interval." Becky acts essentially on this law and its implications, and her system is manifested in her treatment of things. She does hoard things —she accumulates that purse for herself in the little desk—but she hoards them not for their associative value, not for their past significance, but for their future usefulness. She intends to turn them to good account hereafter. The billet-doux from George, the picture of Jos, the banknotes from Steyne—these are her valuable versions of "receipted tradesmen's bills." They are fragments she has shored up against her ruin—and very handy they come in too, when the time comes. Of course in the case of the picture of Jos she *pretends* she has kept it for sentimental reasons, and because it reminds her of her lost love. But Becky is quite unashamed about manipulating time: remember her peculiarly heartless ploy of keeping a little half-made shirt for Rawdy that she takes out to sew when she wants to impress people with her maternal feelings—long after Rawdy has outgrown its size.

We are told of Becky after her grief at not being able to accept Sir Pitt, "Rebbecca was a young lady of too much resolution and energy of character to permit herself much useless and unseemly sorrow for the irrevocable past; so, having devoted only the proper portion of regret to it, she wisely turned her whole attention towards the future, which was now vastly more important to her." One of her snake-like attributes is her ability to slough off the past like an old skin, or like the empty trunks she leaves behind in Paris to make her landlord believe she will come back and pay his bill. And to this talent she owes much of her vitality and charm. Unlike many characters more moral, she bears no grudges. She swallows the fiery curry, and turns a joke. She downs Lady Southdown's horrible bolus, and then acts out a pantomime of the scene. She knows Dobbin is her adversary, but she likes him and does him a good turn.

Amelia, on the other hand, tends to be morbidly fixated on the past. She can muster nostalgia at the drop of a hat. After only nine days of marriage she goes to her parents in Fulham and mourns over her "dear little white bed"—and this in a house that is not the house of her childhood, but has been her family's rented lodging only since the bankruptcy. "Already to be looking sadly and vaguely back," the narrator comments: "always to be pining for something which, when obtained, brought doubt and sadness rather than pleasure: here was the lot of our poor little creature, and harmless lost wanderer in the great struggling crowds of Vanity Fair." And she continues to live up to this character through years of pointless mourning for a bad past husband, when she could have been giving herself to a good new one. It is a measure of Colonel Newcome's moral superiority to Amelia that he is ready to consign his old Stultz coat to the rag-bag when the time comes: "Get me another coat then," he tells his man; "I'm not above learning."

Thackeray maintains that distinction in attitudes to the past between his worldly and his loving characters in the other novels. The long memory is characteristic of the loving soul, but it has its concomitant disadvantage of making forgiveness almost impossible. Henry Esmond has a long memory, yet even his adoring daughter has to own of him that he would never forgive an offense. His grandson inherits this quality, and one of the central themes of *The Virginians* is that of forgiveness, and what one is to do with that awkward affair called a bygone. When young George is urged to forgive Washington, he replies, "Never, sir, as long as I remember. You can't order remembrance out of a man's mind; and a wrong that was a wrong yesterday must be a wrong tomorrow." And years later, though he has reached middle age and a temperate frame of mind, the past is still vivid before him, so that he acknowledges again: "I can't forgive; not until my days of dotage come, and I cease remembering anything." On the other hand, his worldly aunt and cousin, Beatrix and Lady Maria, are not gnawed by the same pangs of lasting resentment. If they can't eliminate the past, they can at least set it aside temporarily, as it were, and for mutual convenience:

> What can there be finer than forgiveness? . . . It was beautiful, for instance, to see our two ladies at Tunbridge Wells forgiving one another, smiling, joking, fondling almost in spite of the hard words of yesterday—yes; and forgetting bygones, though they couldn't help remembering them perfectly well. (*Virginians*, ch. 38)

There is the same opposition between Agnes Twysden and Caroline Brandon, the "Little Sister," in *Philip*. Agnes is ready without regret to "shake hands forever, cancel all her vows" when a more eligible suitor than Philip comes courting: "She will give him up—she will give him up. Good-bye, Philip. Good-bye the past. Be forgotten, be forgotten, fond words!" But the gentle Little Sister has a long memory for a wrong, and she reproaches her father for his past cruelty with some vindictiveness: "I forgive you; but a hundred thousand billion years can't mend that injury, father, while you broke a poor child's heart with it that day!"

So the otherwise good and loving Henry Esmond, Rachel, Helen Pendennis, Laura, Colonel Newcome, George Warrington and Caroline Brandon are all grudge-bearers, and become at some stage moral tyrants, because it is as impossible for them to forgive as to forget.

Between them and the shallow characters like Clavering and Agnes, there is another breed of hybrids whose creed is the world's but whose memories won't die, but chain them to their other younger and more loving selves. Osborne is one of these, and that is what makes him so great a conception. He fervently believes in the pursuit of wealth as a religion, and so sees no alternative but to disown his son when he chooses "to marry a bankrupt and fly in the face of duty and fortune." But he is agonizingly tied to his love and his memories of his son. Even Lord Steyne, the figure in the novels who is closest to being damned, and indeed devilish, has moments of seeming redeemable when his memory connects him with his past:

> 'The young one is in a scrape, [he says of Pendennis.] I was myself— when I was in the fifth form at Eton—a market gardener's daughter— and swore I'd marry her. I was mad about her—poor Polly!' Here he made a pause, and perhaps the past rose up to Lord Steyne, and George Gaunt was a boy again not altogether lost. (*Pendennis*, ch. 14)

A man's estrangement from his own past is powerfully realized in another of Thackeray's portrait images. The rich and irascible old Lord Ringwood doesn't dare to stay in his own grand house when he comes to town because he is surrounded there by his past, the family portraits:

ghostly images of dead Ringwoods—his dead son, who had died in his boyhood; his dead brother attired in the uniform of his day . . . ; Lord Ringwood's dead self, finally, as he appeared still a young man, when Lawrence painted him. . . . 'Ah, that's the fellow I least like to look at,' the old man would say, scowling at the picture. (*Philip*, ch. 21)

Twentieth-century existential literature can scarcely present a sharper image of alienated man. One may be alienated in space, exiled from home or country and at odds with the surrounding society; but one may also be alienated in time like Lord Ringwood, cut off from his past and his own self.

I find when I recall the title of this volume that I have not been addressing myself explicitly to the Victorian experience. But I have been concerned to communicate the Thackerayan experience, which I take to be my part of the business. I have tried to suggest how Thackeray's feeling for the past combines with his vivid apprehension of immediate detail to create a world in which time and space intersect, in which the kind of reality you can lay your hand on in a given moment is rich with philosophical and temporal implications. A study of Thackeray's things and their freight of associations takes us directly into the major themes of his novels—the pursuit of vanity, the process of change, the encroachments of death; and I have intended to reveal some aspects both of his meaning and of his technique. My scope of reference has been the six major novels, and not just *Vanity Fair* and *Henry Esmond*, which are the most familiar, because I take Thackeray's novels to be worth reading as a body. And I have deliberately quoted amply, not to say copiously. Thackeray is splendidly quotable, and I look on the quotations as the plums of the pudding for which my commentary provides the matrix. The Thackerayan experience, after all, is to be found in his text.

If I were asked why we should read and teach Thackeray in this decade of this century, my first answer would be the standard answer, and the same as for any other great writer in any decade. We study great literature because it enlarges our experience, sharpens our perceptions, satisfies our sense of beauty—acquaints us with "the best that has been known and said in the world." But to speak to Thackeray in particular: Thackeray, more than the other writers of the period, addresses himself to the very question of the relation of the present to the past. If he knew that experience is burning with a hard and gem-like flame, he also knew that the flame lives off something, and that to deny the past is as absurd as for the flame to reject the candle. Thackeray reminds us that, both personally and culturally, we are what we have been; that the past, though past, is always latent in the present. Thackeray's present has now become our past, and it "keeps a lingering hold" on us. He ends *The Newcomes* with that tactual image, and with the hope that his time and ours can remain in intimate relation in the world of his novels: "Friendly reader! may you and the author meet there on some future day! He hopes so; as he yet keeps a lingering hold of your hand, and bids you farewell with a kind heart."

---

1. I would like in a single footnote to express my gratitude to the number of Thackeray scholars, past and present, to whose work I feel most indebted: to George Saintsbury, whose edition of the novels I have used as my text; to G. K. Chesterton, John Dodds, Geoffrey Tillotson, Lionel Stevenson, Gordon Ray, John Tilford, Dorothy van Ghent, George Worth, William Marshall, Henri Talon, Myron Taube, Martin Fido, John Loofbourow, Jean Sudranne, Joan Stevens and Barbara Hardy.

EMILY AND NORA AND DOROTHY AND PRISCILLA AND JEMIMA AND CARRY

RUTH apROBERTS

"They lived happily ever after" is a good ending for a fairy tale; how they didn't, is a good subject for a novel. Courtships are the stuff of novels, too, of course, but most typically of the novels called romantic. It is one of the distinguishing achievements of the nineteenth-century realistic English novel that it is often concerned with what happened after the wedding. Courtships are still the subject, too—how could they *not* be! Pairings, sortings, choosings, rejections—form a large part of our lives and interests, if, like the Wife of Bath, we are *nat religious*, that is, not dedicated to celibacy on religious grounds. The Victorian concern with pairings had a new urgency: with the old certainties being questioned on every side, the ways of courtship and marriage were being newly assessed. Certain ways of thinking about sex were available, to be tested one against the other, and mutually adjusted. The legacy of the romantic revival, sexual love as a saving grace, becomes for the most part legitimized in marriage—take the Brownings, for example, both in practice and in poetry. Taken further, in Patmore's Angel-in-the-House poetry, ideal married love is further legitimized, as an earnest of God's love, and so on, and taken so far that theology becomes somewhat embarrassingly sexy. Another strain of woman-worship comes in from an oddly different source—Comte's Religion of Humanity with its emphasis on women as our moral teachers. On the other hand there is the legacy of Jane Austen:

the prudential and economic side of courtship and marriage, bound to emerge with a fresh exigency in an age so bound up with shifting economies as the Victorian. Love, lust, romance, God, and money are all to be newly adjusted to each other in the changing culture of the time. Perhaps Anthony Trollope shows us the ways of the adjustment better than anyone else, with his intelligent awareness of man in society and his detailed psychological realism. Of course if you know women—or people in general—you won't worship them. And one of the recurrently astonishing things about Trollope, then and now, is how well he knows and presents women. George Eliot and Jane Austen are marvelous on women but tend to be weak on men. Trollope seems to have no such limitation sexually. He's weak on rustics, the lower class in general, and avoids children.[1] But with literate men and women, he's one of the greatest.

But all these Victorian men-women relationships, aren't they hopelessly dated? Haven't we changed all that, with female suffrage, divorce laws, property laws, contraception and abortion, the de-fusing of obscenity, and the great contemporary flowering of pornography? Well, we have changed—some. Marriage contracts are less dependent on financial considerations, divorce is easier, parenthood can be planned. How is it then that all our old literatures of love are not invalidated? Dante? Chaucer? Shakespeare? Or older than all these, that *Tale of Genji* that Lady Murasaki wrote at the Japanese court at Kyoto in about 1000 A.D. In the society she describes, courtship proceeds with the two lovers on either side of a screen; one concerns oneself with calligraphy and the texture and color and folding of the paper for a love-letter, with the observation of gardens and with the mixing of perfumes. What could be more remote! And yet the record is so true and witty, Lady Murasaki has been compared not only to Jane Austen but also to Proust! After Genji dies, how the savor has gone out of life! The pleasure of his company and of loving him is so real to us that we can feel nostalgia for those good old days. It would seem indeed that there are qualities called *human* that emerge in pretty well all cultures. If the stone-age men of New Guinea had a literature, we would surely find elements we recognize, just as we recognize familiar processes in the relationship of old earth-father Jupiter and Juno his wife. To discover these familiar processes in their great rich variety of guises is a good part of humane learning. Always these processes are taking place in a cultural context, never isolated; and to observe their interplay with the cultural contexts is finally to be more aware of their interplay with our own culture. We learn better what is the variable and what is the constant, and what are the possibilities. I think that of all Victorian novelists no one was more acutely concerned with the relationship of these variables and constants than Anthony Trollope. He centers on reality with so much concern and awareness that he can be the sympathetic ironist, and can exercise the humor that comes only with complete intelligent control of one's material. So he can write about dead issues like ecclesiastical pluralism or parliamentary reform and still bring us very close to life.

As he is always concerned with men and women, he is never very far away from sex, and saw no reason to stay away. The curious thing is that all the Victorian rules of propriety don't seem to hamper him. I think he is never a prude, never embarrassed or constricted. He manages to communicate in *He Knew He Was Right* just when Emily and Louis Trevelyan break off sexual intercourse. He is able to communicate facts of bastardy, syphilis, calling a woman a *whore* (in *Is He Popenjoy?*) without ever causing a tremor in the typesetter's hand or a blush upon the cheek of the Young Person. He's able to show (in *The Belton Estate*) how Clara Amedroz rejected one suitor because of his sexual inadequacy and took another because he was gloriously adequate. In that book—old proser that he is— he breaks out into a poetic little anti-Puritan hymn; it is not his best writing, but it helps you to know the man.

> Why has the world been made so pleasant? Why is the fruit of the earth so sweet; and the trees,—why are they so green; and the mountains so full of glory? Why are women so lovely? and why is it that the activity of man's mind is the only sure forerunner of man's progress? In listening thrice a day to outpourings from the clergyman at Perivale there was certainly no activity of mind (VIII).[2]

It seems good to celebrate with both mind and body, then. In the *Autobiography* he defends the sexuality of his characters,

89

> downright honest love, in which there was no pretence on the part of the
> lady that she was too ethereal to be fond of a man. . . . Each of them
> longed for the other, and they were not ashamed to say so.[3]

He loves Shakespeare's Rosalind because "she knew herself
and what she was about, and loved her lover right heartily"
(*Vicar of Bullhampton VIII*). He knows and accepts the "right
true end of love" without cavil. When he was in America at
Newport Beach he hated the way they swam in elaborate bath-
ing clothes, for he loved to swim naked himself. "I love to jump
into the deep clear sea from off a rock, and I love to be ham-
pered by no outward impediment as I do so."[4] It is an image to
be cherished. Such a man will treat of sexual relationships, one
feels, in a better way than—Patmore, say. And his treatment of
sexual relationships may still be valid to us even if the mores of
that hundred years ago are very remote.

We are finding these days, anyhow, that even though the
mores have changed, it is enlightening to go back to that time
when the necessity for change was being recognized. Ibsen's
Doll's House seems timely now, and the issues it raised aren't
quite settled yet. And of all Trollope's novels, *He Knew He
Was Right* centers most closely on the marriage relationship,
and it too raises issues that are not quite dead. The novel is
specifically about marriage, the main framework story being a
contest for what the Wife of Bath called the "maistrie in marriage"; and it is literally an internecine contest, in that it results
directly in the death of one of the contestants. It is a case that
brings the issue into the sharpest relief, then. For what seems a
mere crotchet in the husband, a slight and barely blameworthy
crotchet, a tendency to want his own way, which most people of
the time might tend to condone rather than condemn, this crotchet, through a combination of quite believable and probable
circumstances, develops in Louis Trevelyan into a psychosis
that destroys him. The drama of the story is mostly psychological, a series of "games," ploys and counterploys, one-uppings
and down-puttings, that build by delicately traced processes
into a sensational dénouement. Giradoux says somewhere that
Clytemnestra killed her husband because of the way he crooked
his little finger. *He Knew He Was Right* is a demonstration
of how trivialities can build into tragedy that is only too
convincing.

Within the frame of this main story, there are some subsidiary stories that have traditionally been said to have been put
in to "alleviate the gloom" of the main. They do alleviate the
gloom, all right, in case you can't stand a perfectly compelling
and thought-provoking drama of two sympathetic characters
and how their marriage broke up. And these sub-stories are diverting in themselves, often funny, satirical, or moving—the
usual charms of Victorian novels. But as it becomes clear that
this novel is primarily about marriage, all these "alleviating"
sub-stories present themselves very pointedly to show how
women "find themselves" in relation to the marriage question.
We discover, altogether, a great variety of roles in a great variety of situations, all variations on the strong central theme.

There is a sort of urgency about this novel. Trollope was
writing it from November 1867 to June 1868. John Stuart
Mill's *The Subjection of Women* was not to be published until
1869; but he and others had already formulated "The Woman
Question." The essay on "The Enfranchisement of Women"
had been published anonymously in the *Westminster Review*
in 1851; though probably written by Harriet Taylor it was generally thought to be by Mill.[5] And so the association of Mill
with feminism, and with the American movement in particular
as noted in the Essay, was commonly enough known to be part
of the data of the novel. But at the very time of Trollope's writing, Mill was making speeches in parliament, on the admission of women to the electoral franchise, published 1867, and
on the married women's property bill, published 1868.
Trollope was almost certainly following parliamentary debates
at the time. He had given up the Post Office position, had written his study of Palmerston, and was at work on the series of
novels called "parliamentary," in which he demonstrates his
knowledge of contemporary politics both practical and theoretical; and then in November of 1868 himself stood (unsuccessfully) as Liberal candidate in the general election. *Is He
Popenjoy?* is another of Trollope's novels that is primarily
about marriage, again very distinguished for sympathy and intelligence in dealing with role-determination in a difficult
marriage, and it has a satirical picture of the feminists. Written
much later, 1874-75, it has still a great deal of seriousness-in-
humor. But it is less urgent than *He Knew*, more detached and

91

serene. I think *He Knew* in the intensity of its concern relates directly to the contemporary questions as posed by Mill—his name even comes up (see below).

This novel probably has a relevance to Trollope's own life, too, that was proposed by Bradford A. Booth.[6] Trollope had at this period a warm friendship with a bright young American woman, Kate Field—writer, lecturer and feminist—and in his letters to her he shows his concern for the developing role of the professional woman. "I never said you were like W. Petrie,"[7] he writes, W. Petrie being the formidable female American poet in this novel. *He Knew He Was Right* unquestionably reflects the results of his musings on femininism per se, and also on the encounter of the new American ways with the old English ones, in a somewhat Jamesian way—all, I think, with a special concern that came out of care for Kate.

The center of the novel, about which all these concerns are deployed, is the marriage of Louis and Emily Trevelyan. Trevelyan is twenty-four, handsome, well-connected, Cambridge, has already published a volume of poems, has £3,000 a year perfectly secure, when he meets on his travels Emily Rowley, twenty, eldest daughter of the Governor of the Mandarin Islands, and woos her and marries her. The marriage market being what it is and the Rowleys so remote from it, Trevelyan is "a very pearl," well-thought of, honorable and generous: Emily's sister Nora is welcomed into the house in London and shall have her chance at the eligible males of the season. There is just one ominous little note—a cloud no bigger than a man's hand: when Emily's father Sir Marmaduke regrets aloud to Trevelyan that none of his eight girls will have so much as a penny piece for dowry, Trevelyan reassures him:

> "It is my idea that girls should not have fortunes. At any rate, I am quite sure that men should never look for money. A man must be more comfortable, and, I think, is likely to be more affectionate, when the money has belonged to himself" (I).

This is generous and reassuring certainly. The father would have liked, however, to have had money to give, "but having no thousands of pounds to hand over, he could not but admire the principles of his son-in-law." Our conditions must of necessity shape our opinions, Trollope is suggesting. And he is also anticipating already how an economic inferiority may decrease one's leverage. The mother Lady Rowley senses the difficulty; Trevelyan is a pearl, all right, but "he likes to have his own way."

> "But his way is such a good way," said Sir Marmaduke. "He will be such a good guide for the girls!"
> "But Emily likes her way too," said Lady Rowley.
> Sir Marmaduke argued the matter no further, but thought, no doubt, that such a husband as Louis Trevelyan was entitled to have his own way. He probably had not observed his daughter's temper so accurately as his wife had done. With eight of them coming up around him, how should he have observed their tempers? (I)

Everything goes on very well for a while. There is a charming baby boy. Nora is with them in London and meets people. But Emily receives a call from an old family friend, one Colonel Osborne, and Louis Trevelyan objects.

> "If I am suspected [says Emily to Nora], life will not be worth having."
> "How can you talk of being suspected, Emily?"
> "What does he mean then by saying that he would rather not have Colonel Osborne here? A man older than my father, who has known me since I was a baby!" (I)

Emily is very outraged and very righteous and we might well take her side completely; it all comes of her being subject to, as she says, "her master." But Nora, who is full of good sense and sympathy, advises her to forget it. Colonel Osborne is in truth older than her father—by about a month; he did know her as a baby—having glimpsed her briefly. And Emily's words are "more true in the letter than in the spirit." Osborne happens to be rather an old goat—not so bad as to be an adulterer, "not fiendish, not a ravening wolf," but bad enough to enjoy making a little trouble. It flatters his vanity, that he can still do that much—and he has. Everyone knows that Augustus Poole had to take his young wife off to Naples because of the gossip due to Osborne's indiscretion. "He was fond of intimacies with married ladies, and perhaps was not averse to the excitement of marital hostility."

A young husband may dislike the too-friendly bearing of a friend, and may yet abstain from that outrage on his own dignity and on his wife, which is conveyed by a word of suspicion. Louis Trevelyan having taken a strong dislike to Colonel Osborne, and having failed to make his wife understand that this dislike should have induced her to throw cold water upon the Colonel's friendship, had allowed himself to speak a word which probably he would have wittingly recalled as soon as spoken (I).

So the battle lines are drawn up. There are points at which Trevelyan almost relents, but Emily's righteous dignity makes her say, oh, so righteously, those things that further provoke him, and the animosity is kept warm. How these two rational and decent people can quarrel and how the hostility develops, is traced with the most meticulous and delicate art, that really does, as they say, defy summary. Especially in these first five chapters of the book, there is not a word wasted, not a gesture that does not tell. And, most remarkable, we sympathize with both of them. Even that fear of foreign-ness that is part of our psychologies, and plays so large a part in *Othello*, plays a small part here. "He thought he could remember to have heard it said . . . that no man should look for a wife from among the tropics . . ." (V). This seems to me to communicate a breath of a fear of Trevelyan's that Emily might be somewhat oversexed. Her anger, of course, galls him. He makes the mistake of asking his friend dear old Lady Milborough to "speak to" Emily; Lady Milborough is one of those old women whom spirited young women find trying anyway—she had previously been tedious on the subject of Guiness' stout for nursing mothers—and Emily bridles at being "spoken to" and things are worse than ever.

Now Colonel Osborne is an M.P., with connections in the Colonial Office; an investigation of colonial government is afoot, the committee chosen—and two governors are to be chosen to report to the committee. How very nice if he could use his influence to arrange that Emily's father be brought to London, for a visit and holiday, and to report to the committee! He intimates the possibility to Emily, and she naturally and innocently finds it a good plan if he can "manage" it. No, not "manage" it, Emily, he warns. It might appear to be "jobbery" if so referred to. Our conversation on this must be

secret—*even from your husband*. So now there is a secret, and
of course this turns out to be further gall for Trevelyan. We
suspect later, anyway, that Colonel Osborne might have wanted
it kept secret because it had in fact been already settled; if
it was generally known, he is robbed of his credit in Emily's
eyes for "managing" it, and robbed of an occasion for tête-à-
têtes with Emily. Actually, it is so widely talked of that Trevelyan himself hears of it from several sources—in fact "All the
town had heard of it except himself." He confronts Emily with
this, and she is obliged to say she had indeed heard of it, but
it was to be kept a secret between her and Osborne. Poor
Louis of course is furious, rather understandably, but goes too
far: "You shall not see Colonel Osborne. Do you hear me? . . .
by G—, you shall obey me." So now we have an out-and-out
order given, and Emily icily obeys—but explains to him the
nature of the insult: "If I am fit to be told that I must promise
not to see any man living, I cannot be fit to be any man's wife."

Emily is magnificently logical and effective in the sparring
matches, and Trevelyan is pitiable—to a point. He *is* hard driv-
en. After observing a letter, innocent, of course, from Osborne
to his wife, he forbids her to correspond, as well as ever to see
the man. "Of course you will understand that this is not supposed to extend to accidental meetings. . . ." Thereby hangs a
point: accidental meetings do happen in civilized society, and
make uncivilized prohibitions look absurd. There is a sort of
reconciliation, but she gives way "so cunningly that the husband received none of the gratification which he had expected
in her surrender," and he is riled and gives word to the servant that Osborne is not to be admitted to his wife—"and felt
thoroughly ashamed." Osborne addresses a letter to Emily
with a vital piece of information about the parental visit.
Trevelyan is obliged by his own prohibition to intercept and
read it. He asks her to read the letter. She refuses. "As you
have supposed [his letters] to be poisoned I will have nothing
to do with them." Osborne says he will call to report. Trevelyan
asks Emily to receive him; she refuses "because Louis has made
me promise that I will never willingly be in his company again."
"So far he had hardly gained much by the enforced obedience
of his wife." He meant to have acted high-mindedly, but his

actions now appear mean; he vacillates through tenderness, and she takes advantage of his vacillation.

On a Sunday walk together, Trevelyan is

> quite aware that he was being treated as a naughty boy, who was to be forgiven. . . .. Emily worked very hard at her mission of forgiveness, and hardly ceased in her efforts at conciliatory conversation. Women can work so much harder in this way than men find it possible to do! She never flagged, but continued to be fluent, conciliatory, and impossibly wearisome (VI).

And then the accidental meeting happens. They encounter Osborne in the company of Trevelyan's good friend Hugh Stanbury, in whom Nora has a strong interest. Naturally Hugh and Nora join forces, leaving Osborne with Trevelyan and Emily. Osborne addresses Emily with a caressing tone that rubs Trevelyan raw, but it is Emily who makes a scene. "Louis, we will go back if you please." Later, Trevelyan reproves her: "It was quite unnecessary, Emily, that you should behave like that." "Your suspicions," she answers, "have made it almost impossible for me to behave with propriety." In short, Trevelyan is made to feel such a fool for having given an order, that he remands the order, and Emily then takes the most elaborate care to obey the counter-order, and see Osborne quite as though nothing had happened—or with only a little more pointedness.

When Trollope was in the Post Office, he took great care in writing his reports. But, he tells us in the *Autobiography*,

> I do not think that they were regarded with favour. I have heard horror expressed because the old forms were disregarded and language used which had no savour of red-tape. During the whole of this work in the Post Office it was my principle always to obey authority in everything instantly, but never to allow my mouth to be closed as to the expression of my opinion. . . . When carrying out instructions which I knew should not have been given, I never scrupled to point out the fatuity of an improper order in the strongest language I could decently employ. I have revelled in these official correspondences, and look back to some of them as the greatest delights of my life.

And again:

> How I loved, when I was contradicted . . . to do instantly as I was bid, and then to prove that what I was doing was fatuous, dishonest, expensive, and impracticable. And then there were feuds,—such delicious

feuds! I was always an anti-Hillite, acknowledging, indeed, the great thing which Sir Rowland Hill had done for the country [the penny-post, in a word], but believing him to be entirely unfit to manage men or arrange labour. It was a pleasure to me to differ from him on all occasions. . . .⁸

It will be seen from this how well Trollope himself knew how to exploit obedience as a weapon; Emily uses precisely the same ploy. It is a ploy, let it be noted, that can be used with effect by the underling against the "master"; the underling can thereby gain the upper hand, and make the tyrant look a fool, which is perhaps the most painful form of punishment. The Civil Service must be run as a hierarchy, one supposes, but whether a marriage should be so run is the very question here. On another case, in *The Belton Estate* (1866), Trollope comments:

> The theory of man and wife—that special theory in accordance with which the wife is to bend herself in loving submission before her husband—is very beautiful; and would be good altogether if it could only be arranged that the husband should be the stronger and greater of the two. The theory is based upon that hypothesis;—and the hypothesis sometimes fails of confirmation. In ordinary marriages the vessel rights itself, and the stronger and the greater takes the lead, whether clothed in petticoats, or in coat, waistcoat, and trousers; but there sometimes comes a terrible shipwreck, when the woman before marriage has filled herself full with ideas of submission, and then finds that her golden-headed god has got an iron body and feet of clay (XI).

Trollope at the Post Office could exult in advantages won, but Emily can win all the moral victories and still lose all her chance of happiness and even her child. It becomes abundantly clear that the spring of the trouble lies in Trevelyan's assumption of power, his interpretation of the obedience clause in the agreement. In theory he knows equality is right and thinks he grants it, but the economic factor works against it. "In his anger, he could not keep himself from thinking of the gifts he had showered on her." He is a man who is far above extra-marital interests himself; and yet he would feel (with most of his contemporaries) that a sexual peccadillo on his part would be much less culpable than a breath of slander on her. He is a man whose culture has fostered an idea of superiority over women, and circumstances are such that he, with only a slight degree more than ordinary self-importance, is victimized by the assumption of that superiority. Emily's logic is unassailable: ". . . he shall not make me say I have been wrong when I know I have been right." She is surely to be admired for rejecting the martyr's role Trollope describes elsewhere, in a certain Mrs. Morton who is the hero's mistress in *Sir Harry Hotspur of Humblethwaite* (1871):

> The woman was patient to a marvel, long-bearing, affectionate, imbued with that conviction so common to women and the cause of so much delight to men—that ill usage and suffering are intended for women . . . (XI).

But since neither Emily nor Trevelyan will give in, there is no hope. "The truth was that each desired that the other should acknowledge a fault, and that neither of them would make that acknowledgement." Admirable warriors!

A separation is inevitable. Trevelyan makes an arrangement for Emily and the child, and Nora, to live in the country with the family of Hugh Stanbury; and Osborne, quite aware of the trouble he makes, makes a call. Trevelyan has stooped to the hiring of a private detective, Bozzle, the ex-policeman, who spies on Osborne and reports the call, and Trevelyan is further degraded. One might well, when Bozzle first comes on the scene, feel disappointed that Trollope is turning to the comic caricature, doing the Dickensian kind of thing to which he would still occasionally be tempted, although it is so alien to his psychological realism. The name is so offensively cute, the cockney facetiousness so depressing. And yet it all works out with great effect, I believe. Trevelyan in his obsession has alienated all his friends, even Lady Milborough, and is driven in the intensity of his desire for proof to this low means, this low character. Bozzle is the sort of winking comic cynic who is very knowing about how all women sneak off to meet their lovers. Trevelyan hates himself for dealing with such a man and feels defiled. It is part of the nightmare of his degradation that he is reduced to dealing with a Dickensian caricature.

Trollope himself felt he had failed in his intention to create sympathy for the man,[9] but I think he succeeds remarkably.

He does it both by "showing" and "telling"; the "showing" with dialogue and drama is perfectly gripping, and the "telling" with commentary is very remarkable too. We are in these days conscious of the difficulty of defining insanity, and discover that Trollope was, too:

> There is perhaps no great social question so imperfectly understood among us at the present day as that which refers to the line which divides sanity from insanity. That this man is sane and that other unfortunately mad we do know well enough; and we know also that one man may be subject to various hallucinations,—may fancy himself to be a teapot, or what not,—and yet be in such a condition of mind as to call for no intervention either on behalf of his friends, or of the law; while another may be in possession of intellectual faculties capable of lucid exertion for the highest purposes, and yet be so mad that bodily restraint upon him is indispensable. We know that the sane man is responsible for what he does, and that the insane man is irresponsible; but we do not know,—we only guess wildly, at the state of mind of those, who now and again act like madmen, though no court or council of experts has declared them to be mad. The bias of the public mind is to press heavily on such men till the law attempts to touch them, as though they were thoroughly responsible; and then, when the law interferes, to screen them as though they were altogether irresponsible. . . . Now Trevelyan was, in truth, mad on the subject of his wife's alleged infidelity. He had abandoned everything that he valued in the world, and had made himself wretched in every affair of his life, because he could not submit to acknowledge to himself the possibility of error on his own part. . . .
> He came to believe everything; and, though he prayed fervently that his wife might not be led astray, that she might be saved at any rate from utter vice, yet he almost came to hope that it might be otherwise; —not, indeed, with the hope of the sane man, who desires that which he tells himself to be for his advantage; but with the hope of the insane man, who loves to feed his grievance, even though the grief should be his death. They who do not understand that a man may be brought to hope that which of all things is the most grievous to him, have not observed with sufficient closeness the perversity of the human mind (XXXVIII).

Finally, he desires the "proof" beyond anything. He has invested so much, his whole personality, his psyche, in her guilt, he cannot afford to find her innocent.[10]

Emily's parents at last arrive in England, hot with anger and resentment against Trevelyan. Trevelyan abducts the child, and it is learned that they have gone to Italy. The Rowley family follows him there. The pathos of the picture of Trevelyan's retreat drew the special admiration of Mario Praz in his sensitive study of Trollope:[11] Trevelyan's efforts to be a good parent, the physical ravages of his insanity, the apathy of the little boy. As long as the subject can be thought sane, one can be angry; the problem is just where that point is—or *line* as Trollope says—beyond which anger is impossible, and one can only pity—and humor. Emily, at last, in charity, "confesses"! In doing so, she gives up her victory, but she has destroyed him. Or he has destroyed himself; or rather we should say that a certain culture trait has destroyed him. A particular set of circumstances, altogether natural and probable, has developed into a case which reveals the malignancy of a certain power, of a right abrogated.

J. Hillis Miller has observed that Trollope's fiction "concentrates with admirable consistency on the question of what constitutes authentic selfhood. Each novel is a variation on this theme and brings another aspect of it to light," and the subplots, "according to a paralleling usual in Trollope's fiction, are analogous to the main plot and act as a commentary on it." Miller further observes that, in Trollope, "characters come into existence in relation to other people."[12] This surely indicates the particular excellence of Trollope's novels: his people are "realistic" because they exist in relationship to others. They exist fictionally because they exist socially. This is why, as Gordon Ray has said, the *long* novel is Trollope's forte.[13] *He Knew He Was Right* is typical in this way; we see all the characters better for the plethora of other characters about them, in interaction and various degree of linkage or contrast with them. Certainly, Trevelyan's tragedy is a loss of selfhood, as he withdraws more and more from social contact. And all the other story-lines, although they certainly do "alleviate" the grimness of Trevelyan's story, when examined become more apparently analogous to, or commentary on, the main plot. And everyone exists the more, for the presence of the others. We see Emily better because of Nora, and Dorothy and Priscilla Stanbury, and the American girls, and even—remotely—Miss Jemima Stanbury. We see Trevelyan better because of Hugh Stanbury, and Charles Glascock and Brooke Burgess and even—remotely—Mr. Gibson. One may sort them this way, sexually, because the focus and common concern of all the stories is a sexual self-realization, and one can also line them up in couples in a sort of novelistic ark, but the couples overlap and shift in relationships.

Take Nora Rowley first, Emily's sister, because she is there first, with the troubled couple, and invaluable artistically in that she is the third person present, often, in the quarrel, and so is often the occasion of the articulation or verbalization of the quarrel. When it first occurs to Emily, for instance, that Trevelyan might be legally able to take the baby, she thinks she can endure—to avoid that—any humbling, any groveling, and she observes to Nora: "It is a very poor thing to be a woman." "It is perhaps better than being a dog," says Nora, "but of course we can't compare ourselves to men" (V). She is presumably a less exigent character than Emily, but then she has not been tried. She begs Emily to relent. "If I were you I would forget it." But Emily answers, "How can I forget it? . . . He is civil and kind to you because he is not your master; but you don't know what things he says to me." Nora begs that principle be sacrificed to peace, and tries to mediate. Meantime, she has a dilemma of her own. In the marriage market as she is, she has had a great piece of luck: it seems very likely indeed that she is loved by the son and heir of Lord Peterborough, the Honorable Charles Glascock. (How very shameless Trollope is, choosing names that are quite as absurd as those in real life! Note also in this very novel the Reverend and Mrs. *Outhouse*, very respectable people. It is all part of Trollope's realism.) Glascock is good-looking, just under forty, in Parliament, and the family peerage is by no means impoverished. Lady Milborough, and Emily too suggest to Nora that "she ought to fall in love with Mr. Glascock." He is unexceptionable, except that, one, Nora finds his conversation a little limited, and, two, he is not Hugh Stanbury. So Nora's dilemma is a classic Victorian one: marry the approved suitor whom you don't love, or hope the poor man you do love will find you and find some income. All the culture has taught her what her mother has said:

> "Romance is a very pretty thing, and I don't think life would be worth having without a little of it. . . . But you can't be romantic without something to eat or drink." . . . The lot of woman [Nora told herself] was wretched, unfortunate, almost degrading. For a woman such as

101

herself there was no path open to her energy, other than that of getting a husband (IV).

Hugh Stanbury is Trevelyan's close friend from university days. His career had been less distinguished than Trevelyan's, "But he had won for himself reputation as a clever speaker, as a man who had learned much that college tutors do not profess to teach, as a hard-headed, ready witted fellow . . ." (IV). The contrast with Trevelyan is pointed. Where Trevelyan had won the honors, is strong in intellect, and theory, Hugh is as Arnold would say *ondoyant et divers*, sensitive, open-minded, adaptable, and full of sweet reasonableness. Not handsome, he is nevertheless very attractive, and Trollope makes us see him so, self-aware, witty, intellectual and good company. The penniless Hugh has been supported in his education by his wealthy spinster aunt, Jemima Stanbury; he is destined for the bar, but fretted by the slow financial returns, now writes for a radical periodical and his career there promises well. The aunt, however, an arch-conservative, is horrified and cuts him off without a penny. Trevelyan too deplores his friend's new occupation as below him.

When Emily and Trevelyan separate, it is arranged that Stanbury's mother and his sister Priscilla take in Emily and child and sister, in a rented house in Devonshire. There is a chapter (XVI) describing how the three young women, Emily, Nora and Priscilla, make a country expedition with a picnic to the moor near Dartmoor prison. Trollope does not usually go in for symbolic landscape, but there are enough references to the actual prison nearby, and enough suggestions of psychological prisons, for a critic who likes doing that sort of thing to make something of it. Meantime, it is a revealing and diverting interlude. They leave their picnic basket under a bush while they ramble; and oddly enough that day there was no escaped prisoner about and they found it safe.

> A bottle of sherry and water and a paper of sandwiches contained their whole banquet; for ladies, though they like good things at picnics, and, indeed, at other times, almost as well as men like them, very seldom prepare dainties for themselves alone. Men are wiser and more thoughtful, and are careful to have the good things, even if they are to be enjoyed without companionship.

One sees how, in all the varied scenes in this book, Trollope keeps coming round to his subject of culture and sexual differences. (It is amusing to wonder whether this observation is still more or less true.) After lunch Emily and Priscilla sit leaning against a hill and talk while Nora strolls about alone:

> She could be seen standing now on one little eminence and now on another, thinking, doubtless, as she stood on the one how good it would be to be Lady Peterborough, and, as she stood on the other, how much better to be Mrs. Hugh Stanbury.

Again, something might be made of symbolic landscape here. After considering, from the various little eminences of thought, or viewpoints, she concludes that on the whole she had better accept Mr. Glascock, "and tried to make herself believe that in this way she would be doing a good deed."

All this time there is the counter-point of Emily's and Priscilla's conversation. Priscilla is a considerable philosopher, crusty and brusque, presenting in her life-style a determined celibacy and making it seem attractive, too. She rejoices in having come to terms with poverty rather than sell herself in the market. She is uneasy about the arrangement by which she and her mother give a home to the recalcitrant Emily and train, but has to confess the pleasure of the books and cultivated companionship that come with them. She is never anything but frank nevertheless, a courageous and upright woman who has determined her own mode of being.[14]

> "What should I do?" asks Emily.
> "Go back to him. . . ."
> "Ask him to forgive me because he has ill-treated me?"
> "Never mind about that," said Priscilla. . . . "All that is twopenny-halfpenny pride, which should be thrown to the winds. The more right you have been hitherto the better you can afford to go on being right. What is it that we all live upon but self-esteem? When we want praise it is only because praise enables us to think well of ourselves. Every one to himself is the centre and pivot of all the world."

One cannot help but admire Priscilla.

> "I stand alone, and can take care of myself. . . ."
> ". . . and are you contented?"
> "Well, no; I can't say that I am contented. I hardly think that anybody ought to be contented. . . ."

103

> "Why should not you get married, as well as [your sister] Dorothy?
> . . ."
>
> "Who would have me? I am often cross, and I like my own way, and
> I have a distaste for men. I never in my life saw a man whom I wished
> even to make my intimate friend."

But she is very firm in her idea that once married a woman
should submit to her husband.

It turns out to be very timely, all that thinking from various
eminences that Nora had accomplished on the moor, for as soon
as they return from the picnic they find Mr. Glascock has come!
The house is in a flutter. Nora has a chance to wash her hands
and fiddle with her ribbons before the encounter. Emily ad-
jures her to accept—he is faultless. Nora resorts to contrariety:
"I hate people without faults!" "Oh, Nora, Nora, that is foolish. . . . Say you will try to love him, and that will be enough.
And you do love him?" "Do I?" (Obviously equal to—So who
says so? Do I indeed!) "It is only the opposition of your nature
that makes you fight him." (This from *Emily*!) At any rate, in
spite of the feeling that one should resist pressure, Nora does
make up her mind to say yes to "Will you marry me?" and
goes downstairs. "There floated quickly across her brain an
idea of the hardness of women's lot, in that she should be
called upon to decide her future fate for life in half a minute."
Men can mull it over at leisure, and then pop—or not pop—the
question. But she is ready. Glascock, however, plays her false:
instead of "Will you marry me?" he says "Can you love me?"

> "No," she said, and there was something almost of fierceness in the
> tone of her voice. . . . "You are so good, and so kind, and so upright,
> that I cannot tell you a falsehood" (XVII).

She had almost loved him previously for his considerate understanding, as he himself had said, "It has sometimes seemed
to me odd that girls should love men in such a hurry" (XIII).
The good man gives up and goes off bravely and from now on
we notice him more and more as very sympathetic. He is the
archetypal ideal English gentleman, not very bright, but very
civilized and understanding, full of kindness and generosity.
He has the *sangfroid anglais*, a little bit of the Oh-I-Say.
Trollope does this kind of thing wonderfully, the unexagger-
ated character, letting it build up cumulatively with scores of
little touches.

104

Nora reports the outcome to Emily. "I am willing enough, I believe, to sell myself to the devil, but I don't know how to do it." Emily is resigned. Mrs. Stanbury is shocked and incredulous. Priscilla expresses "moderate approval," for to her mind refusals tend to be better than acceptances. And Nora—how vigorously Trollope refuses to let us be heroic!—Nora cries herself to sleep in an agony of regret. "The next morning she came down to breakfast pale as a ghost; and they . . . knew at once that she had done that which had made her a wretched woman." Gentle critics, do not fear. Hugh adores her and will get around to declaring himself. But not for a while, for although he does come to visit the Devonshire household he cannot offer without economic security. There is an excursion to Niddon Park with Priscilla and Nora, and Hugh scrambles down the slope to explore the river. "Come, Miss Rowley," he calls; "will you not show them that a lady can go up and down a hill as well as a man?" But she refuses because she is sore from his feigned indifference to her. After Hugh is gone, Nora persuades Priscilla to revisit the scene of the excursion, and there is some interesting conversation. Nora thinks men must despise women, as dainty and foolish.

> "Sometimes women despise men," said Priscilla.
> "Not very often;—do they? And then women are so dependent on men. A woman can get nothing without a man."
> "I manage to get on somehow," said Priscilla.
> "No, you don't, Miss Stanbury,—if you think of it. You want mutton. And who kills the sheep?"
> "But who cooks it?"
> "But the men-cooks are the best," said Nora; "and the men-tailors, and the men to wait at table, and the men-poets, and the men-painters, and the men-nurses. All the things that women do, men do better."
> 'There are two things they can't do," said Priscilla.
> "What are they?"
> "They can't suckle babies, and they can't forget themselves."
> "About the babies, of course not. As for forgetting themselves,— I am not quite so sure that I can forget myself.—That is just where your brother went down last night."
> They had at this moment reached the top of the steep slope below which the river ran brawling among the rocks, and Nora seated herself exactly where she had sat on the previous evening.
> "I have been down scores of times," said Priscilla.
> "Let us go now."
> "You wouldn't go when Hugh asked you yesterday."
> "I didn't care then. But do come now,—if you don't mind the climb."
> Then they went down the slope and reached the spot from whence

Hugh Stanbury had jumped from rock to rock across the stream. 'You have never been out there, have you?" said Nora.

"On the rocks? Oh, dear, no! I should be sure to fall."

"But he went; just like a goat."

"That's one of the things that men can do, I suppose," said Priscilla. "But I don't see any great glory in being like a goat."

"I do. I should like to be able to go, and I think I'll try. It is so mean to be dainty and weak."

In this way Nora muses over the sexual role. She breaks out:

"When I think of myself, Miss Stanbury, I am so ashamed. There is nothing that I can do. I couldn't write an article for a newspaper. . . . I would sooner write for a newspaper than do anything else in the world."

"Why so?"

"Because it is so noble to teach people everything! . . . I believe there are women who do it, but very few" (XXV).

One senses that Nora would like to be part of a "radical" circle like that of Mill—or George Eliot—whom Trollope knew well.

When Miss Jemima Stanbury cut off Hugh without a penny she found herself lacking a beneficiary, and after some thought invited her niece Dorothy, sister of Priscilla and Hugh, to come live with her in her house in Exeter and be cared for. With some protective clauses insisted on by Priscilla, the agreement is made and Dorothy goes to live with the old curmudgeoness. Dorothy is yet another kind of woman, the mildest and most modest, a *beseeching* woman, Trollope says, the kind that always looks as though asking for help, the picture of feminine dependence. The story of Dorothy is remote from the story of Emily; they never meet in the novel, I think. But by the way the novelist interweaves his strands, we see them as a kind of foil to each other. Hugh Stanbury when he visits the Trevelyans has occasion to talk to Nora and Emily about his little sister's translation to Exeter, and brings Dorothy's letter to show them. Dorothy writes that Aunt Stanbury is not so bad, and she thinks she'll be able to get on, and "of course a girl in my position does not expect to have her own way." Emily fires off:

"Why shouldn't she have her share of her own way as well as anybody else?"

"Poor Dorothy would never want to have her own way," said Hugh.

"She ought to want it," said Mrs. Trevelyan.
"She has spirit enough to turn if she's trodden on," said Hugh.
"That's more than what most women have," said Mrs. Trevelyan"
(IX).

Miss Stanbury finds that Dorothy will do. In fact she does so well that Miss Stanbury finds she will arrange a husband, bought with a small dowry. The lucky man is the clergyman Mr. Gibson—who is a literary descendant of Jane Austen's Mr. Collins, but takes on enough chiaroscuro to appear as a vulgar version of Trevelyan in that he considers himself a great gift to women. We read how the mild Dorothy is first astounded that anyone would think of her marrying, and then that any man should be willing to do it, and then modestly but surely finding herself strong enough to reject the condescending Mr. Gibson (she *has* spirit enough to turn, as Hugh predicted). She faces up to her outraged aunt, and there is some parallel between the self-assertion and integrity of this gentle one, and that of Emily. "I cannot stay where people think I am ungrateful" (XXXVI). But she stays, and her aunt respects her integrity, and there develops a friendship with the delightful Brooke Burgess. Again, conversation tends to turn toward the central issue, as in the genial presence of Brooke, Dorothy unfolds her ideas. There are people, she says, who are just nothing-people, who don't seem to belong to anybody—and why?

> "Because they're just nobodies. They are not anything particular to anybody, and so they go on living till they die. You know what I mean, Mr. Burgess. A man who is a nobody can perhaps make himself somebody,—or, at any rate, he can try; but a woman has no means of trying. She's a nobody, and a nobody she must remain. She has her clothes and her food, but she isn't wanted anywhere. . . . She doesn't earn anything or do any good. She is just there and that's all." . . . She had . . . included herself among that company of old maids who are born and live and die without that vital interest in the affairs of life which nothing but family duties . . . will give to a woman. If she had not meant this she had felt it (LI).

Trollope certainly addresses himself here to the problem of what Gissing calls "The Odd Women." Without proposing any solution, he communicates the sadness of it, and his own sense of the married state as best. But to earn some money, or do some good, would help. On this occasion Brooke Burgess is most anxious to assure Dorothy that she herself is not one of that unhappy company.

The Exeter circle includes the Misses French, Camilla and Arabella, who—it is said—hunt in pairs. They have been closing in on Mr. Gibson for years and are much incensed when the Gibson-Stanbury alliance threatens. But he is flung back to them, and the rivalry and bitterness is very intense. They start as caricatures, but as so often with Trollope, they get believable, in the ferocity of their jealous anxiety. It is both funny and horrifying—the predatory female carried to a terrible extreme, to the physical threat of the carving knife. Gibson must finally capitulate to one and destroy the other, for there are some things even worse than marriage: "Seven years of flirtation with a young lady is more trying to the affection than any duration of matrimony" (XXXVI). The rejected sister must become one of those women who just "go on living till they die."

But by far the most important figure in the Exeter circle is Miss Stanbury herself. Early on, there was a melancholy love affair. She loved, and was forsaken, and quarreled with the lover's family and her own family. The lover, we understand, felt remorse, and dying young left to her his considerable fortune. We never know much about it. "I cannot tell you all that story," she says to Brooke Burgess. "It is too long, and too sad. Romance is very pretty in novels, but the romance of a life is always a melancholy matter. They are most happy who have no story to tell" (XXV). Her surface is very formidable, and Dorothy in coming to Exeter must brave the dragon. "She was as strong as a horse, and had never hitherto known a day's illness. As a consequence of this, she did not believe in the illness of other people,—especially not in the illness of women." I feel sure we have here a pooh-poohing of "female complaints" and the mysterious physical inferiority of women. "You don't have headaches, do you?" she says to Dorothy fiercely. The headache was the usual cover for menstrual malingering,[15] and it seems Miss Stanbury will have none of it, and believes that sensible clothes and lots of outdoor exercise will keep things right. Dorothy must be healthy, then, and wear her hair plain, and drink a glass of beer with her bread and cheese at midday, and port after dinner is good for everyone. She must be regular in religious observance, including daily church services, and the family prayers and the reading of sermons at home. Miss Stanbury is a Tory of the old school and hates Hugh's radical paper and Bishop Colenso. The country is going to the dogs. "They say women are to vote, and become doctors, and if so, there's no knowing what devil's tricks they mayn't do" (XII). But she has a great need to love, and disappointed in Hugh, nervously welcomes Dorothy. Dorothy, though in fear and trembling, braves the dragon and passes the test and is loved, and loves her aunt in return, for the woman is in truth very tender and loving. Her celibacy is accidental—tragic, in fact, and bravely accepted. We see her very susceptible to Brooke's masculine charm and good sense. Furthermore, in spite of the formidable powerful surface, she is very much in need of assurance, and the strong and sensible Martha does much of the guiding of her under pretense of being her servant. Miss Stanbury is the pivotal character in the Exeter story, as Trevelyan is in the main story, and finally she represents the opposite pole to Trevelyan's self-righteousness.

> There was ever present to her mind an idea of failure and a fear lest she had been mistaken in her views throughout her life. No one had ever been more devoted to peculiar opinions, or more strong in the use of language for their expression; and she was so far true to herself, that she would never seem to retreat from the position she had taken. She would still scorn the new fangles of the world around her, and speak of the changes which she saw as all tending to evil. But, through it all, there was an idea present to herself that it could not be God's intention that things should really change for the worse, and that the fault must be in her, because she had been unable to move as others had moved. She would sit thinking of the circumstances of her own life and tell herself that with her everything had failed. She had loved, but had quarrelled with her lover; and her love had come to nothing—but barren wealth. She had fought for her wealth and had conquered;—and had become hard in the fight, and was conscious of her own hardness. . . . there were doubts, and qualms of conscience, and an uneasiness, —because her life had been a failure (LXXXIX).

She does not know she is right, that is. Diffidence seems now a positive grace, to keep in question one's own righteousness. Her life does not seem a failure at the end, for she succeeds greatly in virtue, in generosity, and in yielding.

But before we get to the end there is another set of possibilities presented. A good part of the action moves off into Italy, and we see what it is to be English in Italy, and also what it is to be young and female and American in Italy. Trollope uses an acceptable enough coincidence of travel to put Glascock and Trevelyan together crossing the Alps, and we have the chance to see Trevelyan in the process of rigid withdrawal from society, in contrast with Glascock's easy adaptability. They had known each other of course—Trevelyan knew Glascock's interest in his sister-in-law Nora. There is trouble about the reserved seats in the *diligence* which is to cross the Alps, and two young American women are objecting that they are not getting what they had arranged, "for American ladies understand their rights." The two Englishmen come to their aid, recognize each other, and all more or less join forces for the journey. However independent American women are, they have no scruples about accepting the men's help, and Trollope, ever the comparative anthropologist, allows himself a digression on American women as seat-grabbers.[16] These two women are pretty and witty, however, and the conversation progresses, with a rather comparativist edge. Olivia Spalding, the younger sister, says "I hate being put anywhere,—as if I were a sheep. It seems so odd to us that you here should all be so tame." They also speak of travel companies who don't keep their word.

> "Ah," says Caroline, the elder sister, "that is an affair of honesty. If we want honesty, I believe we must go back to the stars and stripes." Mr. Glascock looked up from his plate almost aghast (XXXVII).

These Americans would be starting to look Ugly, if they weren't so pretty and spirited. When the men are alone:

> "Clever women those," said Mr. Glascock.
> "Yes, indeed," said Trevelyan.
> "American women are always clever,—and almost always pretty."
> "I do not like them," said Trevelyan,—who in these days was in a mood to like nothing. [He wouldn't have, anyway.] They are exigent; —and then they are so hard. They want the weakness that a woman ought to have."
> "That comes from what they would call your insular prejudice. We are accustomed to less self-assertion on the part of women than is customary with them. We prefer women to rule us by seeming to yield. In the States, as I take it, the women never yield, and the men have to fight their own battles with other tactics."
> "I don't know what their tactics are."
> "They keep their distance. The men live much by themselves, as though they knew they would not have a chance in the presence of

110

their wives and daughters. Nevertheless they don't manage things badly. You very rarely hear of an American being separated from his wife" (XXXVII).

Poor Glascock realizes immediately the awfulness of this *gaffe*, and blushes and tingles. He apologizes frankly, and there is at least the advantage of having the subject of Trevelyan's marriage in the open now. This occasions, in their conversation, another vivid picture of another stage of his psychosis. It is part of his anti-social self-righteousness to withdraw from the lively Americans, while Glascock, who should have had a broken heart, is quite enchanted with them.

> And indeed they were very gracious,—as is the nature of American ladies in spite of that hardness of which Trevelyan had complained. They assume an intimacy readily, with no appearance of impropriety, and are at their ease easily. When, therefore, they were handed out of their carriage by Mr. Glascock, the bystanders at Lanslebourg might have thought that the whole party had been travelling together from New York.
> "What should we have done if you hadn't taken pity on us?" said the elder lady. "I don't think we could have climbed up into that high place; and look at the crowd that have come out of the interior. A man has some advantages after all."
> "I am quite in the dark as to what they are," said Mr. Glascock.
> "He can give up his place to a lady, and can climb up into a banquette."
> "And he can be a member of Congress," said the younger. "I'd sooner be senator from Massachusetts than be the Queen of England."
> "So would I," said Glascock. "I'm glad we can agree about one thing" (XXXVII).

The Misses Spalding go to Florence to join their uncle the American Minister there, wondering who their traveling companion was. Olivia says she thought at first that Glascock's servant was his keeper and he a madman, but she likes him, and concludes,

> "It's my belief that he's an English swell, a lord, or a duke;—and it's my belief, too, that he's in love with you."
> "It's my belief, Livy, that you're a regular ass" (XL).

The American Minister, Jonas Spalding, discovers Glascock's identity, and in the course of events they are all in the same circle in Florence,[17] the Rowleys too, now, when their griefs permit them, having heard Trevelyan is in Italy with the child.

111

One of Carry's special friends is Wallachia Petrie, the American poetess and feminist, "the Republican Browning," who is hot against marriage in general, and especially against Carry's marrying Glascock, one of the effete aristocracy of an effete European nation. "They are dishonest, and rotten at the core!" She wants Carry to visit Rome with her.

> "The old stones are rotten too, but their dust tells no lies." That well known piece of hers—"Ancient Marbles, while ye crumble," was written at this time, and contained an occult reference to Mr. Glascock and her friend. . . .
> "Their country, Carry, is a game played out, while we are still breasting the hill with our lungs full of air."

Glascock persists in his courtship, not without trial, for the American Minister, Jonas Spalding, is full of hot air. He's a decent and cultivated man but—especially on the subject of democratic institutions—a crashing (and funny) bore. Most interesting to us, however, is one conversation he captures Glascock with.

> "Your John S. Mill is a great man," said the minister.
> "They tell me so," said Mr. Glascock. "I don't read what he writes myself."
> This acknowledgement seemed to the minister to be almost disgraceful, and yet he himself had never read a word of Mr. Mill's writings. "He is a far-seeing man," continued the minister. "He is one of the few Europeans who can look forward and see how the rivers of civilization are running on. He has understood that women must at last be put on an equality with men."

Glascock counters this with the remark that must have been a ghastly commonplace even then:

> "Can he manage that men shall have half the babies?"

But he can't escape. The minister has him.

> "I have an answer ready, sir, for that difficulty. Step aside with me for a moment. The question is important, and I should be glad if you would communicate my ideas to your great philosopher. Nature, sir, has laid down certain laws, which are immutable; and, against them,—" (LV).

Fortunately for Glascock, and fortunately for the propriety of the Victorian novel, Glascock escapes to the ladies, and we never hear the rest. And so it fell out that Charles Glascock never got the American's secrets of birth control to take back to England and deliver to John Stuart Mill. But he wins Carry, and I think he is so good that Carry will not find the title and the old civilization too onerous. His goodness is especially revealed in the kind offices he does for poor broken Trevelyan and even for the little boy; the chapter is called, significantly, "Mr. Glascock as Nurse" (LXXXVI). With some affectionate humor, Trollope shows him as really noble in "feminine" tenderness. Trollope frequently acclaims "feminine" kindness in men, acclaims it a true "manliness," oddly enough.

Nora, however, probably needed the intellectual excitement of Hugh Stanbury's kind of life. She is something of a New Woman. In the period when she is engaged but not yet married, she is

> somewhat touched with an idea that it would be a fine independent thing to live alone, if it were only for a week or two, just because other young ladies never lived alone. Perhaps there was some half-formed notion in her mind that permission to do so was part of the reward due to her for having refused to marry a lord. Stanbury was in some respects a Bohemian, and it would become her, she thought, to have a little practice herself in the Bohemian line. She had indeed declined a Bohemian marriage, feeling strongly averse to encounter the loud displeasure of her father and mother;—but as long as everything was quite proper . . . she considered that a little independence would be useful and agreeable (XCIV).

When her parents return to the Mandarins, however, she's obliged to go and stay with Lady Milborough, the type of woman who seems to have existed for just such emergencies. But the old lady's benignity and Nora's good humor find common ground, and the marriage isn't far off, anyway.

So like any good Victorian novel, this one has a fair quota of marriages at the end—Glascock and Carry, Stanbury and Nora, Brooke and Dorothy. Before it's settled, however, Trollope threatens us with a novelistic pat ending:

> We will not anticipate by alluding prematurely to Hugh Stanbury's treachery,—or death,—or the possibility that he after all may turn out to be the real descendant of the true Lord Peterborough . . . nor will we speak of Nora's certain fortitude in either of these emergencies (LXXXVIII).

113

And he goes on to hypothesize some other absurd endings for lesser characters, the effect of it all being to make fun of commonplace novels and furthermore to draw attention to his own refusal of any hoked-up ending, to his good faith with his characters and with life. It is part of Trollope's game anyway to pretend he is not writing a novel and thereby to call attention to the fact that it *is* a novel. Olivia and Carry Spalding were talking once about national differences in courtship customs. Carry says,

> "I don't know why there should be a difference."
> "Nor do I;—only that there is. You haven't read so many of their novels as I have."
> "Who would ever think of learning to live out of an English novel?" said Carry (LV).

The question is raised. One doesn't, perhaps, learn to live out of novels.

But whatever it is novels do, they are somehow related to life. Consider in this same book the function of a certain chapter called "Major Magruder's Committee" (LXVIII). It will be remembered that the occasion for Osborne's "managing" the home leave of Sir Marmaduke Rowley was a Government-appointed committee to investigate colonial administration, and two governors are to report. One is to be from a "major" colony—"Bowles, of Canada" is mentioned. Rowley of the Mandarins might not be so expert, "But then two governors were to come, and it might be as well to have one of the best sort, and one of the second best" (III). Representative, that is. One good one and one nonentity. When at last the committee does meet, the "good" governor acquits himself splendidly: "No other lands under the sun were so blessed, in the way of government . . . , and as a natural consequence their devotion and loyalty to the mother country was quite a passion with them." Then it is Sir Marmaduke's turn. Distracted as he is with this terrible trouble of Emily's, and now Nora is refusing to marry a lord, and he is feeling he isn't very good at governing anyway—for him it is a day of martyrdom. In the Mandarins—

114

There was a Court of Chancery, so called, which Sir Marmaduke described as a little parliament. When he was asked whether the court exercised legislative or executive functions, he said at first that it exercised both, and then that it exercised neither. He knew that it consisted of nine men, of whom five were appointed by the colony and four by the Crown. Yet he declared that the Crown had the control of the court;—which, in fact, was true enough no doubt, as the five open members were not perhaps, all of them, immaculate patriots: but on this matter poor Sir Marmaduke was very obscure. When asked who exercised the patronage of the Crown in nominating the four members, he declared that the four members exercised it themselves. Did he appoint them? No;—he never appointed anybody himself. He consulted the Court of Chancery for everything. At last it came out that the chief justice of the islands, and three other officers, always sat in the court— but whether it was required by the constitution of the islands that this should be so, Sir Marmaduke did not know. It had worked well;—that was to say, everybody had complained of it, but he, Sir Marmaduke, would not recommend any change. What he thought best was that the Colonial Secretary should send out his orders, and that the people in the colonies should mind their business and grow coffee. When asked what would be the effect upon the islands, under his scheme of government, if an incoming Colonial Secretary should change the policy of his predecessor, he said that he didn't think it would much matter if the people did not know anything about it (LXVIII).

The poor man is aware of his terrible failure, and feels sure his career is over. But nothing much happens; the instigator of the committee has achieved a gambit as part of a larger scheme, and the government of the Mandarin Islands still muddles along. So much for the "masculine mystique" of governing. Our age, which Lord Snow has called the Age of Committees, might do as well to hold our own self-righteousness in question. "Be not righteous over much." The whole chapter may seem like an excursus, but it is reasonably tied to the main. A lesser novelist would have skimped the committee— it had served its turn in plot arrangement. But the relentless Trollope carries it through, pointing up the irony that after all the fuss in arranging it, it turns out to be—nothing.

Let me take up just one more incident that is specially related to the whole. It is when Jemima Stanbury is gravely ill, and Dorothy is chief nurse, and Brooke Burgess has been sent for. The local doctor has called in the distinguished physician Sir Peter Mancrudy, and now that Brooke has come,

115

> Sir Peter was under some obligation to speak plainly, as being the person whom Miss Stanbury recognized as her heir. So Sir Peter declared that his patient might perhaps live, and perhaps might die. "The truth is, Mr. Burgess," said Sir Peter, "a doctor doesn't know so very much more about these things than other people" (LI).

Of course, it is funny—a not very unusual kind of satire at the expense of the medical profession; and yet it is part of the whole pattern: this doctor is the great one, and the great ones are distinguished for not being sure they are right. They are all very anxious about Miss Stanbury, but Brooke nevertheless declares his love to Dorothy, and Dorothy is surprised beyond her wildest dreams, tremendously fussed, and senses strongly the unsuitableness of such goings-on when her aunt is so ill. But Brooke manages an embrace, and Dorothy thinks she disapproves but is really wildly happy. She escapes to take up her watch by the old lady, and as is the custom, she proceeds to read to her.

> Knowing how important it was that her aunt should sleep, she took up the volume of Jeremy Taylor, and with so great a burden on her mind, she went on painfully and distinctly with the second sermon on the Marriage Ring (LI).

This too can be taken at surface value, a mild and commonplace joke that there's nothing better than sermons to go to sleep by. They were the tranquilizers and barbiturates of our ancestors. On the other hand, it is a pretty specific reference; Trollope didn't *have* to mention any particular sermon. Moreover, most literate households were supplied with Taylor's sermons, and this of the Marriage Ring would be known to many of Trollope's readers.

And known to Trollope. Taylor's name comes up here and there in Trollope's work; see, for instance, *Cousin Henry* (IX) where it may have a particular meaning. I have argued elsewhere that Trollope's art is related to the *casuistic* school of moral philosophy, of that seventeenth-century Anglican kind associated with Taylor, which was being revived in the nineteenth century by Whewell, Grote and Maurice. And I think the sermon mentioned here is part of a larger pattern. We remember Miss Stanbury's piety, the daily services and the interest in

theology; and now she is sick she takes the sacrament weekly
and is calm in the face of death.

> "If it is God's will, I am ready. Not that I'm fit, Brooke. God forbid
> that I should ever think that. But I doubt whether I'll ever be fitter."

We recognize her religion as old "High and Dry" Anglicanism;
she likes best the "unascetic godliness of ancient days." She
rejoices in the fruits of the earth, believes heartily in good
food and wine, and, celibate only by sad accident, believes in
marriage. And Taylor's Marriage Ring is one of the great literary celebrations of the institution. It turns out, moreover, that
it is quite precisely related to the subject of this novel. Perhaps
Taylor keeps a little too much of the *obedience* idea for our
taste today, yet actually, good casuist that he is, the *obedience*
is stringently reduced and modified in his arguments. A wife is
not only wife but friend, too, "for a good woman is in her soul
the same that a man is, and she is a woman only in her body."[18]
Marriage is for both "a school and exercise of virtue." "A
woman indeed ventures most, for she hath no sanctuary to re-
tire to from an evil husband; she must dwell upon her sorrow,
and hatch the eggs which her own folly or infelicity hath produced. . . ." Just so, our poor Emily. Whether it was folly or
infelicity she had indeed to hatch the eggs. But a man suffers,
too, in a troubled marriage: "When he sits among his neighbours, he remembers the objection that lies in his bosom, and
he sighs deeply." So our poor Trevelyan, who cannot hold up
his head and must reject society. Above all, in the early stages
of marriage, when it is yet "unfixed," both should be "equally
concerned to avoid all offenses of each other." "Let man and
wife be careful to stifle little things"; they can "betray us to the
violence of passion." "Let them be sure to abstain from all
those things, which by experience and observation they find
to be contrary to each other."

Louis Trevelyan even in his first hurt and passion is described in terms that are very close to Taylor's; he had

> a feeling that it was his duty to be gentle. There was a feeling also
> that that privilege of receiving obedience, which was so indubitably
> his own, could only be maintained by certain wise practices on his part
> in which gentleness must predominate (V).

117

And in Part II, or the second sermon of the Marriage Ring, this is precisely Taylor's theme.

> The man hath power over her as over himself, and must love her equally. . . . As amongst men and women, humility is the way to be preferred; so it is in husbands, they shall prevail by cession, by sweetness, and counsel, and charity, and compliance. So that we cannot discourse of the man's right, without describing the measures of his duty. . . .

This, along with Taylor's delight in the joys and securities of marriage, is surely the *unascetic holiness* of old Anglicanism that Miss Stanbury loved. And I don't think she slept through all of the sermon, and I think she wanted Dorothy, at this stage of her life, to be well persuaded of the values of the honorable estate. The sermon itself has a great deal of that seventeenth-century poetry and intelligence that occasioned the Victorian new edition—and it is not quite inaccessible now. How interesting, finally, that in this glancing reference, Trollope invokes the theme and center of his novel, ringed round with the many variations of the subsidiary stories.

Finally we see in this realistic novel of Trollope's a testing of principle and culture by cases, and a great rich variety of ways to find oneself in a social context. Like Miss Stanbury, Trollope is diffident, and his diffidence extends into art. He refuses to be doctrinaire, insists on the reservation of judgment and the ironic multiple perspective. He cannot be said to be pro-feminist, certainly, but neither can he be said to be against. What he does do, is present some current possibilities, weighing and considering with a great tolerant breadth of sympathy and understanding. His novels are "experimental" indeed, in Zola's sense. He did not at all "know" he was right. As it appears that our good is, for all we know, a social good, the ways of realizing ourselves in the most intimate, perhaps most important and most difficult social relationship—marriage—that "school of virtue" as Taylor calls it—is really quite vital. Reading a novel like this of Trollope's is a social act.

1. But the Brattles in *The Vicar of Bullhampton* are good; and in the unfinished, posthumously published *Landleaguers* there is a very promising portrait of a child.
2. References to novels are by chapter number.
3. Anthony Trollope, *Autobiography* (Berkeley and Los Angeles, University of California Press, 1947), p. 121.
4. *North America*, eds. D. Smalley and B. A. Booth. (New York: Alfred A. Knopf, 1951), p. 28.
5. F. A. Hayak, *John Stuart Mill and Harriet Taylor* (Chicago: University of Chicago Press, 1951), especially p. 167; and Alice S. Rossi, ed., *Essays on Sex Equality* by John Stuart Mill and Harriet Taylor Mill (Chicago and London; Chicago: University of Chicago Press, 1971), p. 41. The text of the essay is on pp. 91-121.
6. *Anthony Trollope: Aspects of His Life and Art* (Bloomington, Ind., Indiana University Press; London: E. Hulton and Co., Ltd.), 1958, pp. 127-28.
7. See *Letters*, ed. Bradford A. Booth (London, New York, Toronto: Oxford University Press), 1951, p. 262, *et passim*.
8. Trollope, *Autobiography*, pp. 115, 236-37.
9. *Ibid.*, p. 266.
10. I once heard a distinguished psychiatrist who very much admires Trollope's psychological observation, diagnose Trevelyan's trouble as being really that he is in love with Colonel Osborne. This is so far out of my field that I cannot agree or disagree. What I find noteworthy, though, is the fact that the psychiatrist had a sufficiency of clinical detail on which to make a diagnosis, a diagnosis which seems to the layman quite as arcane as real psychiatric diagnoses of real people.
11. The chapter "Anthony Trollope" in *The Hero in Eclipse in Victorian Fiction*, trans., Angus Davidson (Oxford: Oxford University Press, 1956), pp. 261-318.
12. *The Form of Victorian Fiction* (Notre Dame and London; South Bend, Indiana: University of Notre Dame Press 1968), pp. 123, 130.
13. "Trollope at Full Length," *Huntington Library Quarterly*, XXXI, August, 1968, pp. 313-40.
14. Although Priscilla is very gruff and perhaps "masculine" in manner, I don't think there is any suggestion of lesbianism. I know of one such suggestion in Trollope. It occurs when Lizzie Eustace of *The Eustace Diamonds* reappears some years older in *The Prime Minister*, having descended to the demimonde where Ferdinand Lopez is at home. She lives now with a widow, a Mrs. Leslie, who has "attached herself lately with almost more than feminine affection to Lady Eustace" (XLVIII). To those who know Lizzie this may seem a brilliantly consistent touch. She was emotionally impotent, one remembers; her love affairs and marriages were play-acting. The very strong revulsion Emily Lopez and her father feel toward Mrs. Leslie and friend, apparently as *such*, corroborate the point. It is another case where Trollope seems able to indicate just what he wants, unhampered by the rules of propriety.
15. See "Victorian Women and Menstruation," by Elaine and English Showalter, in *Suffer and Be Still*, ed. Martha Vicinus. (Bloomington and London: Indiana University Press, 1972), pp. 38-44.

119

16. Trollope does this in his *North America*, too; and he also devotes a chapter (XVII, "The Rights of Women") to the feminist movement in the United States.
17. Trollope knew this circle well personally (*see*, for instance, *The Golden Ring: The Anglo-Florentines 1847-1862*, by Giuliana Artom Treves, trans. Sylvia Sprigge, London and New York; New York: Longmans, Green and Co., 1956). His brother Tom's "Villino Trollopè" was well known, and Trollope visited there often, and the aged but still formidable mother lived there. It was a smart place to visit, and their parties were quite the rage, and they made it chic to serve lemonade. (The lemonade was such a success I think there must have been gin in it.)
18. The sermon is available in the edition that Trollope probably used, edited by R. Heber (London: Longman, Orme, Brown, Green and Longmans, etc., in 15 volumes, 1839, V, pp. 248-79).

THE BRONTËS: THE SELF DEFINED, REDEFINED, AND REFINED

FREDERICK R. KARL

In an analysis I wrote of Doris Lessing's *The Golden Notebook* and *The Four-Gated City*, I tried to locate her work in what I called the "literature of enclosure," a literature we usually associate with Kafka, Proust, and Beckett. The antecedents of such a literature are lengthy, however, and the Brontës, with their intense preoccupation with the unfolding of the self and the protean self, appear to fit well into the early development of this important literary theme. It is a theme we can more precisely place in fiction a full hundred years before their own work, in Richardson's *Clarissa*, where the room or enclosure becomes the arena for the epistolary drama. Without enclosure, there could be no method, and, therefore, locale and narrative manner are intertwined.

In *The Golden Notebook*, such an intertwining of locale and method recurs, since Lessing's "notebooks" are not appreciably different from letters, both being part of an introspective, solipsistic process of self-analysis. In the Brontës, to return to them momentarily, the use of the first person narrator is a variation on epistolary and "notebook" conventions, narcissistic and self-revelatory as all such methods are. Significantly, enclosure serves with special effectiveness as backdrop for that unfolding, protean self we find, then, in letters, notebooks, and "I" narratives.

In those we usually associate with the later development of

121

"enclosure," Kafka, Proust, Beckett, their stress would appear at first to be a direct response to the Freudian reliance on the regressive tendencies of the adult to return to the womb, that quasi-sacred place where needs are met without effort and without external threat. Such a literature probably would not have developed in this manner without the influence of psychoanalytic thought. The condition, nevertheless, existed in a social context long before it was identified psychoanalytically. In Doris Lessing's handling, which appears to owe less to Kafka or Proust than to the female line—for example, Clarissa and the Brontës—the room or enclosure is a mixed experience. Even though it is a place of refuge, it is also the locale of one's descent into hell. Its physical desolation or emptiness is indeed a counterpart of the character's psychological state. The enclosure fixes the limits of sexuality, threatens and reassures within bounds, freeing as it limits. The novel around the room becomes, perforce, subjective, solipsistic, even when externals such as political or social events are of significance.

The room bottles up rage, leaves no escape for anger except when it is directed back into the self. The lair is itself a physical symbol of impotence—lack of choice, will, determination; identity is indistinguishable from one's furnishings. Like Kafka's mole-like creature, one does not even know what events are shaping outside one's enclosure. One struggles with the parts, for the whole is unrecognizable, unseizable. Clearly, the panoramic novel is snuffed out, for adventure is lost; there is no overt struggle for external goals. The room or house is battleground. Family relationships are symbiotic. In such a room, Eros becomes sex, spirit becomes physical, idea or theory becomes fact. Whereas once space was used for repetition of a holy act, the act of creation itself, now its repetition is one of staleness, of folding anxiety into neurosis. Lessing, like Beckett, provides rooms whose air is foul; space is not infinite, but geometric, and it signifies the final vestiges of the profane city.

Later, we will see how the Brontës concerned themselves almost solely with profane resolutions—good Victorians that they were in this respect—but here it is sufficient to note how they exploited the theme of enclosure. The most famous example, surely, is the red room of *Jane Eyre*, and later I discuss that conception in detail, demonstrating its thematic centrality for the novel. The red room, however, has several counterparts: the hothouse atmosphere of Wuthering Heights (the house itself as well as the novel); the various schools in *Jane Eyre* and elsewhere where pupils are persecuted and homes where governesses are imprisoned—enclosures for the imprisoned heart; Wildfell Hall, where Mrs. Graham "hides," victim, hunted, prey for her male pursuer, Mme. Beck's Pensionnat in *Villette*, the entire Pensionnat but especially its attic; the Reverend Helstone's home for Caroline in *Shirley*; the Bretton home also in *Villette*, a refuge and a source of anguish; the office of William Crimsworth's brother in *The Professor*. Perhaps so much of the "action" in a Brontë novel is interior-directed and occurs in enclosed places because they were, as females, themselves enclosed and restricted, limited in whatever social movement they were allowed to schools, houses, positions as teachers and governesses.

There is, however, surely more to the idea than that. For if their movements as females were limited, then we should ask why we have almost no domestic scenes and almost no enclosed scenes involving married couples and children? Why, indeed, do so few children have living parents? Or parents at all? If the primary intent had been to reflect the realities of female life, then we should have more scenes of domesticity. Evidently, the point lies elsewhere, not simply in enclosure itself, but in a *particular* kind of enclosure. For the Brontës have another scene or angle of vision which is, in their usage, curiously allied to enclosure, and that is the theme of the observer, the outsider, to the extent that the characters and we as readers participate in acts of voyeurism and Peeping Tomism. The voyeur cannot really exist without rooms, enclosed space, restricted movement; she or he must peek in through chinks, windows, small openings, much as the person being observed moves within enclosures, peeks out, peers through chinks. It is a matter of positioning; for often the person peering in, the voyeur, is searching for herself, is looking at the person peering out.

123

The image here is a double one, like Narcissus looking at himself, lover in love with the loved one, all of them himself, or herself. We have, then, a curious play of forces: on the one hand, the enclosed area which can be both prison for the self and staging area for the unfolding of the protagonist's identity; and, on the other, a counterpointing theme, of the same character always looking in-looking out from her isolated point of vantage. Lucy Snowe, in *Villette*, is the perpetual spectator, watching from her various enclosed points of vantage, stifled and yet growing, as much a voyeur in her role as Mme. Beck and M. Paul are more obviously in theirs. Similarly, Jane Eyre, "imprisoned" at Gateshead, an alien observer of the Reeds, suffocated by the atmosphere, uses the experience to develop her inner resolve.[2]

Jane Eyre and Lucy Snowe are joined by Markham and Mrs. Graham (*The Tenant of Wildfell Hall*), Heathcliff, Agnes Grey, William Crimsworth, and others. Enclosure and perpetual peering: these are the twin modes of lonely existences lived far from the eyes of others; as if one's existence were on a strange planet beyond human ken. In Lucy Snowe's Brussels, all events take place in a different arena from hers; she listens, watches, steals out unobserved, makes no waves, is small and unnoticeable—how often Charlotte Brontë catches her in this way. The enclosure and observation are part of her lonely role: to be an eye and an "I," not to do, not to impinge. This would appear to be her fate, to be the fate of all the Brontë protagonists; and yet, if they are to survive they must unfold, they must become identified, they must forsake observation and enclosure for involvement.

Starting from sacred assumptions, the Brontës ranged out into the most profane conflicts, encompassing inner and outer, individual and society, subject and object. Their foreshadowing of several aspects of the current struggle for women's rights was merely one side of their awareness of the individual's rights, or the individual's struggle for identity. What makes the Brontës' sense of struggle intense is their own uncertainty about the terms of the conflict; their own dubious commitment to it. By that, I mean they are themselves caught up by the romantic possibilities of conflict as much as they are by its practical terms. Put another way, they have their daydreams in the world of Cinderella, while they have their actions in the world of hard-fought struggle.

In Freudian terms, they think of themselves as creatures in a "Family Romance," which is to say they act out fantasies of courtships, marriages, birth rites, and parentage which involve transformations of themselves. In their fantasies, they are fairy princesses, Cinderellas, tied to myths and tales which evade reality. Yet, at the same time, they are also involved in tough decisions about present and future, choice of husband, or not, difficult work possibilities, and all the other dilemmas of people trying to exist as individuals.

So much of the Brontë self-made legend involves transformation—myths of change, metamorphosis, and the like—that we have to view the conflicts of their characters from a long perspective. Conflict in their work is never quite what it is in a novel of Dickens or Eliot. It is rarely based on a matter of will, a decision of the conscious self. Their characters do not freely choose, although choice is not ruled out. The Brontës move in and out of the nineteenth-century preoccupation with the individual will; at times accepting the Victorian conception of happiness, on occasion embracing Providence, at other times rejecting both will and Providence in favor of the inner demon which precludes happiness. As authors, they are not to be pinpointed here or there. Struggle and adversity do not by any means lead to unalloyed happiness, for there are nearly always significant catches which derive from within.

When we note, for example, Shirley Keeldar, from the flawed novel *Shirley*, we can see how a Brontë character is often as a created thing more significant than the novel itself. Shirley is herself involved in an extremely difficult problem of self-definition, stemming from her parents' expectation of a boy child, their giving her an ambiguous Christian name, and her own assumption of a certain duality because of her very desire for self-definition.

Shortly after we meet her, almost one-third into this long novel, she is insisting on roles which her society has traditionally assigned to males, such as churchwarden, magistrate, captain of yeomanry. Mrs. Pryor, her former governess, gently reproves her for such talk, asserting that her habit of alluding to herself as a gentleman is a "strange one." Those around Shirley apparently treat her manner of talk as frivolous, especially since her appearance is femininely attractive. Yet even as we go this far, we are deep into a Brontë dilemma which involves the whole range of enclosure and self-definition: the distinction between outer cool and inner passion, the longing for role playing and role changing, the yearning for activities which transcend traditional situations and positions, the recognition of potential powers which are destined to atrophy, the great sense of individual loss, dissatisfaction with human boundaries and reaching out toward limits. Locked into these issues is the Brontë sense of tragedy: the individual scaled down to fit into a universe which negates his/her pride and yearning.

Like Jane Eyre and Lucy Snowe, Shirley straddles more issues and roles than her consciousness can contain. For even as she yearns for a male involvement in society, she is unwilling to forsake her female role. To be unmarried means one can pursue "hard labour" and "learned professions"; to be married, one must be "womanly." The very middle ground she seeks—that is, to realize both senses of her Christian name—is lacking, and she knows she will have to choose her future by way of a man. That is, despite her own sense of worth, she will ultimately have to choose her roles through men's attitudes toward her, not through any final choice of a role for herself. Toward this decision she feels only contempt and voices the injustice of such restrictions. In a dramatic, exultant passage, she strikes out at the male arbiters and referees who have "decreed" the female role and seizes upon Milton as blind in more ways than one:

> "Milton's Eve! Milton's Eve! I repeated. No, by the pure Mother of God, she [Nature kneeling 'before those red hills'] is not! Cary [Caroline Helstone], we are alone: we may speak what we think. Milton was great; but was he good? His brain was right; how was his heart? He saw heaven: he looked down on hell. He saw Satan, and Sin his daughter, and Death their horrible offspring. Angels serried before him their battalions: the long lines of adamantine shields flashed back on his blind eyeballs the unutterable splendour of heaven. Devils gathered

their legions in his sight: their dim, discrowned, and tarnished armies passed rank and file before him. Milton tried to see the first woman; but, Cary, he saw her not." (Chapter XVIII)

What Milton failed to see, in this extraordinary passage, is that Nature kneeling on the far hill is woman herself, Eve herself, Jehovah's daughter as much as Adam was His son. Later on, to complete the reconstruction, Shirley repudiates St. Paul and the Pauline view of women.

Yet through it all, even while she exalts women, Shirley wants to be known as "Captain Keeldar." Further, even as she exults in being as capable as a man, she is surrounded by those who insist on her being a woman. Somewhere, between self-knowledge and repudiation of assigned roles, she must find who she is and what roles she is going to play, a question not at all difficult for Caroline Helstone, who defines herself traditionally, even though she suffers physically and mentally from deprivation. Shirley's desire may be to become a lawyer or a magistrate, but her fate is to become Mrs. Moore, a fate no different from Caroline's, although the two young women could not be more unlike each other. Enclosure—the enclosed heart—a frustrated self-bounded activity: all of these qualities come together even in a character as well situated as Shirley, seemingly the least anguished of Brontë females.

In this desire for self-definition we find the theme the Brontës posed with such anguish and determination. In *Villette*, a novel far more intensely felt and seen than *Shirley*, Lucy Snowe limns a great image of the "beast in the jungle" waiting to pounce even as she enjoys moments of respite. Near the beginning of Chapter 7, she is traveling into the unknown, toward Villette (the fictionalized Brussels), on the offhand remark of Ginevra Fanshawe. Friendless, without much money, unable to speak the language, yet prepared to explore the darkness, Lucy starts her journey; and, surprisingly enough, she feels a certain hope amidst the grey sky and stagnant atmosphere. ". . . yet amidst all these deadening influences, my fancy budded fresh and my heart basked in sunshine."

We enter now the heart of a typical Brontë image of contrasts and opposites. Lucy has made a decision, she is moving toward some fate, and she is able to let in a little light; yet the

127

beast is present. "These feelings, however, were well kept in check by the secret but ceaseless consciousness of anciety lying in wait on enjoyment, like a tiger crouched in a jungle. The breathing of that beast of prey was in my ear always; his fierce heart panted close against mine; he never stirred in his lair but I felt him: I knew he waited only for sun down to bound ravenous from his ambush."

James's Marcher gains his identity from a false belief that he has once lived; and the beast waiting to spring, crouching for the leap, and finally springing as Marcher throws himself onto May's tomb, is the beast of unfilled hopes, of wasted vigils, of a jungle of doubts. For Lucy Snowe, the tiger "crouched in a jungle" is an indication of what she must always face. Unlike Marcher, who turns away from his beast, Lucy must never settle into passive happiness or moments of unthinking bliss. For intertwined with every moment of joy is its opposite, that image of a beast of prey which reminds her of what she is and where she is, of her limited expectations for fulfillment. The tiger reminds her she is indeed split, between those moments in which she can lose herself and forget her identity and those in which she must be on guard lest she be devoured.

There is little relaxation in a Brontë novel. The tension we experience in reading is the consequence of the intense guardedness all characters must exhibit both to enclose themselves and to provide self-definition. They must always be in the process of creating themselves, regardless of the beast waiting to spring or the tiger that has already sprung. Wary, tuned in to survival, hopeful of happiness, they find their moments of joy always compromised by moments of challenge. Ultimately, their sense of happiness is just such a joining of elements; they often, like Jane Eyre, perform best under adversity. And, therefore, they often seek adversity so as to test their own development. What is extraordinary is the steel that lies within, although, ultimately, whether Shirley Keeldar, Lucy Snowe, Jane Eyre, or Catherine Linton, they buckle under to a Victorian resolution that disguises their unfilled hopes and aspirations, as well as their elements of anarchy and passion.

As part of the "enclosed-unfolding" image, all Brontë heroines must be tested by their confrontation with a male. They must, in a sense, pass through the male experience and somehow let their existence be absorbed thereby. Much of the Brontë ambiguity, of course, lies just here: in the oscillation between female identity, a fierce desire for a unique self, and the demands of the other side of the female appetite, the urgency of fulfillment by a male, and frequently not by a particularly sympathetic or pro-feminist male. Although we normally think of Jane Eyre and Catherine Linton, Lucy Snowe of *Villette* has the most dramatic, extended confrontation. Her relationship with M. Paul, somewhat based on Charlotte's own experiences with Constantin Heger at the Pensionnat Heger in Brussels, runs the gamut of male-female processes in a society which tries to foreclose the female experience.

However, in discussing this relationship, we should see it not only from Lucy's point of view; that is, we should view it not solely from her attempt to gain a self in a miniature world which prescribes female selflessness. We must also see the relationship as part of a changing male process, in which M. Paul—chauvinist, worried by any semblance of female equality, full of pique and self-importance—must realign some of his attitudes in order to provide an umbrella for Lucy.

Part of the Brontë's genius lies in their delineating a process and not solely one side of a relationship. Only Heathcliff fails to alter his assumptions, and that is readily explicable by the fact he sees love as itself immutable, going beyond himself and Catherine into a spiritual region where male-female do not even exist. As pure spirits, they would transcend their bodies and, as well, their earthly roles; equality or subservience would not be at issue, nor would even sexual passion. It is this journey, this spiritualizing of self and roles, which Catherine evidently rejects, much as later Lawrentian protagonists, male and female alike, either accept or reject such relationships depending on how they feel about their bodies and "other selves."

Heathcliff aside, however, virtually every Brontë protagonist must himself "unfold" a hidden self which is the reciprocal of change in his female opposite. Such factors crystallize in *Villette*, in M. Paul, who fears and detests women who do not

129

demonstrate weakness. His reliance on his manhood is virtually pathological in its implications, for his defense of masculinity is attached to several other aspects of his character: his stance as Bonaparte; his constant voyeurism—beyond the call of an inquisitive schoolmaster; his need to keep others dependent upon him—disguised as charity; his priestly devotion to a long-lost love, a girl who took up the vocation of a nun. Chapter 30 of *Villette* focuses on M. Paul: especially, his dislike of Madame Panache, who shows independence of spirit. Her voice, which angers him, indicates her indifference. M. Paul sets out to defeat and frustrate her, and, as soon as she is vanquished, he rushes to her aid. In his reaching out for supremacy, he is a scholarly Bonaparte.

He carries over the same attitudes to Lucy. As he informs her, a woman of intellect is a sort of "lusus naturae," a freak of nature. He goes on to say that a woman's role is "passive feminine mediocrity," which should eschew work and active roles as manly. Although M. Paul appears to be sporting with Lucy, his bantering tone barely disguises very deeply felt attitudes which he has carried over into every other aspect of his life. Even his role as a charitable man is couched in strange, secretive terms, for his charity goes to support a scene which has strong Gothic overtones. When Lucy is tricked into visiting Madame Malraven, at Numéro 3, Rue des Mages, she passes a church with "dark, half-ruinous turrets," she crosses a "deserted 'place'," she sees as the sole evidence of life an "infirm old priest"; when she enters, she notes a picture on the wall which involves passages, winding stairs, a donjon, and so on through typical Gothic atmospherics, all against the background of a developing storm.

Finally, someone approaches Lucy: "I began to comprehend where I was. Well might this old square be named quarter of the Magi—well might the three towers, overlooking it, own for godfather three mystic sages of a dead and dark art. Hoar enchantment here prevailed; a spell had opened for me elfland—that cell-like room, that vanishing picture, that arch and passage, and stair of stone, were all parts of a fairy tale." Or, rather, a nightmare, since this "scene" is supported by M. Paul, and Lucy, we later discover, has been sent here as a way of warning her off marriage to him. The next figure to appear is that of Cunégonde, the sorceress, or Malevola, the evil fairy: three feet tall, shapeless, with a wand-like ivory staff, gowned in brocade, with bejeweled ears, ringed fingers. "Hunchbacked, dwarfish, and doting, she was adorned like a barbarian queen."

Since this scene is presented with great care and yet is tonally such a departure from the relatively realistic development of the surrounding chapters, Charlotte Brontë is making some metaphorical statement well beyond the actual scene. M. Paul, who is directly identified as the benefactor of Numéro 3, Rue des Mages, is psychologically attached to the house and its inhabitants: the dwarf, the old priest, the donjon-like quality. Its interiors are his interiors; its existence part of his. As a voyeur, a man intensely connected to secrets and secret lives, M. Paul preserves his masculinity through oppression, whether through charity or that gained by his superior position at the Pensionnat.

While Charlotte Brontë later mutes this view of him, nevertheless he is this type of creature *when* Lucy becomes attached to him. She does not become attached to the man who will later give her a school of her own to operate while he is away; she attaches herself to someone who, with affinities to Rochester and Heathcliff, will enter her life like a wraith, seize her imagination, and imprison her senses. The Gothic, specter-like trappings, then, of Madame Malraven's establishment amidst the three Magis are a vague equivalent of Wuthering Heights and Thornfield in their physical and spiritual characteristics; further, the "scene" indicates how deeply obsessive and secretive M. Paul really is, so that when he does change under Lucy's influence—as she changes under his—he has come back from a Gothic-Jesuitical existence far from human eyes, exactly as she has returned from the deadness of life which she felt before meeting M. Paul.

The development of self, or at least the definition of self implicit here, is typical of the Brontë way of proceeding. Each element, both male and female, must evolve from a secret and secretive core, from an "other" which may not be at all pleasant. We find almost always the resonance of an interior

131

existence—whether Lucy's crouching beast or Paul's dwarf—
and the literary experience is evidently a fictional representation of the double life the Brontës themselves lived, that life
on the functioning surface of things and that secret existence
which contained the intense reality of the living imagination.

To seek the self, then, is to experience a burrowing process,
somewhat different in degree and kind from the procedures of
Brontë contemporaries like Dickens and Thackeray. Through
her own kind of personal wound, George Eliot approximates
the Brontë type of reality, especially in her probing of experience gained through pain and suffering. Even George Eliot,
however, differs in that she probes a wider range of feeling,
something less feral, something more peculiar to mid-Victorian humanism than to the wilder Romantic assumptions of the
three sisters. Further, by grafting pain and suffering on to a
socio-political scene, Eliot diluted the purity of feeling which
we experience in the Brontës, for whom socio-political considerations simply did not exist.

Before moving more specifically to certain Brontë novels,
we can see how Charlotte's view of pain is tied to her views
of female independence, so that social issues can never pre-
empt individual attitudes even when the two are attached. In
a letter to Mr. Williams (May 12, 1848), the Smith, Elder
literary advisor and reader, written at the time of both *Jane
Eyre* and *Shirley*, Charlotte spoke about the "condition of wom-
en" question. She asserted that women should earn their own
living: "Most desirable then is it that all, both men and women,
should have the power and the will to work for themselves—
most advisable that both sons and daughters should early be
inured to habits of independence and industry." She then
chronicles how painful such a transplantation of a young woman
among strangers may prove to be, acknowledging that a "governess's experience is frequently indeed bitter." Nevertheless,
the very bitterness challenges one's discipline, so that the results as well as the process are precious. Each step in independence, no matter the pain, is a stage in the unfolding of the
self, whose development is irresistible. To be a governess, or
something comparable, is an ordeal one must pass through, so
that one is "strengthened and purified, fortified and softened,

made more enduring for her own afflictions, more considerate for the afflictions of others."

The outlook here is more unflinching than George Eliot's, whose own views these words of Charlotte appear to foreshadow. There is, of course, as in George Eliot, a compensatory view: discipline for physical beauty, pain for careless ease and leisure; but there is also an insistence on the purity of the experience, *for itself*, which we do not feel in George Eliot, and which remains unique in English fiction until Hardy and Conrad.

In this area of pain and suffering, where relief is virtually impossible, where relief is often illusory and insufficient to balance the pain, in this area we can come close to defining Brontë tragedy.[3] Let us attempt some general formula: While redefinition, testing, trying-out, seeking new frontiers for the self are all thematic for Charlotte, Emily, and Anne (in varying degrees), each individual must come up against the limitations of her own mortality. That is, the individual yearns for redefinition and is willing to experience the intense pain of novelty; she yearns for some mythical, transcendent experience, as later Hardy protagonists were to do. And yet, even as she yearns, suffers, reaches out, she approaches the outer limits of the possible and must face the realities of her own limitations.

Put another way, we alluded at the beginning to how the Brontës approximate in their fantasies of love and romance the situation Freud wrote about as "family romances," a brief paper he published in 1909. "Family romances" are particularly appropriate to the Brontës since their early Gondal and Angria tales—romances of the most compulsive sort, even down to the minute, almost microscopic holograph—are intense, far-reaching fantasies. Sex—romance—marriage—transformation—rebirth: all of these are implicit in those early tales, as they are in Freud's definition.

The condition Freud has called to our attention is so appropriate to the early Brontë experience *and to their subsequent development* that we should quote at some length from his essay.[4] "The later stage in the development of the neurotic's estrangement from his parents," Freud writes, "begun in this manner [with hostile impulses toward the father], might be

133

described as the 'neurotic's family romance'. . . . For a quite specific form of imaginative activity is one of the essential characteristics of neurotics and also of comparatively highly gifted people. This activity emerges first in children's play, and then, starting roughly from the period before puberty, takes over the topic of family relations. A characteristic example of this particular kind of phantasy is to be seen in the familiar day-dreams which persist far beyond puberty." Such daydreams, Freud continues, serve as wish fulfillments and as correctives of actual life, with two primary drives: eroticism and ambition. As these dreams work out, the child will replace his parent or father by others of better birth. "The technique used in carrying out phantasies like this (which are, of course, conscious at this period) depends upon the ingenuity and the material which the child has at his disposal." Charlotte's intense admiration for the Duke of Wellington, as reflected in her Angria tales, contains much of this conscious and subconscious fantasy, although we should be careful not to equate a general interpretation with a specific result. The presence of the Duke as both lover and father-figure, nevertheless, indicates something very close to the fantasy-romance outlined by Freud, especially important to us because it becomes so closely allied to Charlotte's literary development.

The fantasy is much more complicated than this, since Charlotte's admiration for the Duke may not be a displacement of her father, but an exaltation of him, a desire to resurrect a happier time when the father was indeed comparable to the Duke. So, too, the fantasy would relate to the brother figure of Branwell, the father's favorite, the only son in a family of five girls and, therefore, the one expected to carry the family's fortunes. Precisely how the sisters' attitudes toward Branwell worked is unclear, but we can suggest that the transformation of males which produced Heathcliff, Rochester, M. Paul, among others, was not an act of reproduction of reality, but a transmutation of reality toward the wish fulfillment Freud speaks about.

Since fantasy is one extremity of the Brontë polarity, the other extremity must be limitation and deprivation. A protagonist yearns for myth, transformation; yet she must settle for

134

long stretches of pain and for a mixed sort of fulfillment, if any at all. In this movement toward outer reaches beyond material rewards, the Brontës defined an area almost completely lacking in their Victorian contemporaries, who eschewed tragic disproportion in favor of more moderate goals. The intensity we sense in a Brontë novel is the intensity of dangerous feelings as they brush the possible (or impossible), and there is no more appropriate beginning than *Jane Eyre*, where myths of rebirth, transformation, and unfolding are always coming up against realities which require unrequited suffering.

Jane Eyre is cast in terms of rebirth, although one uniform imagistic pattern does not define the entire novel. Nevertheless, the pattern involves an unfolding of self which begins with a rebirth image, the famous "red room" scene. Before we arrive at that scene, however, we have noted Jane (as, also, Heathcliff, Lucy Snowe, Mrs. Graham, Caroline Helstone) as the outsider. She is "outside" not only the Reed family experience, but especially John Reed, the first in a line of male figures whom she must hurdle. At ten years old, Jane is physically inferior to John, Eliza, and Georgiana Reed, a physical inferiority that symbolizes her situation. She desperately wishes to be elsewhere and to be "other," wherever that may lead. We begin, here, the Cinderella pattern.

The red-room or chamber, which comes only five pages after the novel starts, has mythological overtones: its redness, its silence and chill, its former use as a resting place for Mr. Reed's coffin, its attachment to tradition, the past, to secrets, to jewels, to a former grandeur. It is foreignness itself to the timid, fearful Jane, and it has sufficient overtones of death and regression within it to make Jane become fetal within its confines. "No jail was ever more secure," Charlotte writes. When Jane peers into the looking-glass, she sees a "strange little figure" gazing back at her, the face white, the eyes glittering, and she thinks of "tiny phantoms, half fairy, half imp"—that is, fairy images coming out of strange dark places.

In order to survive the particular moment and general situation, Jane has regressed so that the red-room becomes both the place for her present death and the staging area for her rebirth. She is, in any event, changed by the experience and

135

by the results of her emergence; the room, we can say, has elements of mythological ordeal, elements of the womb, elements of (re)birth of hero(ine) after underground journey. Within, Jane examines her own status, the fact she is always accused, blamed, condemned. Pursued, persecuted, oppressed, she resolves some form of escape from her predicament: the first stage of her rebirth. Fears, nevertheless, pile up; suffering intensifies. Jane expands to fill the room so that she must come out or burst. Help comes. She emerges, and, when confronted by the wicked stepmother, breaks down in a convulsive fit.

Awakening, she experiences the confused awareness of an infant, the foetus who "sees" the light. "The next thing I remember is, waking up with a feeling as if I had had a frightful nightmare, and seeing before me a terrible red glare, crossed with thick black bars. I heard voices, too, speaking with a hollow sound, as if muffled by a rush of wind or water: agitation, uncertainty, and an all-predominating sense of terror confused my faculties." (Chapter III) The red-room episode having been passed through, Jane is now in a different relationship to herself and to those around her. Although she still sees other people as larger than she is—the experience of Swift's Gulliver is brought into focus—nevertheless, she has clarified the first stage of her new self, and she is ready to achieve the primary level of her rebirth. Shortly after, she sets out into the dark, leaving the distasteful womb-like existence of Gateshead, a lantern providing light for the next stage of her development.

The imagery here is quite complicated and not always consistent, but it has much of the same chiaroscuro of *Wuthering Heights*, and it evidently carries some of the burden of meaning. Just as contrasts of color, situation, character type categorize Emily Brontë's novel as well as Charlotte's *Villette* and *Shirley*, so here, in *Jane Eyre*, the use of contrast signals content. If Jane and her quest represent the need for "coming out," unfolding, then she has placed herself in an adversary position, like Heathcliff in Emily's novel, Mrs. Graham in Anne's *Tenant*, Lucy Snowe in *Villette*, Caroline Helstone in *Shirley*. Each place for Jane, whether Gateshead, Lowood, Thornfield, or Moor End (St. John's), has the potential and ac-

136

tuality of shackling her. Helen Burns, at Lowood, with her stoical endurance of pain, which precludes development or unfolding, indicates what Jane must reject; just as, earlier, she has rejected Mrs. Reed and Gateshead, and, later, she will decline aspects of Thornfield. None of this is easy, for even as she moves out into her major quest, she has regressive tendencies, dreams that return her to "infancy" at Gateshead and Lowood, seasonal relapses in which, like Persephone, she retreats to her underworld seeking either renewed strength or retreat from all challenge.

In that remarkable series of water-colors Jane paints while still at Lowood, we have several aspects of her struggle, the conscious wish to stay afloat and unfold as against the subconscious desire to give it all up and withdraw into the warm sea and death. As she spreads her portfolio before Rochester (Chapter XIII) in the form of a triptych, we see in the first a wreck, a drowned corpse, a fair arm extended from the sea, a cormorant with a gold bracelet in its beak, evidently from the raised arm. In the second, the gigantic figure of a woman stretches into the dark blue sky, a figure with streaming hair, eyes dark and wild, foreshadowing madness and probably Rochester's mad wife, Bertha. In the third, a colossal skeletal head rests against an iceberg which pierces the winter sky, with a ring of white flame, "gemmed with sparkles."

The paintings are stages of Jane's life, with herself drowning in the first, or at least an inner vision of herself as drowning; then a foreshadowing (in keeping with her dream material) of her situation at Thornfield as long as Bertha is alive, and, by extension, possibly of herself as a double or duplicate of Bertha's insane condition. Finally, we find an apparent shift to Rochester, another of Jane's prefigurations while she was still at Lowood, part of that underground lore she acquired when she retreated into her own visions and images. In that third water-color, the figure is neither male nor female, but evidently with dual characteristics: the hollow eye, the colossal head, a look of despair recalling Rochester, while the veil and diadem imply a woman, although not clearly Jane. Perhaps the third is purposely unclear, since Jane in her movements between vision and reality did not have a sharp focus while still

137

at icy Gateshead and Lowood, and predicament had not yet become prophecy.[5]

In any event, these water-colors, like dreams, visions, and prefigurations, are stages of Jane's own journey, between her regressive desire for death and burial and her inner urgency to emerge from behind the veil. Not surprisingly, Rochester leads into this scene by toying with Jane's emerging sexuality, by referring to her as having "lived the life of a nun." What is emerging, then, in Jane is an entire pattern of unfolding: sexual, personally expressive, societal. She is, indeed, attempting to emerge from behind the veil, or curtain.

I have devoted this much space to *Jane Eyre*, a novel normally well defined by scholars and critics, because it apparently contains the basic premises and movements of all seven completed Brontë novels. While we can say the same of *Villette* and, to a lesser extent, of *Wuthering Heights*, each of these raises special questions which divert us from the underlying quest: the unfolding of a secret self, the emergence of a most volatile sexuality, the need to break out into expression, physical or otherwise, the necessity of definition and redefinition. These urges bring terrible intensity to the Brontë's sense of fiction, and it is this desire for multiple, polymorphous lives which connects them so startlingly with our own age. All the great Victorian novelists live for us in varying ways, but the Brontës survive and impinge upon us for their insistence on the intensity of their inner lives and their almost mythical reconstruction of a self. To strike out, however fearfully, was for them virtually an existential act.

For variations on this theme, we can turn to Charlotte's *Shirley*, Emily's *Wuthering Heights*, and Anne's *The Tenant of Wildfell Hall*. *Shirley* is the least known of Charlotte Brontë's three major novels, and rightfully so, since its artistry is considerably flawed by the lack of a clear line of development or sharp enough focus. It is, nevertheless, remarkable as a "handbook" of the developing self, of both the titular character and of her friend, Caroline Helstone. *Shirley*, like *The Golden Notebook* of Doris Lessing, is a novel about women and how they can survive, if they are to survive, in a male world. The novel is shot through with dominant males: from the unpleasant curates at the beginning, whose joviality barely disguises their distrust and scorn of women, to virtually all the male figures in the novel, with the exception of Louis Gérard Moore. And Shirley herself, as we have noted, appears torn between the two sexes, since, theoretically at least, she appears to desire both the male and female worlds.

While *she* does not really unfold or develop, she does reveal a self which she has already achieved. That is to say: Shirley moves toward us in a way opposite to Jane Eyre, for while the latter heroine does unfold as we read her narrative (a first person narrative, for that effect), the former heroine is defined for us (in the third person) in terms of what she has, in her own mind and body, already achieved. There are, as it were, two sides here: the uncertain young girl who must seek herself in exploration and in new territory, and the certain young woman who has already achieved the new territory, has pioneered in forbidden ground, and has returned to tell us what she has found; as it were, Telemachus and Odysseus.

Shirley has found nothing less than a way to live. Of course, she has both money and a favorable appearance, so that her choices are considerably lightened by her relatively easy acceptance. She is, we recognize, something of a wish-fulfillment figure for Charlotte, even though Shirley, Gérin tells us, was modeled on Emily, as Caroline Helstone was based on Anne Bronte. Whatever the intention, Shirley is not Emily, nor is she Charlotte except in some magic mirror reflection or as part of a "family romance." She has close affinities with a long line of "heroines," not the least of whom derive from Jane Austen, but she has, of course, the added ingredient of a Brontë mystique: that canker sore at the heart of her emotional life. The most telling parts are concerned with Shirley's "sore," while the least effective are devoted to the socio-economic conditions peculiar to north of England mill owners in 1812.

The image of enclosure, of blackness, of the stifled self (which defines Caroline Helstone) is not for Shirley, for, as we have noted, she has already resolved what and who she is. She needs neither red rooms, nor weathering stations, nor lonely refuges in alien homes to act as spring boards for her own developing self. Shirley, unlike the other half of the novel, is concerned almost solely with self-definition, with expressing attitudes about roles, individual dignity, relationship to self. The reason the novel splits so badly is the antithetical quality of the halves: one directed outward, the other directed inward. Shirley has little "social self," as opposed to social responsibility, which she has in abundance.

Like the later Dorothea Brooke of George Eliot, Shirley has a charitable and humanitarian heart, but her sense of social responsibility is secondary to the primary area of combat, which is solipsistic. Shirley must settle in her own mind what it is to be a woman, what roles she may play as a woman, and what reactions she will allow herself to an eligible male. Thus far she is not unlike a Jane Austen heroine. Shirley, however, goes much further. When she says she cannot marry Samuel Fawthorp Wynne because "His intellect reaches no standard I can esteem . . . his views are narrow; his feelings are blunt; his tastes are coarse; his manner vulgar"—when she says this, she is in the line of Clarissa rejecting Solmes and Elizabeth Bennet mocking Collins' proposal.

When, however, she answers Robert Gérard Moore's proposal, she has broken with her female predecessors:

> You insinuate that all the frank kindness I have shown you has been a complicated, a bold, and an immodest manoeuvre to ensnare a husband: you imply that at last you come here out of pity to offer me your hand because I have courted you. Let me say this:—Your sight is jaundiced: you have seen wrong. Your mind is warped: you have judged wrong. Your tongue betrays you: you now speak wrong. I never loved you. Be at rest there. My heart is as pure of passion for you as yours is barren of affection for me.

Her response is, in a sense, that of a culture heroine, one who has spoken for all women who want to reject the wrong male but cannot because of familial pressure or economic fear. Shirley's aim is to redefine Eve. Earlier, she had asserted Milton failed to "see" the first woman, for Eve is Nature herself, and it is necessary to revive Eve in her glory, not in her sinful or penitential state.

Shirley, then, is a remarkable intermediate creation between Jane Eyre and Lucy Snowe, an anomaly in Charlotte Brontë's

140

own method of proceeding. One can only speculate that the resolute quality of the heroine is Charlotte's way of hanging on to forcefulness to mitigate the personal tragedies occurring in the Brontë household: the decline and deaths of Branwell and Emily in 1848 and Anne in 1849. Most of Shirley's strongest statements about self, marriage, and males come toward the end of the manuscript, supporting the view that Charlotte Brontë used her as emotional compensation for the disintegrating Brontë household; or, even more likely, that Shirley was the singular focus of an author seeking meaning in a protean-narcissistic mirror image of herself, strength amidst decline, force among the weak and dying, "masculine" certainty amidst "female" irresoluteness. Even Shirley, however, does not represent reality for Charlotte, but reflection: Shirley, appearing between less certain characters as Jane Eyre and Lucy Snowe, is a wish-fulfillment female, the product of a dream about oneself.

To dream about oneself: such is the road that leads us back to Emily Brontë, whose one novel has thus far in this essay received little attention. Emily of course differs from both Charlotte and Anne in her commitment to a ruling passion, rather than to the more normalizing "unfolding" process we have cited in their work. She set for herself an impossible ideal, most imposing because of its impossibility. The "unfolding" we have spoken of before does occur in her novel but as the consequence of a self-defeating impulse. She is attuned to magnificent failure, to unscalable heights and passions. Since she was concerned with an ideal, her novel moves from one frustration to another, while for her sisters at least the possibility of "opening up" and succeeding was ever present. Both in her verse and in her novel, Emily foreshadows a poet like Hopkins. In a poem such as "No Coward Soul Is Mine," dated January 2, 1846 (either written or transcribed on that date), overlapping with the writing of *Wuthering Heights*, she mixes divine and human in a way that foreshadows Hopkins' mixture of God and gall, divine presentiment and human inadequacy.[6] In their overlapping views, the individual may unfold relentlessly, but the end is always the same: one falls far short of

141

divinity, to the precise extent that mortality falls short of the divine.

Emily reached for the unattainable, and therefore we note her contempt for all mortal events, her defiance of all attempts to keep her alive, and, in her novel, Heathcliff's refusal to compromise with his feelings even when the feeling no longer had an object. Yet despite her seeming intractability, which Charlotte noted in her Preface to the 2nd Edition, *Wuthering Heights* does fit into the general patterns we have established for her two sisters. Emily, in fact, exploits the "enclosure" theme to a far greater extent than either Charlotte or Anne, utilizing an enclosed space-time concept in her very narrative method. The story of Heathcliff and the Lintons is inset into the "outer" narrative scheme of Lockwood and Nelly Dean. Such a narrative device is more than a convenience or a way of achieving aesthetic distance. Like all effective forms of narration, the device is part of Emily's way of envisioning her material: as isolated in space and time, caught as a moment in history, in suspension apart from the normal, regularizing world. It is dream, fantasy, Freudian "family romance," the quest for the impossible and the unattainable in a world unimpeded by clock and calendar.

Although Heathcliff has such implacable force and although Catherine Linton is cleaved by conflicting feelings, neither would have existence without the "outside" narrators; for in her narrative Nelly brings back the reality of Heathcliff's feral nature. The older Heathcliff whom Lockwood meets has little of the ferocity Nelly relates to us from the past. Since Catherine is herself dead, she can exist only in Nelly's words. Thus, the "outer" creates the inner, although the inner is the greater and more compelling story, *is*, in fact, the story. We can say, then, that for Emily the development of her compelling tale is itself the unfolding process we have found in all the Brontë works. Certainly, the inner place is both a lair and a trap. Heathcliff finds a refuge in Wuthering Heights as a child and then, like a demon guarding the gates of hell, proceeds to ensnare everyone who enters it.

In one sense, its enclosed nature makes it a sacred place where particular ceremonies are celebrated, ceremonies of

142

initiation and baptism by fire. No one who enters the Heights is ever the same again; life is itself intensified, like a hot-house which becomes a special kind of place because of its relationship to something we normally take for granted, the sun. To enter the Heights is to force a choice: whether to remain in its intense, extreme form of atmosphere or to leave for the tepid, more normalizing world. Only Heathcliff seems to under-stand the full potential of the Heights, both the intensifica-tion of life and its enervation, both the exhilarations and the fear and trembling; only Heathcliff remains perfectly true to the vision of the Heights. All others, including Catherine, who even while marrying Linton denies she has ever forsaken Heathcliff, all others temporize with the essential nature of the place and try to shield themselves from its tempestuous blasts. Heathcliff remains on the wind side, while they seek the lee for protection.

The nature of the inner story also fits well into the connection we have made of "enclosure" to voyeurism. The use of an outer narrative device, the use of a narrator who has carefully ob-served whatever she relates, the use of an inner story as if viewed through a telescope—all of these are voyeuristic devices employed as ways of conveying meaning. Lockwood is, of course, the ultimate voyeur, almost literally, reading Cather-ine's diary, staying on, peering, returning to the Heights to pick up details of a story which he has, perforce, to observe from without. Even his attraction to young Cathy is a voyeur-ist's; he watches her and fantasizes as she and Hareton carry on a ritualistic ceremony of courtship. He notes her qualities, as Hareton observes her, and as she, with full awareness, watches Hareton watch her. Argus-eyed, each character moves in a slow ballet, peering at the other's inner drama.

In a related matter, Heathcliff wishes the ultimate in "in-ner" imagery: to be buried alongside Catherine, to burrow not only into her body but into her dust, and to seek in that inner place of ashes to ashes and dust to dust a final celebration of his impossible ideal of love and loyalty. We note an extra-ordinary vision of secrets, secret lives, secret wishes, secret shames. The Gothic, Romantic frenzy we usually associate with Emily is really not the result of literary influences, but of a hard, unshakable core within her; she refused to compromise with her vision because compromise meant relinquishment of what sustained her. Gérin speaks of Emily's intractability in dealing with the corrupt publisher Newby even when she might have known better; but Emily was intractable as a way of surviving. She held on. She never revealed herself the way Charlotte and Anne did; she never embraced the "actuals" of the world, neither its pleasures nor rewards.

She was a burrower who, like Kafka's mole-like creature, found her sole pleasure in her Castle Keep hole. "All that can be seen from outside," Kafka writes, "is a big hole; that, however, really leads nowhere; if you take a few steps you strike against natural firm rock." Emily would have agreed: enclosure, peering, concentration, no compromise—these were the stuff of her conception of the self as she tried to find the precise line between sanity and insanity, between order and disorder, between pleasure and pain. If the self unfolded, it did so in isolation, in a feral atmosphere of tempests and blasts, far from the more moderating influences of normal people and events. How appropriate Kafka's words are to Emily, when he says, in "The Burrow":

> But you do not know me if you think I am afraid, or that I built my burrow simply out of fear. At a distance of some thousand paces from this hole lies, covered by a movable layer of moss, the real entrance to the burrow; it is secured as safely as anything in this world can be secured; yet some one could step on the moss or break through it, and then my burrow would lie open, and anybody who liked—please note, however, that quite uncommon abilities would also be required —could make his way in and destroy everything for good.

Whether in "Gondal," her poetry, or *Wuthering Heights*, Emily knew her refuge lasted only until death.

Anne's *The Tenant of Wildfell Hall* was part of that remarkable Brontë two-year burst of energy: *Wuthering Heights*, *Agnes Grey*, and *Jane Eyre* in 1847; *Tenant* in 1848; *Shirley* in 1849. While *Agnes Grey* is by far the slightest of the Brontë novels, *Tenant* warrants attention both for itself and for its affinities to the Brontë syndrome. Once again, as in *Wuthering Heights*, we become aware of a narrative method which at-

144

tempts to become a way of seeing. Since Anne is less of an artist than Emily, her methodology is less meaningful; nevertheless, she eschewed a straightforward narrative, as she did the uniformity of a female point of view. In keeping with the ambivalence of the Brontës presenting themselves as three male writers under the name of Bell, Anne begins this ambitious novel with a first person narrator, Gilbert Markham, an example of sexual transference that continues for the first 125 pages. Such a sexual transference for purposes of narration are extremely rare in English fiction, the notable rarity being Richardson's Pamela.

Part of the reasoning behind Anne's utilization of Markham, we can speculate, was to "hide" Mrs. Graham, whose own diary-narrative occupies the middle 250 pages of the novel. By beginning with Markham and establishing his voice, Anne was able to work in toward her main subject, the actual "tenant" of the Gothic Wildfell Hall. The process, as we have seen with other Brontë novels, is enclosure and observation or voyeurism. Markham is the constant observer; his opening narrative is virtually a post of observation, in the Jamesian sense. He peers in, stares, prowls around, hides in lanes and paths, does all except peep into open windows. He collects data (imperfectly, it is true), for all he knows must come from the outside—as if Lockwood had had to gather information without Nelly Dean.

Markham fills the gap in his information when he reads Mrs. Graham's diary or "golden notebook," which becomes the middle of the book. A self-enclosed unit, it is a tale of a female's oppression by her husband and other men, a now familiar Brontë preoccupation. Through it all, Mrs. Graham strives to find her own center, to make sense of events, to hold on to her true feelings, to preserve her sanity, a situation not too different from Jane Eyre's, Lucy Snowe's, or Catherine Linton's. Her journey is from innocence through experience (of the male and of marriage). In all aspects of her quest, she must coil herself into a small bundle of active energy and resist breakdown; victimization must not destroy her. She hangs in and on. As she almost drowns in a sea of marriage ills, the question of identity haunts her.

145

All the Brontës present protagonists who undertake journeys in order to see themselves and then to change, or to be destroyed because they cannot change. The journey is usually "underground," into some enclosed place, the refuge and snare noted above. Wildfell Hall serves both functions in *Tenant*. Since the enclosure offers the allurement of a place of rest, the protagonist is encouraged to remain; after all, what except the quest itself drove Jane from Lowood once she had become a respected teacher at the institution? Enclosure, we have seen, provides calm, retreat from life, passivity, acceptance of one's fate; and yet, simultaneously, it entices with a false image of oneself. It offers both sides of the "narcissus" coin. One can remain in the refuge and make love to oneself, without fear of rejection; or one can forsake the mirror image and seek one's life amidst others, where there is always the fear of indifference, rejection, ridicule, exploitation.

Like Maturin's Melmoth, a Brontë protagonist embodies a demon which drives him or her into an "adversary" life. Heathcliff insists that Catherine be true to her real feelings and leave the refuge of a marriage with Linton. Jane insists that Rochester face his full situation, both for her own purposes and for his. Lucy "educates" M. Paul into what kind of woman she is, and what kind of woman she will remain, even though Paul, like so many Brontë males, is fond of a particular woman but scornful of the sex in general.

Valuable for us as readers 125 years later is the Brontës' urgency to explore the outer limits of experience, their cult of self. Even though Richard Chase (in "The Brontës: A Centennial Observance") tries to show that the Brontës "were essentially Victorian,"[7] nevertheless in both their males and females they explored existentially. The dialectic of a Brontë novel, as we suggested above, is almost always between that happy resolution (the refuge and lair) which Chase mentions and the unknown which lies outside the burrower's warm, safe hole. There are always other entrances to and exits from that Castle Keep.

In sounding out the unknowns of the Victorian experience, the Brontës explored some startling elements: psychosomatic illness and hypochondria; surrealism of character and event;

savage, almost uncontrollable sexual passions; sexual dislocation—impotence, sadism, masochism, voyeurism; extremes of
emotion within the person and within human relationships;
intimations of lesbianism, ambiguous male-female roles, unful-
filled desires. Mixed in with these extremes are several experi-
ments in narrative: use of inner and outer narrators, utilization of post of observation, cross-referred male-female narrators.

For an evident example of Brontë "adversary-ness" even
within Victorian happy resolutions, we can note how they responded to the parent-less condition of their major characters.
The point is this: most Brontë protagonists, male and female
alike, are parent-less; if they do have families, the latter are
foster or step. This is a condition we normally associate with
Dickens, the archetypal novelist of the "wandering child."
The Brontës, in fact, plumbed this theme more daringly, for
while Dickens sought surrogate parents for his orphans, they
more realistically confronted the consequences of what it is to
be alone, isolated, and rejected. One need not attempt to match
the Brontës against Dickens, but to demonstrate they faced the
enormous consequences of such a theme—their basic theme—at
a time when family inspired stability and moderation.

They moved, as did Dickens, into the interstices of society,
and what they discovered was the terrible disorder of isolation. Like their other contemporaries, Carlyle, Ruskin, Arnold,
but especially Carlyle, they forced their characters to seek
deep within for their best selves, to grapple with the insanity
that lies under the surface, to bring forth a new self, and to
be transformed in the process. Perhaps our best example would
be Lucy Snowe of *Villette*, whose icy name contrasts with the
directionless passion of her nature. We recall that Harriet Mar-
tineau disagreed with Lucy's all-consuming greed for love, but
Charlotte knew that the lack of love dislocated all other feelings and created an oceanic wave of illness and anguish.

Despite the frigid connotation of her name, Lucy attaches
herself to a succession of males and females. Feeling herself
drowning because she lacks love, family, support, connections
of any kind—she always awaits that "beast in the jungle" to
spring—she acts out her need in several conflicting ways. Her

147

need is so great she seeks family/lover without regard for clear choice. Young John Bretton—Polly—Madame Beck—Ginevra Fanshawe—Dr. Bretton—finally M. Paul: Lucy attaches herself to all of them, children and adults, male and female, as possible supports for her agonizing loneliness and loveless condition. In the course of some very astute remarks on *Villette*, Kate Millet comments on how Lucy, through the amateur theatrics, makes love to Ginevra on the stage, so that role-playing and inner need come together. Millet possibly intends to shock us, but Lucy's need is palpable, whether male- or female-directed.

Without love, even if based on someone she dislikes as intensely as Ginevra, she must float aimlessly, as she does during the Pensionnat vacation, as she did earlier when she left England, as she would later when she secretly observes the fête.[8] Our image is of a figure wandering alone through a large, bustling city, a stranger to it even if she remained a lifetime. All connections are a temptation to her, all responses; even Ginevra's disdain and contempt feed her masochism, which is a form of love in a time of need. None of this quite fits into Victorian resolutions; none of this is "acceptable," and yet this example, one among several, indicates how a Brontë protagonist exploits existence before settling the conflict.

It is indeed a process, the unfolding of a self that had burrowed into the ground, the rejection of what Dostoevski's Underground Man was to call "cheap happiness." The Brontë women, in this respect, are culture heroines, speaking chiefly for women, but also for all "selves" which must find their own levels despite privation. To emerge from the red room hysterical but undefeated is to hang on to oneself by the slimmest thread, but it is that slim thread of hope, of faith in the salving power of pain and suffering which defines Brontë characters. They forerun Lifton's "protean man," Fiedler's "new mutants," Laing's "genuine" schizoids. They understand hallucination, alien experience, bizarre extremes. Here, both Victorianism and Modernism collide.

---

1. See Richard Chase's "The Brontës, or Myth Domesticated" (*Kenyon Review*, IX, Autumn 1947) for a discussion of how their "profane" domes-

ticity smothered their "sacred" mythopoeia. Intent upon Brontë resolutions, Chase at times loses sight of Brontë process, which is another matter.

2. The dominant colors of the opening chapters of *Jane Eyre* are whites— frosty, icy—and rich reds, signifying the extremes of Jane's experience: frigid isolation and passionate rage, with no middle ground or resolution. In a curious updating of these themes and colors, Ingmar Bergman in "Cries and Whispers" utilizes frozen, isolated characters against all-red interiors, symbolizing dislocation and failure to connect.

3. Part of Lucy Snowe's emotional dislocation as the result of trying to understand herself and her situation is manifest in the naming of characters in *Villette*. Robert Bernard Martin comments on this point in a brilliant analysis of "naming difficulties": "Young Bretton is variously called Graham in his domestic aspect. Isidore as Ginevra's suitor, John in his adult, professional life. Polly Home becomes the Countess Paulina Mary Home de Bassompierre, and ultimately, of course, Mrs. Bretton. M. Paul most often speaks of himself as Emanuel and on occasion has the full, sonorous name of Paul Carl David Emanuel." (*Charlotte Brontë's Novels: The Accents of Persuasion*, p. 177, n.1) One may add "Wolf"—Mme. Beck's term for Dr. John; Missy—another name for the child Polly; and others indicating a disarrangement of identity. In Dickens, one recalls in *Bleak House* the names John Jarndyce conjures up for Esther Summerson: "Old Woman, and Little Old Woman, and Cobweb, and Mrs. Shipton [a witch and prophetess], and Mother Hubbard, and Dame Durden [a ballad figure who kept five male and five female servants]," among many others. By having Jarndyce make Esther into an old woman by means of names, while all the time planning to marry the young girl, Dickens indirectly keyed into the sexual dislocation of these characters, part of the overall pattern of fog and dislocation which the novel insists upon.

To return to *Villette*: naming patterns extend well beyond the characters. Even the place "Villette" is really Brussels and "Labassecour" is Belgium, while Mme. Beck's establishment is M. Heger's Pensionnat. Naming difficulties are, clearly, one aspect of disarrangement.

4. Carefully researched and presented as Winifred Gérin's studies of the Brontës are, the reader must still wish for a heavier psychological orientation, at least to the extent of probing how the early Gondal and Angria themes offered keys to Brontë neuroses and, thus, to Brontë themes in their later work.

5. For a somewhat different reading of the water-colors, see Mark Kinkead-Weekes' excellent essay, "The Place of Love in *Jane Eyre* and *Wuthering Heights*" (*The Brontës: A Collection of Critical Essays*, ed. Ian Gregor, pp. 79-80).

6. In discussing Hopkins' Sonnet 69, beginning "I wake and feel the fell of dark, not day" and containing the line "I am gall, I am heartburn," R. D. Laing moves in and out of Emily Brontë's world as well. He writes: "Hopkins knew that this taste, of ale or of gall, was *him*. To be 'cured' of this is more problematical than any other cure, if the cure is to become estranged from one's self-being, to lose one's very self. The loss of the experience of an area of *unqualified privacy*, by its transformation into a quasi-public realm, is often one of the decisive changes associated with the process of going mad." (*Self and Others*, p. 21)

Later, Laing has another passage which remarkably fits both Emily and her Heathcliff: "In that study [*The Divided Self*], descriptions were given

149

of a *modus vivendi* with some forms of anxiety and despair. In particular I described that form of self-division which involves a split of the person's being into a disembodied mind and a de-animate body. With this loss of unity, the person preserves a sense of having an 'inner' 'true' self which is, however, unrealized, whereas the 'outer,' 'real,' or 'actual' self is 'false'. We tried to reveal this position as a desperate attempt to come to terms with one form of 'ontological insecurity'. (p. 35)

7. Chase asserts that the end of a typical Bronte novel represents the triumph of "the moderate, secular, naturalistic, liberal, sentimental point of view over the mythical, religious, tragic point of view. The moral texture of these novels is woven whole cloth out of the social customs of the day." My stress, however, is on the journey, which is mythical, religious, and at some stages quasi-tragic, rather than on the resolution. If we indeed seek our point of view in resolutions, then all Victorian journeys end up the same way, and imaginative exploration becomes self-defeating.

8. Several commentators have picked up the "surrealism" of the fête episode, the best of them being Robert Heilman (in "Charlotte Brontë's 'New' Gothic," *From Austen to Conrad*, ed. Rathburn & Steinmann, pp. 118-132). The strange quality of the scene, its dream-like components, for example, is the result of Charlotte's exploration of new sensations and bizarre experiences, part of the need to bring forth a new self, all presented, incidentally, as an act of voyeurism.

ON FIRST LOOKING INTO GEORGE ELIOT'S
MIDDLEMARCH

JEROME BEATY

For Royal Gettmann

In chapter 15 of *Middlemarch* the narrator describes how the ten-year-old Lydgate one day reached down from the topmost shelf of his family's small library a volume of an encyclopedia and how, before he got down off his chair he had found his vocation:

> The page he opened on was under the heading of Anatomy, and the first passage that drew his eyes was on the valves of the heart. He was not much acquainted with valves of any sort, but he knew that *valvae* were folding doors, and through this crevice came a sudden light startling him with his first vivid notion of finely adjusted mechanism in the human frame. . . . [T]he moment of vocation had come, and before he got down from his chair, the world was made new to him by a presentiment of endless processes filling the vast spaces planked out of his sight by that worldly ignorance which he had supposed to be knowledge. From that hour Lydgate felt the growth of an intellectual passion.[1]

Middlemarch itself performed the function of the dusty old encyclopedia when, twenty-five years ago, I read it for the first time. It immediately and directly planted the seeds of an intellectual passion; it more gradually and indirectly led to a vocation.

Lydgate comes to want to "alter the world a little" by his new vocation. I had decided two years earlier to alter the world a little by writing that universally anticipated work, The Great

151

American Novel. At twenty-one, I had emerged from World War II with a few hours more combat experience and a couple more years of formal education than Hemingway had had at the end of World War I, and that seemed like a good start. By August 1948 I had completed my undergraduate work and an M.A. in "creative writing." Just before completing the degree, still following in the bootsteps of Hemingway, I applied for a newspaper job, but the Baltimore *Sun* chose to hire instead a Johns Hopkins classmate of mine named Russell Baker. I had had no favorable replies as yet to my letters offering my services to the teaching profession. Then, very late, the University of Illinois wired an offer of a "full-time assistantship": $2400 p.a. for teaching three courses a semester and the right to take free one or two graduate courses.

Still not resigned to be "shapen after the average," the first course I took at Illinois was one of those rare "impractical" courses not aimed directly at preparing students for prelims. "The History and Theory of Prose Fiction," I surmised, might accidentally contribute to the composition of The Great American Novel. "Theory" might help my practice; "History" was a bit embarrassing, for no one under thirty was anything other than a New Critic, and I detected in myself anachronistic historical yearnings. The technical analysis inherent in the New Criticism first of all appealed to those of us who thought we were interested in literature primarily as craftsmen and creators. It appealed secondarily because having come from war and in some cases command, we were not anxious to resume inferior or apprentice roles, and, in rendering knowledge, scholarship, and critical experience irrelevant, the New Criticism put us on a par with our elders. Thirdly, its concreteness, particularity, and demonstrability appealed to our vision of ourselves as worldly, "experienced," pragmatic. There were, moreover, many who were tired of history, of "social significance" (our then-term for "relevance"); and finally, formalism was a refuge for many in the year of the Alger Hiss case and the turn into the 'fifties.

Luckily the professor teaching the seminar was Royal Gettmann. He was probably the most sympathetic of the senior professors at Illinois to the new critical methodology, though himself a trained and committed literary historian. His own historical scholarship, however, centered on seeing literature from the inside: the advice, judgment and influence of the publisher's reader; the effects of serialization on the novel; study of the aesthetic and pragmatic reasons behind authors' revisions, etc. Though his political views were perhaps not precisely the same as mine and his interests more ethical than societal, he saw literature as vitally related to the rest of life. A learned, humane and engaged concretist, he could serve as a role-model in a way no one else could, should I slough off Hemingway as I already had Ted Williams and Ed Murrow.

But I had not as yet abandoned plans for The Great American Novel. Two recent novels seemed to promise a new direction, a new golden age of fiction. The earlier had perhaps appealed to me initially because of its reporter-narrator Jack Burden, but *All the King's Men* also seemed to fuse the political, the psychological and the aesthetic. My newspaper experience as copyboy and cub was adolescent, my war experience was prematurely adult, so *The Naked and the Dead*, when it appeared in 1948 spoke not to an ambition but to an achieved experience, of sorts; its political overtones harmonized with my political ideas, and its echoes of Joyce and Proust and Dos Passos and Crane and Hemingway convinced me that it was "literature" and that Norman Mailer was as worth watching as Robert Penn Warren. It was from these writers and not from Bernanos, Djuna Barnes, Ronald Firbank or the precious progeny of Woolf and James that I looked for the shape of the New Novel. Though I was not prepared to say amen to the many funeral orations intoned over the corpse of the novel, I felt that fiction had gone astray somewhere, and that most of the more or less recent novels I read pretended to be either a social documentary or a seismograph of a cork-lined consciousness. Man had an unconscious life, a conscious internal life, and a life expressed in words and actions, but he also had a familial, cultural and temporal context. He was neither a determined chemical nor a disembodied will. The New Novel—of Warren? of Mailer? of ——?—would hold a multifaceted mirror up to the complex reality of human life. The greatest novelist of the twentieth century, Proust, had done so, but with a little

153

too much of the air of the greenhouse. Joyce had tried, but Stephen was too little Daedalus and too much Icarus, plunging into the Liffey of the unconscious. The sons and daughters of Tolstoy—Roger Martin du Gard and Romain Rolland, Dos Passos, Undset, Sholokhov—had somehow splintered his world. And Tolstoy, like Shakespeare, was too monumental to serve as a model. Was there no novelist who had an integral view of life without the crushing weight of Tolstoy?

Then, early in 1949, I read *Middlemarch*. Not because I expected to find in it the undivided stream or anything relevant to my "real" interests, but because Royal Gettmann had said, almost casually one day, that it was a great novel. My admiration of Royal Gettmann's human and critical judgment was already such that, despite my unpleasant memories of *Silas Marner*, and despite the fact that I had never heard the novel mentioned at The Hopkins, and despite the fact that it was not even a Modern Library Giant, I sat down to read the first of the three volumes of the Cabinet Edition. I can hardly say that I had found a vocation before descending the library ladder but well before that first volume was finished I knew I was in the grips of a new literary passion.

2

What, then, were the *valvae* revealed in *Middlemarch*?

My interest in literature from the point of view of a would-be practitioner, reinforced by Royal Gettmann's "George Moore's Revisions of *The Lake, The Wild Goose,* and *Esther Waters,*" *PMLA*, 59 (1944), 540-55, and comparable published and unpublished observations of his on the various stages in the writing of fiction, led me quite naturally to focus on the planning, composition and revision of novels. In my next Victorian course, with Gordon Ray, I read *Daniel Deronda* and reported to the seminar on Leavis's famous bisection of it in *The Great Tradition* (New York: George W. Stewart, n.d.). One of the central issues in George Eliot scholarship and criticism at the time was, roughly, this: were the "good" parts of the Eliot canon the product of the unconscious, emerging from the deep well of experience and the "bad" parts the consciously contrived (essentially the position of Joan Bennett, *George Eliot*

[Cambridge: The University Press, 1948])? Or were the "good" parts the product of the conscious intellect and the "bad" parts the emotive, the unconscious, and the self-indulgent (essentially the position of Leavis)? If this seems now somewhat irrelevant, the corollary will seem incredible: was it the feeling and feminine Mary Ann Evans or the profoundly learned, masculine George Eliot who was the great novelist struggling to free him/herself from the incubus/succubus of The Other? *Deronda* seemed the appropriate novel on which to test at least the genetic hypothesis in this description. If the "Gwendolen" parts of the novel were heavily revised and the "Deronda" parts virtually uncorrected in manuscript, Dr. Leavis would be right; if the reverse were true, Mrs. Bennett would be right. My hunch—based on my own attempts at writing fiction—was that neither was right, and that a study of the manuscript would reveal no significant variation in the kind or quantity of revision in the various parts of the novel.

The British Museum catalogue description of the manuscript did not seem promising. It suggested that the Museum manuscript was that which George Eliot submitted to the publisher; it seemed unlikely to me that a publisher would accept or a printer set type from heavily revised copy. Still, it seemed worth investigating. The University of Illinois agreed, and generously awarded me a Traveling Fellowship. In the Fall of 1951 I sat in the Manuscript Room of the British Museum waiting for the holograph manuscript of *Daniel Deronda*.

Four leather-bound volumes, each about seven by nine inches, arrived at my desk. I opened the first volume with fingers numbed both by the chill of the unheated reading room and by excitement. There was George Eliot's handwriting. Her very words. Violet ink, tiny letters, two lines of writing to each ruled line on the paper. And many, and extensive, changes! This was my first acquaintance with a major writer's manuscript, my first vivid notion of the finely adjusted mechanism of the creative process.

I had what I wanted. Now I was not quite sure what to do with it. The duty that lay nearest my hand was to collate and to transcribe changes into my Cabinet edition of *Deronda*, and so, not so much as the embryonic writer of The Great

American Novel but as a good Victorian, that is what I began to do. There were no revisions in the first paragraph of the manuscript but the first sentence differs from that of the printed text reading, after "glance," "and made it an epoch?" There were but two changes in the second paragraph: "Belonging, in great part, to the highest fashion" read "in great part fashionable," and "at last" had followed "elsewhere" and been deleted. These were not monumental changes nor was a pattern evident, but the game itself was engrossing. I played on. In the third paragraph "August day" seems to have been written over something else, then both were deleted and "a September day" inserted; "broken only" had been "only broken." I was now on the second manuscript page: "little boy" had been inserted in favor of "child"; "for the rest of his person" for "otherwise," and "now and then be observed" for "occasionally be seen." Onto the third page, the fourth, fifth. At the bottom of the fifth page (the eighth paragraph of the novel) the changes became more frequent and more extensive—and more illegible. After Gwendolen's eyes are "arrested" by Daniel's, the phrase "—how long?" was inserted and a full line of manuscript deleted, perhaps after a second version was written over the first. What had it said? ". . . made . . . ————-ible by their quick [or was it "quiet"?] . . . ————-ies." In the next sentence, after "inferior," another three-quarters of a line of manuscript plus a couple of insertions had been deleted and are illegible. The whole next page, the middle of the long paragraph, had been heavily revised and is largely indecipherable; on the page after that, most of the rest of the paragraph—"objects of defiance. Since she" to "Vanity's large family, male or female"—is free of changes. At the top of the next, the eighth page of manuscript one line was deleted and "find their performance received coldly, they are apt to believe that a little more" inserted, so that the "clean" p.7 seems to have been recopied. The concluding pages of the first chapter are also relatively free of revision, but the last is numbered "11a," suggesting that some or all of these too had been recopied.

I went through the first volume and the first two chapters of the second volume (through chapter 22) word by word. I found minor changes of a word, phrase, or order the purpose of which

I could not always infer. I found considerable evidence of re-writing and recopying and a number of extensive, often inde-cipherable, revisions. Not all the extensive revisions were il-legible, however. In chapter 16, for example, a lengthy passage that was deleted is legible and reveals a rather significant change. In the final version, Daniel sacrifices his chance at a mathematics scholarship in order to help his friend Hans Mey-rick with his classical studies. Hans, at that crucial time, had "a severe inflammation of the eyes" because of his having im-prudently bought an engraving he could not afford, which ex-travagance then forced him to ride in a third-class carriage exposed to a bitter wind. The sacrifice is real—Daniel fails; but it is worthwhile—Hans wins his scholarship.[2] But the two pages in the manuscript describing Meyrick's imprudence, the sacrifice and the result seem a later version. The preceding page now ends "Meyrick was going in for a classical scholar-ship, and his success, in various ways momentous, was the more probable from the steadying influence of Deronda's friendship" (*DD*, p. 222); but the eleven words following "momentous" have been substituted for a much longer and rather different passage:

> would be the more secure for Deronda's companionship. By an engage-ment that they should read together Meyrick could be better kept in harness, and with that condition few men could have a better chance.
> However, the needy man missed the prize, and the man who could do without it won. When the result was made known and Deronda saw that Meyrick being bracketed with a winner would come in for a va-cancy, he at once made up his mind to resign [the . . . *deleted*] his scholarship and allege his half-formed intention of quitting the

The page ends at this point with no evidence of a link to the page that presently follows it. This passage is deleted and there follows the episode of the inflamed eyes, Hans' triumph at Daniel's expense.

There are other renumbered pages, indications of recopied or rewritten pages, evidence of late decisions to divide chapters, and even a change in the division into books. Book III—"Maid-ens Choosing"—now begins with chapter 19, but at this point in the manuscript there was originally not even a chapter break. Book II was to have ended with the end of the first

157

manuscript volume, at the conclusion of what is now chapter 20 (*DD*, p. 268).

As I began working on the second manuscript volume I realized I had a decision to make. If, as I had once intended, I were to attempt to go through the manuscripts of all George Eliot's novels in such painstaking detail, it would take not nine or ten months, but at least that number of years. If I merely wanted to prove that, whatever their relative merits, the "Deronda" and "Gwendolen" portions of the novel were similarly revised, and that, therefore, neither was more or less "consciously" created or more or less contrived than the other, I had already done so to my own satisfaction. "Gwendolen" chapters 6 and 7—Rex's accident—and 10 and 11—the archery meet and Grandcourt's proposal—were quite extensively revised, but so were "Daniel's" chapters 16—in which he seeks to learn his parentage and discover a vocation—and 20—in which Mirah (originally "Miriam") recounts her life with her father.

Since the more ambitious project was clearly impractical, the question then became how to objectify my clear but "subjective" inference. Could my estimate of comparable revision be quantified? Could I identify each chapter as "Gwendolen's," "Daniel's" or "mixed," count the number of changes in the chapter, or changes per page, or per hundred words? or should I count not the number of changes but the number of words changed? or combine the statistics so that both number and extent could be demonstrated? And what about the illegible passages? Would a sample of chapters serve? Finally, a sinking doubt about the premise: do the number and extensiveness of revisions prove whether a passage was written "consciously" or "unconsciously," out of feeling and memory or through intellectual contrivance?

What I needed was an apparently authoritative, apparently acceptable, and unequivocal statement that (1) would link revision and consciousness or unconsciousness and clean copy; (2) would identify specifically some passage or passages as written entirely consciously or unconsciously, and (3) be demonstrably wrong!

And I found it. The authority was none other than George Eliot herself as reported by her husband John Cross. He identified a scene which he called one of her best, and which, like all her best scenes, he said, she told him she had not planned but had written "exactly as it stands, without alteration or erasure, in an intense state of excitement and agitation."[3] Here was a passage, specifically enough identified, authoritatively describing "unconscious" writing, and linking the mode of composition to revision or lack of revision. It could be checked.

I checked. The passage was considerably revised; from what I had seen of George Eliot's manuscript so far, it seemed typically or characteristically revised. There existed, moreover, notebook entries that revealed that the specified scene had been planned and that George Eliot had taken pains with its timing.

There was only one catch: the passage was not in *Daniel Deronda* but in *Middlemarch*.

So I closed my *Deronda* and opened my *Middlemarch*, the object of my first Victorian intellectual passion. For the next four years I read through the manuscripts, notebooks, corrected proof, printed books, unpublished and published letters, all sorts of -ana, returning periodically to the text and variants of *Middlemarch*. I was so steeped in George Eliot's life and writings I could sometimes almost infer her thoughts. When, for example, I read that A. W. Kinglake, author of *Invasion of the Crimea*, wrote to his and George Eliot's publisher in terms that suggested that Blackwood had, apparently with George Eliot's authority, described her writing process in terms similar to Cross's, I "knew" that something was wrong. So I went back through my record of the George Eliot-Blackwood correspondence and found reference to a letter in the National Library of Scotland that both Gordon Haight and I had missed. The letter, put back into context, showed that Blackwood interpolated from what George Eliot had actually written in order mildly and indirectly to rebuke Kinglake for his constant revision of proof.[4] But that was an easy inference, closely related to my study of the manuscript and notebook and readily demonstrable. The immersion also meant hunches, wild surmise, "knowledge" that I was certain of but could never demonstrate. I "knew" years ago—and am still convinced—that

George Eliot's pseudonymous surname originated in the alias of another plain young woman: Jane Eyre, fleeing Rochester, tells the Rivers family that her name is Jane Elliott.[5] A more important hunch is my inference that in the 1860's and into 1870 George Eliot very nearly abandoned the writing of fiction for poetry and poetic drama. Here there is evidence but not proof.

Romola is clearly a watershed in George Eliot's career. She began it, she later told her husband, a young woman and finished it an old woman (Cross, II, 352), yet from conception to completion was a scant three years (May 1860–June 1863). This Florentine historical romance clearly breaks with her first three novels of Midland domestic realism. Indeed, at first she planned to publish it serially and anonymously in *Blackwood's Edinburgh Magazine*, to test its reception divorced from her name and reputation.[6] She set off for Italy on March 24, 1860, a few days after finishing *The Mill on the Floss*, with confidence and expectation, seeking new life and new ideas; within two months she conceived an Italian story. Three months later, not having begun to write the Italian work, she quickly wrote the short story "Brother Jacob," and in another three months interrupted her simmering towards *Romola* to write *Silas Marner*, finishing it in March 1861. Here the first small cloud of poetry appears on the horizon: She writes to John Blackwood on February 24, 1861, "I have felt all through as if the story [*Silas*] would have lent itself best to metrical rather than prose fiction, especially in all that relates to the psychology of Silas. . . . It came to me first of all, quite suddenly, as a sort of legendary tale . . . , but, as my mind dwelt on the subject, I became inclined to a more realistic treatment." She starts the actual writing of the "historical romance" in October, but by the end of the month is despondent (*GEL*, III, 461n.). She stops for more plotting, and starts again in January 1862. Near the end of February, when she had written only about seventy-seven pages, George Smith offers her the unprecedented sum of ten thousand pounds to serialize her new novel in *Cornhill*, but because he wants it to begin appearing in May and she cannot agree to begin publication until she can see her way clear to the end of the novel, she refuses. Less than three months later, however, with fewer than 180 pages written, she accepts a considerably reduced but still handsome offer. When the novel began to appear in July she was a scant three months ahead of the printer, and she stayed just two or three months ahead, finishing the novel early in June 1863, the final part appearing in the August issue of *Cornhill*. For a writer of George Eliot's lack of confidence and fitful writing pace this narrow and occasionally shrinking distance between composition and print must have been harrowing, enough to turn a young woman into an old woman. Despite the psychically taxing work and despite the fulsome praise that flowed in from some quarters, she soon knew that *Romola* was a relative failure, both commercially and, probably, artistically. In 1862 George Smith had offered two hundred and fifty pounds for "Brother Jacob," but in 1864 she gave the story to him gratis (*GEL*, IV, 157n.). In July of that year she wrote in her journal, "Horrible scepticism about all things—paralyzing my mind. Shall I ever be good for anything again?—ever do anything again?" (*GEL*, IV, 158n.). George Eliot had frequent bouts of self-doubt and dejection, but her mood here seems closer to despair than usual. She began turning elsewhere than fiction: in September she began a poetic drama set in Spain, "But I have little hope of making anything satisfactory" (Cross, II, 388).

Now that she had turned to poetry, however, her pace quickened. By the end of the year she had written three acts and read them to Lewes. On New Year's day 1865 she called the last three months "an epoch," "for the first time in my serious authorship, I have written verse" (Cross, III, 394). During the first week of the New Year she was converting some prose material into a poem, and on January 28 she completed "my poem on 'Utopias'" (Cross, II, 396).

But even writing poetry, she faltered. Late in February Lewes takes her drama away from her, and she turns to nonfiction prose. Early in March she writes two essays, "A Word for the Germans" and "Servants' Logic" for the *Pall Mall Gazette*, and on the twenty-fifth records in her journal that she is "in deep depression, feeling powerless. I have written nothing but beginnings since I finished a little article for the

161

Pall Mall on the Logic of Servants." Four days later, still another beginning, this time a novel, *Felix Holt*.

Still she cannot revive her spirits or her confidence. During the Spring she writes two more articles, reads the opening of her novel to Lewes and during the Summer works "doggedly at my novel, seeing what determination can do in the face of despair." During the rest of the year she barely finished the first volume.

A few months later, however, her pace picks up: she writes more than one hundred pages in the last three weeks in March, completing the second volume early in April. There was some hesitation on the part of publishers that could not have been too encouraging: George Smith would not pay Lewes's asking price of five thousand pounds (*GEL*, IV, 240n.); Blackwood would not accept the novel sight unseen. When John Blackwood read the first two volumes, however, within forty-eight hours the firm offered five thousand pounds. The offer and the fulsome and sincere praise John Blackwood heaps upon her makes her glad she resisted "the tempter Despondency" (*GEL*, IV, 248). When she finished the novel at the end of May, her earlier despondency gives way to her usual "distrust and anxiety." The letters from Blackwood's—where her sensitivity to adverse criticism is well known—are full of reports of reviews and personal opinions of the great and the common amounting to a universal chorus of praise.

On the tenth of September, however, four hundred copies of the first printing of 5250 remain, and John Blackwood is clearly disappointed, though he blames the book trade in general for the poor sale: "The libraries have starved the book, or rather their customers, as is proved by the fact of some of them buying quite recently in small numbers. The next time we take the field together I think we must experiment in a new form, but we can keep our own council about this." The burst of hope and energy that resulted in the completion of *Felix Holt*, sustained by early praise, must have seemed illusory in the light of the poor sales and cool reception, some of which must have infiltrated through Lewes's guard. What did her future as a novelist promise? After four quick successes, two failures. What next?

In the middle of that Summer (July 19, 1866), Frederick Harrison, the Positivist whom she had consulted frequently about the tangled legal problems in the plot of *Felix*, wrote thanking her for a presentation copy of the novel. He reported having read the novel through again and again, as if it were a poem; indeed he considers it "a really new species of literature . . . (a romance constructed in the artistic spirit and aim of a poem)," wonders if such care and finish are not wasted on a prose narrative, and, he asks, "Are you sure that your destiny is not to produce a poem—not a poem in prose but in measure—a drama? Is it possible that there is not one yet existing or does it lie like the statue in the marble block?" Whether this letter is cause or coincidence, in August George Eliot returns to her Spanish poetic drama determined to recast it, as she reveals confidentially to Harrison on August fifteenth: "At present I am going to take up again a work which I laid down before writing 'Felix.' It is—*but please let this be a secret between ourselves*—an attempt at a drama, which I put aside at Mr. Lewes's request, after writing four acts." There is virtually no mention of the dramatic poem for seven months, until, upon her return from Spain, she records in her journal her intention to "go to my poem and the construction of two prose works—if possible" (Cross, III, 13). Blackwood, in a letter on the twentieth of March, asks rather gingerly whether the work on Spain is a Romance, fearing perhaps that it is on the order of *Romola*, and he quickly follows that question with an inquiry about a short work, about the length of *Silas*, on "home life" that she had once mentioned to him. She responds the next day: "The work connected with Spain is not a Romance. It is—prepare your fortitude—a poem," but to soften the blow she adds that she does not expect to make money from it and that "I have also my private projects about an English novel, but I am afraid of speaking as if I could depend on myself." In mid-Summer she tells George Smith that her new book is not a novel and that it is unsuitable for *Cornhill*. In August she writes her famous hymn, "O May I Join the Choir Invisible." On the tenth of October she begins "the scene in the Gypsy Camp" (*GEL*, IV, 394n.), and, except for taking a few weeks out at the end of November to write "Address to the Working Men, by Felix

163

Holt," she is totally absorbed in the poem until completing it on April 29, 1868. The reviews were mixed but the sales gratifying: the first edition of two thousand copies was virtually sold out in two months; a third edition at a reduced price is planned in October, and by the end of that month five thousand copies had been sold in America (*GEL*, IV, 480n.). All in all, she found *The Spanish Gypsy* "a great source of added happiness to me—all the more, or rather principally because it has been a deeper joy to Mr. Lewes than any work I have done before. I seem to have gained a new organ, a new medium that my nature had languished for" (*GEL*, IV, 465).

On her forty-ninth birthday (November 22, 1868) she is mulling over the subject of Timoleon for another long poem with no mention of a prose work in her mind. The new year opens with a journal entry projecting "A Novel called Middlemarch, a long poem on Timoleon, and several minor poems."

For the unwary, that would seem to ring down the curtain on any thoughts of George Eliot's turning her primary attention away from fiction to poetry—we know what became of a novel called *Middlemarch* and what did not become of "Timoleon." So it seemed at first. In January, George Eliot made some progress in constructing her new novel and finished sketching the plan by the nineteenth of February. Then, for five months, nothing. In Summer there is another burst of activity: in mid-July she is writing the introduction; between the second and fifth of August she writes the first chapter; by the eleventh of September, she has finished three chapters, about fifty pages. Until that final burst the year has been punctuated primarily by the completion of poems: "Agatha" on January 23; "How Lisa Loved the King" on February 14; the "Brother and Sister" sonnets on July 31.

Thornton Lewes, who had returned from Natal quite ill in May, died on October 19. For more than a year after his death, there is virtually nothing about the novel. On March 7, 1870, she writes Blackwood that the novel "I suppose, will be finished some day; it creeps on." Her first journal entry after Thornton's death, May 20, is similarly despondent: "I am languid, and my novel languishes too" (Cross, III, 110). What little there is about writing during the year deals with poetry: she completes "The Legend of Jubal" in mid-January and writes "Armgart" between the eighth and twenty-ninth of August.

The few months before Thornton's death and the year that followed are almost wholly unproductive and it does not seem entirely evident that George Eliot was interested in or confident about writing poetry any more than about writing novels. Still, her first real emergence from despondency came in August with the writing of a poem, "Armgart." And how did her career seem to her, looking back almost a decade? Two novels failed and a third all but stillborn. A successful long poem the adverse criticism of which she could blame on the critics' slowness to adapt to the unexpected. Reinforcement from Lewes and friends like Harrison. Serious study of prosody and language. A succession of poems of varying lengths completed. And, recently, no fiction at all. *Middlemarch*, an English novel, not historical or foreign like *Romola* nor yet political like *Felix Holt*, still seemed powerless to be born. What kind of novel to write? Could she ever again write a long novel? Surely in these months, if not for several years, she must have thought of abandoning fiction altogether and plunging fully into her new career. Shorter works, like poems, she could complete. Perhaps a short piece of fiction. She had mentioned such a project to Blackwood some time ago and he seemed interested.

Early in November 1870 she begins "Miss Brooke," and though she intended it to be short, by the end of the year she has written one hundred pages. This story will, of course, flow into the meandering "Middlemarch" and from mid-March 1871 to early October 1872 the four-volume *Middlemarch* moves relentlessly if not torrentially towards completion, poetry left far behind. Even when she records the first significant progress on "Miss Brooke"—a hundred pages in less than two months—the first surge of fiction-writing in four and one-half years, however, she seems somewhat less than enthusiastic, seems almost to regret the interruption of her poetic career:

> We found the cold here [London] more severe than at Ryde, and the papers tell of still harder weather about Paris where our fellow-men are suffering and inflicting horrors.[7] Am I doing anything that will add the weight of a sandgrain against the persistence of such evil?

165

Here is the last day of 1870. I have written only 100 pages—good printed pages—of a story which I began about the opening of November, and at present mean to call "Miss Brooke," Poetry halts just now.

Middlemarch, of course, was to be an unexpected, gratifying, almost overwhelming success—her first real success, remember, in more than ten years. Characteristically, though, the anxious novelist found even her success a reason for concern—"I am slowly simmering towards another big book," she wrote John Blackwood on November 5, 1873, "but people seem so bent on giving supremacy to M[iddlemarc]h that they are sure not to like any future book so well." The big book was *Daniel Deronda*; poetry was pushed into the background where it would thenceforth remain.

3

My interest in George Eliot's writing practices or "creative process" began with my own ambitions to write fiction, and only gradually became transformed into a scholarly interest in her life and works which led to such hunches and inferences as I have indicated. Another thread in my Victorian experience also spun out from my viewing her novels with the eyes of a would-be practitioner. Indeed, what struck me as I first looked into *Middlemarch* metaphorically perched upon a library ladder was not some trancelike vision of the novelist as she planned, wrote, and revised, but the "valve" of the rich social or historical texture of the novel. If what I missed in contemporary fiction was a serious novel that mentioned President Truman or Prime Minister Attlee, here was a novel that was not generically political or historical, one that focused on private lives and even on the psychological in human life, but that mentioned George IV, Peel, Wellington, and Huskisson; the opening of railways; the July Revolution in Paris, and all of this presented so subtly, so indirectly, that few readers are conscious of the historical background and wealth of detail.

I first set about investigating the craft, the technical means by which George Eliot had created a depth of historical texture while weaving the history so subtly into the private lives of the fictional characters that that strand did not force itself on the attention or distract from the fiction. I isolated a number of elements. The major event of the period happens just outside the time-frame of the novel, the First Reform Bill having been passed a couple of weeks after the fictional action ends. When important events do occur within the fictional time—like the death of George IV or the opening of the Liverpool to Manchester railway—they are not reported directly in the fiction as "news." Historical events and the date are never mentioned together and indeed at times the historical event is the only indicator of date. On the rare occasions when events are reported they are put in the context of "momentous" fictional events and so are overwhelmed by them: thus when the House of Lords throws out the Reform Bill Dorothea's uncle approaches his Tory friends—the Cadwalladers, Sir James Chettam and his wife and mother—with a dejected look which they interpret as political disappointment but he is actually upset about having to break the news of Dorothea's betrothal to the socially unacceptable Will Ladislaw (M, pp. 871-72).[8]

There are a few passages which place a fictional event directly by reference to historical background, for example the opening of chapter 19: "When George the Fourth was still reigning over the privacies of Windsor, when the Duke of Wellington was Prime Minister, and Mr. Vincy was mayor of the old corporation in Middlemarch, Mrs. Casaubon, born Dorothea Brooke, had taken her wedding journey to Rome" (M, p. 219). In this early stage of the novel the passage seems to serve primarily to link the Miss Brooke and Middlemarch strands rather than to link either to the historical period (and the imminent death of the monarch and the disfavor and early fall of the prime minister may serve to foreshadow the course of the Casaubon marriage). More often history serves as a macrocosmic background, almost as a pathetic fallacy in which the larger events are projections of the personal, fictional situation: so Peter Featherstone's death is rapidly followed by that of George IV, and the relatives waiting to hear the terms of the will talk "of the last bulletins concerning the King" (M, p. 369). Fred's disappointment in Featherstone's will is similarly linked to the political macrocosm, the dissolution of Parliament, and both are related to the cosmos itself by the apocalyptic vision of Mr. Vincy. Rosamond has come to him to express her wish that she and Lydgate can be married soon; he replies,

> "I hope he knows I shan't give anything—with this disappointment about Fred, and Parliament going to be dissolved, and machine-breaking everywhere, and an election coming on—"
> "Dear papa! what can that have to do with my marriage?"
> "A pretty deal to do with it! We may all be ruined for what I know—the country's in that state! Some say it's the end of the world, and be hanged if I don't think it looks like it. Anyhow, it's not a time for me to be drawing money out of my business, and I should wish Lydgate to know that." (*M*, p. 388)

Rosamond's "Dear papa! what can [socio-political conditions] have to do with my marriage?" is one of the central questions of this novel—and of many of George Eliot's other novels. In *Adam Bede*, those who live in Loamshire where the living is easy are themselves easy-going, complacent, but intolerant of those who fail or fall; while the hard life in the mill town of Stoniton virtually necessitates more understanding and pity for the poor or weak, more looking beyond the self, often, indeed, beyond this sublunary life. In *The Mill on the Floss* "steam" and the growth of international trade make it possible for Tom to pay the family debts and restore its solvency much more rapidly than even his successful uncle Deane could anticipate; modern conditions make the "Protestant ethic" of the Dodsons anachronistic and drive a wedge between generations and split the psyches of the young. This is the frequent and inevitable price of progress: in the onward tendency of human things [many generations] have risen above the mental level of the generation before them, to which they have been nevertheless tied by the strongest fibres of their hearts. The suffering, whether of martyr or victim, which belongs to every historical advance of mankind, is represented in this way in every town, and by hundreds of obscure hearths."[9] Social conditions not only have something to do with one's actions but history creates responsibilities, offering perhaps the only definition available in the nineteenth century of "duty" and "morality." Dr. Kenn deplores the relaxation of "ideas of discipline and Christian fraternity" (*Mill*, p. 432) that once were central to the functioning of the Church and finds the source of that failure in contemporary society: "At present everything seems tending towards the relaxation of ties—towards the substitution of wayward choice for the adherence to obligation, which has its roots in the past" (*Mill*, p. 433). As Maggie cries out in her crisis: "If the past is not to bind us, where can duty lie?" (*Mill*, p. 417). Romola, fleeing from an intolerable marriage, is turned back by Savanarola who tells her that she owes a duty not just to her own father but to "Florence, where there are the only men and women in the world to whom you owe the debt of a fellow-citizen."[10]

It is in this novel that the generalized relationship of individual to society is first explicitly described: "as in the tree that bears a myriad of blossoms, each single bud with its fruit is dependent on the primary circulation of the sap, so the fortunes of Tito and Romola were dependent on certain grand political and social conditions which made an epoch in the history of Italy" (*Rom*, p. 213). The connection is defined in less metaphorical, more precise, and yet more sweeping terms in *Felix Holt*:

> These social changes in Treby parish are comparatively public matters, and this history is chiefly concerned with the private lot of a few men and women; but there is no private life which has not been determined by a wider public life, . . . [I]f the mixed political conditions of Treby Magna had not been acted on by the passing of the Reform Bill, Mr. Harold Transome would not have presented himself as a candidate for North Loamshire, Treby would not have been a polling-place, Mr. Matthew Jermyn would not have been on affable terms with a Dissenting preacher and his flock, and the venerable town would not have been placarded with handbills . . .—conditions in this case essential to the "where," and the "what," without which, as the learned know, there can be no event whatever.[11]

In *Daniel Deronda*, Gwendolen Harleth, like Rosamond in *Middlemarch*, has no understanding, literal or metaphorical, of the relationship of the world and its conditions to her personal lot. Determined to "do as she likes" Gwendolen has rejected Grandcourt, socially the most eligible of suitors, and has fled to the Continent. She is called back, however, because her mother's investments have failed: "The conduct of those uninteresting people who managed the business of the world had been culpable just in the points most injurious to her in particular. Gwendolen Harleth, with all her beauty and conscious force, felt the close threats of humiliation: for the first time the conditions of this world seemed to her like a hurry-ing roaring crowd in which she had got astray, no more cared for and protected than a myriad of other girls, in spite of its being a peculiar hardship to her" (*DD*, p. 278). Forced by ex-ternal circumstances to choose between the life of a governess and marriage to Grandcourt, Gwendolen, after much writhing and self-delusion (contemplating a career on the stage, for ex-ample), chooses to marry Grandcourt as the lesser evil—even after learning of the existence of Mrs. Glasher and Grandcourt's illegitimate children makes the marriage morally repugnant. She still believes she can master him and continue to do as she likes. It is he who is master, however, and he who does as he likes. Gwendolen endures not only subjection and humilia-tion but self-hatred, now that she recognizes that she is capable of immoral actions. She finds herself capable even of murder, and feels justifiably if excessively guilty when her hatred of her husband freezes her at a moment of crisis so that she makes no attempt to rescue him from drowning.

Her marriage has educated her, but the lesson that initiated the marriage—the relevance of the larger world to her personal lot—she has not yet learned. She has learned that she is not perfect, even perhaps that she cannot always have her way, but she has not yet learned that she is merely one center of consciousness and claims among hundreds of millions. Daniel has for a long time served as her conscience, her confessor and her moral mentor. He has awakened her to the insufficiency of her egocentric world-view, but it is only when she learns she is to lose Deronda himself to broader claims and respon-sibilities she has been wholly ignorant of, that she sees how vast the world is and how small her part in it:

> The world seemed getting larger round poor Gwendolen, and she more solitary and helpless in the midst. The thought that he might come back after going to the East, sank before the bewildering vision of these wide-stretching purposes in which she felt herself reduced to a mere speck. There comes a terrible moment to many souls when the great movements of the world, the larger destinies of mankind, which have lain aloof in newspapers and other neglected reading, enter like an earthquake into their own lives—when the slow urgency of growing generations turns into the tread of an invading army or the dire clash of civil war. (*DD*, p. 875)

Just as Mr. Vincy placed Rosamond's marriage in the context of the dissolution of Parliament and machine-breaking, and placed both in a still larger, cosmological, apocalyptic context, so Gwendolen's vision extends from the personal to the political and to the cosmological. Her earlier fear of wide horizons, insisted upon in imagery that is apparently psychological, even Freudian, is all too justified by events: inside the closed circle of her family and its environs she controls or feels she can control her destiny—she can do as she likes. In the larger, almost unbounded sphere she is only one among many, not the center of the universe but a speck.

This larger vision—one that does not exclude but subsumes the smaller spheres of self and society—is ultimately religious. The reality of God—whether the god of theology or of the religion of humanity—becomes most apparent at great historical moments. When the great movements of the world thrust themselves into the individual life in the form of war, for example, "it is as if the Invisible Power that has been the object of lip-worship and lip-resignation became visible" (*DD*, p. 875); and when "the good cause" seems to be losing, then

> the submission of the soul to the Highest is tested, and even in the eyes of frivolity life looks out from the scene of human struggle with the awful face of duty, and a religion shows itself which is something else than a private consolation.
>
> That was the sort of crisis which was at this moment beginning in Gwendolen's small life: she was for the first time feeling the pressure of a vast mysterious movement, for the first time being dislodged from her supremacy in her own world, and getting a sense that her horizon was but a dipping onward of an existence with which her own was revolving. (*DD*, p. 876)

The societal tree of which the individual is a leaf in *Romola*, the private lives in Treby parish determined by the wider public life, the invasion of the soul by the world's great movements (all strongly suggesting a rigid determinism)[12] have their counterpart in the famous "Prelude" to *Middlemarch*, where the individual, though he or she may be by nature and aspiration a saint, is born into a society where there is "no coherent social faith and order which could perform the function of knowledge for the ardently willing soul" (*M*, p. 25), where society blocks significant action: "Here and there is born a Saint Theresa,

171

foundress of nothing whose loving heart-beats and sobs after an unattained goodness tremble off and are dispersed among hindrances, instead of centering in some long-recognizable deed" (*M*, p. 26).

Middlemarch nonetheless seems to suggest an efficacy of individual social action, no matter how limited, that goes beyond the implications of the earlier novels. Romola's tending plague victims is not a negligible achievement, but it is a personal rather than social action, not even taking place in Florence, among whose populace, according to Savanarola, the chief social responsibility lies. In Florence she rears her husband's illegitimate children. The exemplars of self-sacrificing nobility involving feeling for the world outside our selves are Bardo in scholarship and Savanarola in his struggle against powerful wrong. But Bardo worked in poverty and obscurity, his library was sold away, and there is no evidence in the novel of his effectiveness as a scholar or, indeed, of scholarship in general. Savanarola was himself a powerful wrong at times: to a considerable degree he was corrupted by the evil he faced; and in any case, in Eliot's novel he does not seem to have effected very much good. It is difficult for the leaf to affect the tree. Neither do Felix or Harold seem to have been able to do much for their society:

> As to all that wide parish of Treby Magna, it has since prospered as the rest of England has prospered. Doubtless there is more enlightenment now. Whether the farmers are all public-spirited, the shopkeepers nobly independent, the Sproxton men entirely sober and judicious, the Dissenters quite without narrowness or asperity in religion and politics, and the publicans all fit, like Gaius, to be the friends of an apostle—these things I have not heard, not having correspondence in those parts. Whether any presumption may be drawn from the fact that North Loamshire does not yet return a Radical candidate, I leave to the all-wise—I mean the newspapers. (*FH*, pp. 486-87)

Felix, on probation, has left Treby and politics, his attention directed now to Esther—and to mending watches. Even the future in the two novels does not seem to promise effectiveness: Romola lectures Tito's son, Lillo, on how to live nobly, so that if—or when—calamity comes he will have no regrets, and "There is a young Felix, who has a great deal more science than his father, but not much more money."

The "Finale" of *Middlemarch* returns to the theme of the later-born Theresas announced in the "Prelude": the "mixed results" of Dorothea's acts are attributable to the "imperfect social state," "For there is no creature whose inward being is so strong that it is not greatly determined by what lies outside it" (*M*, p. 896). This indeed seems as deterministic as the passages cited in *Romola* and *Felix Holt* (p. 169) and seems even darker than the "Prelude": there society simply lacked a coherent faith and order to guide and structure the aspiring heroine—conditions which if not present in 1829-1832 and still absent in 1871-1872, may be present at some future date; but here in the "Finale" society needs not merely faith and order but the unattainable perfection. "A new Theresa will hardly have the opportunity of reforming a conventual life, any more than a new Antigone will spend her heroic piety in daring all for the sake of a brother's burial: the medium in which their ardent deeds took shape is for ever gone. But we insignificant people with our daily words and acts are preparing the lives of many Dorotheas, some of which may present a far sadder sacrifice than that of the Dorothea whose story we know." Did Theresa and Antigone, then, live in social states whose perfection we can neither recapture nor equal? or did their "medium" shape their heroism and ardor into particular deeds which cannot (even need not) be repeated, though other, equally significant achievements may be possible? Dorothea, potentially a Theresa or Antigone, is denied heroic action and heroic results by social conditions, but even in this imperfect state she was able to exert an "incalculably diffusive" effect on those around her and half the world's progress can be attributed to such unheroic and unhistoric noble lives. Will is a Member of Parliament working for reforms at a time "when reforms were begun with a young hopefulness of immediate good which has been much checked in our days" (*M*, p. 894). His struggles, too, may not achieve heroic results, but, presumably, do achieve some not insignificant good, ultimate if not immediate good. So Dorothea's unhistoric life is nonetheless a public one, measurably if only slightly more socially effective than those of Romola and Felix. And later-born Dorotheas may be still more effective. We unheroic, insignificant people through words and deeds prepare the social conditions for the heroic, and our effect too can be incalculably diffusive if unhistoric, preparing a medium, a culture for the growth of historic heroes.[13]

If *Middlemarch* seems ambiguous as to the possibility of effective social action in the contemporary world, *Daniel Deronda* is clear. Daniel finds a medium for his ardent and heroic action, the founding of a Jewish state in Palestine. He finds in his racial past not, like Maggie, bonds, but opportunities, a role, a social faith and order, and passional fulfillment as well. George Levine, p. 271 of the essay cited earlier, finds Deronda's heroism and Mordecai's incompatible with George Eliot's vision, and Leslie Stephen, *George Eliot* (London: Macmillan, 1904), p. 189, finds Daniel's achievement inapplicable to our lives: "As we cannot all discover that we belong to the chosen people, and some of us might, even then, doubt the wisdom of the enterprise, one feels that Deronda's mode of solving his problem is not generally applicable." But George Eliot's vision does allow for the hero, not as one who tampers with history but whose career coincides with it, the right man in the right place. There was a Saint Theresa, after all. If there are unhistoric lives, there are also a few historic ones. Saints and heroes may be rare, the exception and not the rule of human life and lot, but that does not mean that they have not existed or cannot exist. Their lives are not meant to be "generally applicable." Our insignificant lives are the rule. But we can prepare for the heroes. That is why Gwendolen's story is related to Daniel's.

There is another reason as well. If our lives, our decisions, can make things a little better for those who follow, and if our words and deeds can prepare the social soil for heroic actions and achievement, the moral struggles of the inner and personal life are not only ingredients but microcosms of the battles on the national and world-wide scale. Though Gwendolen's ultimate moral vision shows her that her own life is only one among many, that she is but a speck in the universe, her history is important because each life is a microcosm. The great movements of man are the aggregate and abstraction from the miniscule movements of individual men and women. The microcosmic personal battle and the macrocosmic humanity-wide battle is the same, the war between good and evil:

174

Could there be a slenderer, more insignificant thread in human history than this consciousness of a girl, busy with her small inferences of the way in which she could make her life pleasant?—in a time, too, when ideas were with fresh vigour making armies of themselves, and the universal kinship was declaring itself fiercely: when women on the other side of the world would not mourn for the husbands and sons who died bravely in a common cause, and men stinted of bread on our side of the world heard of that willing loss and were patient: a time when the soul of man was waking to pulses which had for centuries been beating in him unheard, until their full sum made a new life of terror or of joy.

What in the midst of that mighty drama are girls and their blind visions? They are the Yea or Nay of that good for which men are enduring and fighting. In these delicate vessels is borne onward through the ages the treasure of human affections. (*DD*, pp. 159-60)

War as an image of the struggle between good and evil and as a theater for heroic action did not seem so unsuitable to young veterans of World War II as it does for those of Vietnam. Eradication of slavery and its consequences, the founding of a Jewish state after Auschwitz did not seem either impossible dreams or unheroic acts. And the significance and relevance of diapers and doctoral degrees needed definition and reinforcement for those who had so recently felt themselves to have had a part, no matter how small a part, in a somewhat larger theater of operations. George Eliot's alternating microscopic and telescopic vision, her moving back and forth from the near to the far, has been spoken of fairly often, usually in imagistic or formalistic terms. A quarter century ago this systole-diastole was the functional heart of her work for us, more vital than *valvae*. Her stereoptic vision still illuminates. It can still serve as a corrective for the myopia of a decade like the 1950's or the short-lived hypermetropia of the 1960's.

1. George Eliot, *Middlemarch*, ed. W. J. Harvey (Harmondsworth, Middlesex: Penguin Books, 1965), p. 173. Subsequent references will be to this edition with page numbers preceded by *M*, indicated parenthetically.
2. George Eliot, *Daniel Deronda*, ed. Barbara Hardy (Harmondsworth, Middlesex: Penguin Books, 1967), pp. 222-23. Subsequent references to this edition with page numbers, preceded by *DD*, are indicated parenthetically.
3. John W. Cross, ed., *George Eliot's Life as Related in Her Letters and Journals* (London and Edinburgh: William Blackwood and Sons, 1885), III, 425.
4. See my "Into the Irrevocable: A New George Eliot Letter," *JEGP*, 57 (October, 1958), 704-07.

5. Gordon S. Haight, *George Eliot: A Biography* (New York and Oxford: Oxford University Press, 1968), p. 220, lists this as one of the possible sources of the name.

6. Gordon S. Haight, *The George Eliot Letters* (New Haven, Conn.: Yale University Press, 1954), III, 339. The final four vols. were published in 1955. The letters are arranged in chronological order. Where date is in text I will not give page reference; where it is not clear or for some reason is out of order, I shall indicate page numbers, preceded by *GEL*, parenthetically.

7. Paris was beseiged by the Germans and suffering famine.

8. See my "History by Indirection: The Era of Reform in *Middlemarch*," VS, 1 (1957), 173-79.

9. George Eliot, *The Mill on the Floss*, ed. Gordon S. Haight, Riverside Edition (Boston: Houghton Mifflin Company, 1961), p. 239. Subsequent references are to this edition with page numbers, preceded by *Mill*, indicated parenthetically.

10. George Eliot, *Romola*, World's Classics Edition (London: Oxford University Press, 1949), p. 371. Subsequent references are to this edition with page numbers, preceded by *Rom*, indicated parenthetically.

11. George Eliot, *Felix Holt*, ed. George Levine (New York, W. W. Norton, 1970), pp. 51-52. Subsequent references are to this edition with page numbers, preceded by *FH*, indicated parenthetically.

12. George Levine, "Determinism and Responsibility," *PMLA*, 77 (1962), 268-79, brilliantly defines the precise nature of George Eliot's determinism, and argues convincingly that despite its rigidity it does not necessarily obviate human choice and moral responsibility. I am here more interested in the question of the results of that responsibility, the possibility of effectiveness of individual action in a determined world, a subject that Levine touches but does not emphasize.

13. In the first edition the next-to-last paragraph in the novel specifies some of the imperfections of current social conditions and blames society for Dorothea's marrying Casaubon. W. J. Harvey's chapter, "Contemporary Reception," in *"Middlemarch": Critical Approaches to the Novel*, ed. Barbara Hardy (London: The Athlone Press, 1967), persuasively argues (pp. 133-34), that George Eliot revised the paragraph because contemporary reviewers leapt on the passage, pointing out that the novel does not *show* the society to blame for Dorothea's decision at all. Coincidentally, in "A Study of the Proof," a chapter in the same volume, I discuss the same change (pp. 59-62), pointing out that the manuscript offers a third version of the passage and a somewhat different version of the final sentence in the novel, the over-all effect of the changes from manuscript to revised edition being to darken the tone, moving from meliorism toward tragedy. Harvey shows that contemporary reviewers saw a discrepancy between the narrative and the narrator, the teller and the tale, and a consequent crux in the theme: is society or Dorothea herself to blame for her first marriage? I, too, find something of a discrepancy but in terms of effectiveness of action rather than in terms of responsibility, the first versions seeming to urge social change, the final version leaning more toward resignation to the imperfections of society: "This is more congenial to the modern sensibility," I conclude, "though I am not so sure it as adequately suggests the moral vision of the novel" ("A Study of the Proof," p. 61).

MEREDITH AND THE ART OF IMPLICATION

LIONEL STEVENSON

Undeniably Meredith is an acquired taste; and all acquired tastes, whether gastronomic or aesthetic, evoke contrary responses. The persons who have cultivated one are complacent in their superior sensitivity; those who reject it sneer at the enthusiasts as pretentious poseurs. Two recent volumes on Meredith aptly illustrate the diversity. The one edited by Ioan Williams, in the *Critical Heritage* series, shows that throughout his career the critics were irreconcilably divided between admirers and disparagers; the one entitled *Meredith Now*, edited by Ian Fletcher, brings together a clutch of young scholars whose respectful chorus is conveyed in the full panoply of currently fashionable critical terminology.

There are a number of reasons why Meredith's status has always been ambiguous. First of all, he is hard to classify as to literary genre. Critics and literary historians prefer to deal with authors who can be readily labeled and pigeonholed. Is Meredith a novelist or a poet? For the first five years of his literary career he wrote only in verse, and again for his last decade he confined himself to the same field. Throughout his life he insisted that he wished to be evaluated primarily on his poetry, implying that his novel writing was an uncongenial task required by the vulgar necessity of earning a living.

In studies of the Victorian period he is apt to be uncomfortably partitioned between the two categories; and yet it is essential that his work be considered as a whole. As a poet, he is often novelistic. His dramatic monologues, such as "Juggling

177

Jerry" and "The Old Chartist," might have been uttered by characters in his fiction. Some later poems, such as "Earth and Man," follow the logical structure of prose discourse more than the emotional movement of poetry. His only poem to be widely admired by present-day critics, *Modern Love*, is the nearest approach that has ever been made to that elusive chimaera, a novel in verse. By deletion of realistic details, rigorous condensation, collage of snapshot dramatic scenes, and patterning of significant symbols, he created a complex psychological study of an intense emotional crisis, confining it to less than seven thousand words.

In *The Egoist*, by a converse process, he expanded what might have been a three-act comedy of manners into a full-scale novel by retarding each episode through accumulation of gesture, phrase, and allusion. In that novel as in his others, his methods were essentially poetic. Far more than any other Victorian novelist, he used the devices of metaphor, symbolism, archetypal myths, emotional tone, and rhythmic movement. In consequence, his readers found his poetry difficult because it partook so much of prose, and his novels even more difficult because they were saturated with poetry. Was it aesthetically defensible to mingle two basic modes that are ordinarily considered to be mutually exclusive?

Since critical consensus has identified Meredith as novelist, he is included in the present volume. Hence arises a series of further ambiguities. What sort of novelist is he? Last of the old tradition or first of the new? Realist or romanticist? Cynic or sentimentalist? Chronicler of the mind or of the passions? His persistently ironic attitude left serious-minded people in doubt as to his basic opinions on the dominant ethical and social controversies of his period. Readers are apt to feel frustrated and annoyed by the apparently inconsistent qualities of his work.

If Meredith's fiction is to be classified, it must be put into the category of "the novel of intellect." This is not the same thing as "the novel of ideas," which implies a didactic purpose. Meredith was certainly not deficient in opinions, which became more assertive as he grew older; but his primary objective in writing his books was to make his readers think for

178

themselves. This assumed that they were capable of independent mental exertion and might even enjoy it. Such an elite group would merely be bored by the obvious and hackneyed material of popular fiction.

To find Meredith's antecedents one has to go back to previous generations: Sterne in the eighteenth century and Peacock as a belated child of the Enlightenment. The vast expansion of readership in the Victorian age entailed a lowering of the literacy level in the novel. This did not prevent the major authors from including elements that might be appreciated only by well-informed and sophisticated minds; but even so learned and philosophical a writer as George Eliot accepted the obligation of being comprehensible to the multitude.

Among his contemporaries, then, Meredith was an anachronism, harking back to the elegance of the eighteenth century, when literature was a prerogative of cultivated gentlefolk. His attitude toward such popular novelists as Dickens and Trollope was the amused contempt of Fielding toward Richardson. To be sure, Meredith conformed with the Victorian premise that the basic function of the novel was to be an anatomy of society, displayed by means of interwoven plots and a wide spectrum of characters. Indeed, he provides some of the best surveys of mainly upper-class English society, with considerable extensions to the Continent—Italy in *Vittoria*, Germany in *Harry Richmond*, France in *Beauchamp's Career*. But we can now see that he was even more a forerunner of the twentieth century, when writers regard themselves as possessing esoteric sensibilities and communicating only with a small coterie of kindred spirits. If Meredith cannot be termed "alienated," he has taken a step in that direction by insisting on being detached.

He was preoccupied with the minute gradations of pretence and self-deception that emerge from the tension between natural impulses and the rigid code of morality and conduct that has developed in a formally structured social system. With this objective, it was essential that he should probe into the inmost depths of mental states; and his purpose could not be achieved through Henry James's technique of limitation to a single recording consciousness. Meredith wanted to demon-

179

strate the relativity of truth by moving from one mind to another, revealing in each a baffling mixture of veracity and falsehood, intelligence and stupidity, perception and prejudice. It was a disquieting experience for a reader to realize that he could not complacently identify himself with the values and judgments of one particular character.

In Meredith's first novel, *The Ordeal of Richard Feverel*, the dogmatism and self-righteousness of Sir Austin precipitate the disasters that ensue, and yet his aphorisms often express genuine wisdom. The irony resides in the incompatibility between his theories and their application. Similarly, Adrian Harley is the most despicable character in the book, and yet the reader cannot be immune to the persuasiveness of his worldly logic. Readers were even more exasperated to find that the ostensibly impeccable hero, Richard (like Nevil Beauchamp in a later novel), was highly fallible, willful, and obstinate, incapable of relating his cloudy ideals to the actualities of the human condition. Lacking a secure anchor of identification, the reader was precipitated into the uncomfortable necessity of judging for himself. As an efficient means for producing that result, the author constantly manipulated the devices of implication.

Meredith's techniques of implication function on several levels. As a consistent ironist, he must be approached with vigilance to make sure whether or not he means what he appears to say. Seemingly favorable language may mask contempt, or pejorative terms may carry overtones of approbation. His highly metaphorical language and his wealth of scholarly allusion demand all his reader's resources for recognizing connotations. His representation of dialogue is particularly elusive through its fidelity to the discontinuities of talk: sentences remain unfinished, or leap from one topic to another without transition. A speaker often seems oblivious to what his interlocutor is saying. In the larger units of narrative presentation, Meredith sometimes capriciously foreshortens or omits a scene that any other novelist would consider obligatory, and it devolves upon the reader to construct it for himself out of preparatory foreshadowing and subsequent retrospect. The fragmentation and distortion of experience, the frustrating sense of inadequate observation or ambiguous interpretation, even the flexibility of the sense of time, are thus carried over from actuality into the novelist's methods. Behind the mask of apparently candid authorial comment, Meredith perpetually tantalizes his readers with hints, insinuations, and ambiguities, which render his fiction almost as elusive as real life.

Seen from this angle, his work is a recognizable step in the movement of Victorian fiction in the direction of realism; but in other respects he seemed to be arrogantly defying it. The adverse or uncomprehending reactions of his contemporaries demonstrate how remote his methods were from those prevalent when he began to write. The extent of his innovations can best be appreciated by regarding them in the context of what other novelists were doing at the time.

If the principal object of a novelist is the depiction of ordinary events in contemporary surroundings, plausibility demands that this material shall be conveyed in language entirely familiar to the reader. Any discrepancy will be objectionable on two counts: it will weaken the convincingness of the record, and it will be aesthetically indefensible through incongruity. The simplest of all forms of comic burlesque is the inflated narration of trivialities, and any serious realist wishes to avoid such absurdities at all cost.

It was in style as much as in choice of subject that Thackeray signaled a major turning point with *Vanity Fair*. Disgusted by what he considered to be the vulgar bombast of Bulwer and Dickens and the tawdry flamboyance of Disraeli—qualities that he had parodied in *Mr. Punch's Prize Novelists*—he scrupulously maintained a quiet, informal manner to suit his restrained and ironical picture of upper-class society. His readers were startled and sometimes antagonized by the illusion of carelessness. As late as 1879 we find William Cory, the fastidious Eton classicist, declaring contemptuously:

> I do not in Vanity Fair see anything that might not have been written by a blind man to whom people had read novels aloud and to whom clubmen had talked freely. I can understand insular people, with no Academy to correct their taste, being bewitched by Dickens; but Thackeray is not even clever, not even strong; it is all of it just the stuff 'easy to understand' which one would serve up for the common idlers of watering places and parsonages in second-rate magazines.

To most people, however, Thackeray is a master of the relaxed manner, that of an urbane gentleman chatting with a friend rather than an orator addressing an audience. This does not mean, of course, that Thackeray was actually insensitive to subtlety of suggestion. The peculiar flavor of his irony resides in his ambiguity of attitude, in which an apparently innocent remark often conveys baffling complexities of feeling.

Whether it was a direct result of Thackeray's influence, as he sometimes complacently imagined, or whether other novelists were independently responding to the same pressures that made for realism, there can be no doubt that by 1850 the rhetorical style has become archaic. The extent of the change can be gauged by comparing the previous books of Bulwer-Lytton with *The Caxtons*, which he began to write in the year following *Vanity Fair*. Nor did Dickens, in *David Copperfield* and thereafter, ever revert to the melodramatic fustian of *Oliver Twist*, or of the death of Little Nell, or even of such a recent chapter as the parting between Carker and Edith Dombey.

The decade of the fifties was the great era of the domestic novel, which found its most gifted exponent in Trollope. Admirer of Thackeray though he was, Trollope acquired little if any of the subtlety and elegance of Thackeray's style. Instead he wrote in a homespun and pedestrian prose that gave his novels their unique persuasiveness, as though they were not the work of a creative author at all, but were a plain man's honest report of other plain people's doings.

George Eliot, too, though she commanded a much stronger power of moving her readers' feelings, retained a sort of puritan suspicion of stylistic display. This can be attributed to two principal causes: first, her ethical earnestness obliged her to strive for the illusion of literal truth; and second, her familiarity with current scientific thinking and writing impelled her to present her observations with the precision and impartiality of a clinical report. During that generation the reading public was acquiring a grasp of scientific method and an enthusiasm for scientific discovery, and so in their various ways Wilkie Collins and Charles Reade and George Eliot all sought to give the impression that their novels were produced by a process of collecting and organizing evidence, as scrupulous as that of any scientist in his laboratory. Under the influence of Herbert Spencer and subsequently of George Henry Lewes, George Eliot was certain that the road to knowledge of the human heart led through the well-cultivated fields of scientific rationalism.

Her purpose, as she stated it in a famous chapter of *Adam Bede*, was "to tell my simple story, without trying to make things seem better than they were; dreading nothing, indeed, but falsity. . . . It is for this rare, precious quality of truthfulness that I delight in many Dutch paintings, which loftyminded people despise. I find a source of delicious sympathy in these faithful pictures of a monotonously homely existence." Naturally, then, her techniques are those of a Ter Borch rather than those of a Rembrandt. Sometimes, indeed, she indulges in a figure of speech or in a sarcastic or a jocular phrase; but even these seem conscientiously excogitated and soberly explained, rather than being spontaneous imaginative excursions.

By 1860, therefore, the evidence indicated that domestic realism was the particular province of the English novel, and that its style and technique must accordingly be of the placid, unassuming sort that Mario Praz has dubbed "Biedermeier." But in the same year as *Adam Bede*, another new novelist had appeared on the scene with a recalcitrant determination to invest prose fiction with poetic beauty, emotional evocativeness, and intellectual acumen. It was not that Meredith wanted to go back to the turgid rhetoric of the previous generation. He was emphatically a man of the new age, quite as keenly alive to the importance of scientific progress as George Eliot was; but he believed that the function of the novelist was not so much to ape the impassive and literal accuracy of the scientist as it was to impart some imaginative conception of the infinitely complicated relationships that psychology was beginning to recognize. In order to achieve this effect, he felt that he must abandon not only the old stereotypes of melodrama and mystery but also the detailed reproduction of external phenomena which seemed satisfactory to his competitors and which later earned from Henry James the epithet of "saturation." As a matter of fact, Meredith abandoned even more than this: J. B. Priestley goes so far as to say that he was the first novelist to attempt a form of communication that was not essentially narration at all.

There were several reasons why Meredith was able to shatter the accepted molds of the craft of fiction. He had become an author because no other vocation offered a comparable opportunity for him to overcome social and educational handicaps. The son of a provincial tailor, he could not claim to be a gentleman; and since the tailor had gone bankrupt and emigrated to the colonies there was no financial recompense for the stigma of his origin among tradesmen. It followed that the boy had not enjoyed the advantages of a public school and a university, but had picked up some erudition haphazardly. No wonder he wanted above all things to demonstrate his intellectual superiority and his fund of information.

Having begun unsuccessfully as a poet, he turned to fiction with a disconsolate sense of defeat, for which the only remedy was to endow his prose with as many poetic values as possible. From its beginnings, the English novel had been the particular literary medium of the bourgeoisie. It emerged along with the prosperity of the businessman and was given its basic forms by three egregious representatives of the moralistic, materialistic middle class—Bunyan, Defoe, and Richardson. The readers of the novel were predominantly the solid citizens and their wives, people for whom poetry was too elusive and serious prose too abstract. They were of the type that had earlier been affectionately ridiculed in *The Knight of the Burning Pestle*, the type that enjoyed meeting their own familiar surroundings in a story and finding their own virtues and values extolled, with no inordinate strain upon their imaginations or their range of knowledge.

In this context another element in Meredith's personal heredity is significant. Positive that his father's family was purely Welsh in origin and his mother's equally purely Irish, he possessed all the Celtic conviction of that race's imaginative and emotional superiority over the phlegmatic literal-minded Saxon. Furthermore, his father had transmitted the notion that the Merediths were descended from Cymric princes, and though George Meredith affected to laugh at the legend, it probably helped to endow him with disdain for the smug and sluggish bourgeoisie.

It is worth noting that his literary career was synchronous with Matthew Arnold's, though he was eight years younger. They published their first books of poetry only two years apart, and both turned from verse to prose in the late fifties. They are much alike in their use of oblique irony and witty phrases to mock the Philistines, in their faith that the widest possible culture and the most disinterested critical intelligence are the best weapons against English stolidity and parochialism. Just as Meredith resembles Arnold in his contempt for Philistinism, he is a precursor of Bernard Shaw in his mischievous ridiculing of the English predilection for blunt common sense and "middle-class morality."

His own immediate literary mentors were Richard Hengist Horne, a picturesque adventurer, and Thomas Love Peacock, a witty Sybarite. From Horne's *Orion* Meredith acquired a habit of embodying philosophic concepts in classical myths, with a Keatsian floridity of natural setting; from Peacock a taste for the very different classical quality of intellectual clarity and sceptical detachment. Much of his distinctive manner derives from the uneasy alliance of these two almost antithetical elements.

Regarding himself primarily as a poet, Meredith reserved the most serious statements of his creed for such baffling, symbolic poems as "The Woods of Westermain," "The Day of the Daughter of Hades," and "A Hymn to Colour." Familiarity with his poetry is the best guide to the sincere meanings lurking within the capricious texture of his fiction. Yet, though he was first and foremost a poet throughout his novels, he united this trait with another which delighted his friends in all periods of his life. This was his amazing conversational fluency, particularly a knack of phrase-making and a wild gift of comic improvisation that enabled him to elaborate fantastic sagas about his neighbors. The apparent obscurity of his prose style is due largely to these two elements. Like poetry, it conveys its meaning through imagery, and dispenses with the normal logical and factual explanations and transitions; like conversation, it is full of digressions and parentheses, echoes and elisions.

Often a passage that seems unintelligible on the printed page will become lucid when read aloud with the oral devices of emphasis, pause, and inflection that are automatically employed by a good talker.

Meredith insistently declared that his chief purpose was to force his readers to think, and that conventional methods and style rendered fiction so easy to absorb that the mind scarcely functioned at all. The effort to grasp Meredith's meaning produces a collaborative relationship between the novelist and his audience which is stimulating to the brains of the latter. In his first novel, *The Ordeal of Richard Feverel*, he stated his objective hopefully:

> At present, I am aware, an audience impatient for blood and glory scorns the stress I am putting on incidents so minute, a picture so little imposing. An audience will come to whom it will be given to see the elementary machinery at work; who, as it were, from some slight hint of the straws, will feel the winds of March when they do not blow. To them will nothing be trivial, seeing that they will have in their eyes the invisible conflict going on around us, whose features a nod, a smile, a laugh of ours perpetually changes. And they will perceive, moreover, that in real life all hangs together; the train is laid in the lifting of an eyebrow, that bursts upon the field of thousands. They will see the links of things as they pass, and wonder not, as foolish people now do, that this great matter came out of that small one.

In *Sandra Belloni*, somewhat less confidently, he offered a mock apology for his digressive comments and oblique suggestions:

> Right loath am I to continue my partnership with a fellow who will not see things on the surface, and is blind to the fact that the public detests him. I mean this garrulous, super-subtle, so-called Philosopher. . . . He maintains that a story should not always flow, or, at least, not to a given measure. . . . He points proudly to the fact that our people in this comedy move themselves—are moved from their own impulsion —and that no arbitrary hand has posted them to bring about any event and heap the catastrophe. In vain I tell him that he is meantime making tatters of the puppets' golden robe—illusion; that he is sucking the blood of their warm humanity out of them.

Later, in *Beauchamp's Career*, he returned to the defense of his method:

> My way is like a Rhone island in the summer drought, stony, unattractive and difficult between the two forceful streams of the unreal and the over-real, which delight mankind—honour to the conjurers. My people

186

conquer nothing, win none; they are actual, yet uncommon. It is the
clock-work of the brain that they are directed to set in motion, and—
poor troop of actors to vacant benches!—the conscience residing in
thoughtfulness which they would appeal to; and if you are impervious
to them, we are lost.

The effect that Meredith defines in the foregoing pronounce-
ments could not be produced by laborious lists of "minute inci-
dents" and explicit narration of "the invisible conflict." He had
to adopt a complete system of devices that I am summarizing
under the term "implication." By employing implication on
every level, from individual phrases to the total construction of
a novel, he was able to convey multiple levels of meaning to a
degree surpassed only by James Joyce (who, incidentally, read
Meredith assiduously in his youth). Among earlier novelists,
the only one who indulged in anything like Meredith's implicative vagaries was Sterne, and the reviewers of *Richard Feverel* were prompt to accuse Meredith of "Shandyism."

There were several valid justifications for Meredith's adoption of his devious manner. For one thing, he found the elaborate and artificial behavior of the upper class vastly more interesting and significant than the elementary reactions of
peasants, such as (in succession to Wordsworth) George Eliot
considered the best material for a philosophical author's study.
An elaborate and artificial style was logically appropriate.
Cultivated English people were apt to indulge in classical allusions and literary tags. More importantly, in the mid-nineteenth
century, English fashionable society had brought the suppres-
sion of emotion and the avoidance of plain speech to the level
of a fine art. The only technique adequate for reproducing
such conduct, while at the same time revealing the suppressed
crises, was some form of equivocation.

A more practical influence upon Meredith was the excessive
verbal delicacy of his period. In spite of all his reliance upon
implication, *The Ordeal of Richard Feverel* struck many readers as intolerably coarse and lewd. Several reviewers condemned it on this count, and Mudie's library withdrew it from
circulation. The only way the author could hope to avoid a recurrence of this disaster was to phrase his subsequent books so
evasively that readers could not be sure whether an improper

meaning was intentional. In *Richard Feverel* Meredith had already described this technique: "Adrian ventured to make trifling jokes about London's Mrs. Grandison: jokes delicately not decent, but so delicately so, that it was not decent to perceive it."

Further, in the light of Meredith's declaration that "our people in this comedy move themselves, and that no arbitrary hand has posted them to bring about any event," it followed that the reader must interpret for himself the sometimes inadequate evidence that is all we ever have as a basis for judgments in real life. Anything but a totally invisible narrator, Meredith is an all-pervasive presence, elaborating every gesture, philosophizing on every event; but his commentary usually serves to intensify the ambiguities of human intercourse rather than to dissipate them.

Finally, and most important, Meredith wanted to convey the relativity of truth, the extent to which every impression is fragmentary and biased. It became a critical cliché, after Meredith gained tardy fame, to compare him with Browning—a cliché that led Oscar Wilde to remark, "Yes, Meredith is a prose Browning—and so is Browning." The concern over the relativity of truth caused Browning to develop his technique of the dramatic monologue, and finally to expand it to epic proportions in *The Ring and the Book*. Only thus could he hope to give his readers the illusion of entering other people's minds and looking out through their peculiar eyes. Meredith sought to achieve a similar effect by his elusive shifting from mind to mind and from tone to tone, so that the apparently simple sunshine of everyday observation was fragmented into the whole spectrum that actually comprises it.

Analysis of Meredith's art of implication can begin with the largest unit—the over-all structure and tone of a whole book. On this scale the simplest device of implication is allegory; and it is significant that Meredith's first two long works of prose fiction, which cannot properly be designated as novels, were in traditional allegorical form. In a preface to a reprinting of *The Shaving of Shagpat*, it is true, he disclaimed allegorical intent; but the disclaimer is so equivocally phrased that it is undoubtedly itself a specimen of implication, meant to call the reader's attention to hidden meanings that might otherwise be overlooked. In later life Meredith admitted that "I suppose it does wear a sort of allegory, but it is not as a dress-suit, rather as a dressing-gown, very loosely." Both in *Shagpat* and in his next book, *Farina*, he set forth many of the general concepts that reappeared throughout his later work.

Nevertheless, neither of these books was a readily recognizable allegory in the manner of *Everyman* or *The Pilgrim's Progress*. An ingenious imitation of the *Arabian Nights*, the first book could be read merely as a fantastic fairy tale, full of thrilling adventure and breathless suspense. Then its rhythmic prose was so richly encrusted with jeweled words and luscious metaphors that a connoisseur of style could enjoy it as a work of verbal art. But furthermore, these very qualities were from time to time subtly exaggerated beyond the bounds of artistic restraint, and the whole thing seemed to be a burlesque upon heroic exploits and exotic beauty of style rather than a choice example of them. The reviewers were so baffled by these levels of meaning that they disagreed as to whether any deeper significance lay buried below the shimmering surface. It remained for the pertinacity of a Scottish Presbyterian minister, half a century later, to produce a whole book erecting a systematic interpretation of Meredith's fantasy. No such effort has yet been made for his second work, *Farina*, in which he turned from oriental visions to the quaint superstitions of German folklore, and created an almost equally ingenious pastiche of romance and absurdity.

Never thereafter did Meredith undertake a formal allegory; but traces of fable and apologue survive in *Richard Feverel*, as in the recurrent echoes of the story of Eden and the Fall; and even in Meredith's last major novel, *One of Our Conquerors*, installments of Colney Durrance's satiric romance, "The Rival Tongues," serve as a sort of allegorical counterpoint to the main story.

Another device of implication on the large scale of a total book is the mingling of modes; and this was displayed in full measure in *Richard Feverel*. The prevalent tone is that of high comedy, which is so well recognized a dramatic genre that it establishes certain positive expectations in the reader's mind.

189

In this novel, however, the sophisticated, faintly cynical attitude repeatedly gives place to totally different effects: the rhapsodies of young love in the first Richard-Lucy scenes, the deeper emotional tension of Richard's solitary night among the Rhineland hills, the bitter pathos of Lucy's death. The author enhances these effects by abrupt changes of style. The famous love chapter entitled "A Diversion Played on a Penny-Whistle" is in ornate free verse, the deathbed is described with such grim taciturnity that the reader can scarcely realize what has happened. But the author is not satisfied with mere juxtapositions; he mingles the modes even within the individual scene. The shepherd lad with his pipe is in one sense an appropriate Arcadian figure for the idyll of the young lovers; in another he suggests the god Pan and thus helps to emphasize the note of sexual passion that is latent under the naïve idealism of the boy and girl; and yet at the same time he sheds a faint aura of ridicule over all the ecstatic poetry by being so completely an English clodhopper, making uncouth noises with his trophy from some penny stall.

Most critics seem to feel that the mingling of modes in *Richard Feverel* is a piece of youthful bravura that is not aesthetically defensible. Certainly Meredith never attempted it again so extravagantly, though it can be recognized in one of his most mature novels, *Beauchamp's Career*, and even in the last two that he wrote, *Lord Ormont and his Aminta* and *The Amazing Marriage*. Yet in spite of critical strictures, the lavish heterogeneousness of *Richard Feverel* does succeed in producing an effect of depth and richness which is not wholly compensated for by the rigid adherence to unity of mood in *The Egoist*.

The variety of styles and tones in *Richard Feverel* is directly concerned with displaying the relativity of truth. Sir Austin is a pompous autocrat who obstinately provokes the whole tragedy; but he is also a sincere and magnanimous gentleman with an uncommonly able mind. The excerpts from his book, *The Pilgrim's Scrip*, not only enable Meredith to display his own skill in another and difficult form, the apothegm; they also embody some of Meredith's cherished beliefs. One of the basic themes of his poetry is summed up in Sir Austin's maxim: "Nature is not all dust, but a living portion of the spheres. In aspiration it is our error to despise her, forgetting that through Nature only can we ascend. . . . St. Simeon saw the Hog in Nature, and took Nature for the Hog." Thus Meredith is able to smuggle some of his graver opinions into the novel, while at the same time deriding all such solemn generalizations. But the real irony of this particular maxim is that Sir Austin's blind disregard for this very view of Nature is the central theme of the book.

Nor is Sir Austin the only surrogate for the author in supplying commentary from various angles. Diametrically opposite to his sententious aphorisms are the cynical epigrams of Adrian Harley, the unscrupulous worldling, whose charm is so affectionately conveyed that one cannot help believing that he utters some part of the author's own mind. Portions of his introductory description may be quoted as a good example of Meredith's implicative style:

> Some people are born green: others yellow. Adrian was born yellow. He was always on the ripe sensible side of a question. . . . Adrian had an instinct for the majority, and, as the world invariably found him enlisted in its ranks, his appellation of wise youth was generally acquiesced in.
>
> The wise youth, then, had the world with him, but no friends. Nor did he wish for those troublesome appendages of success. He caused himself to be required by people who could serve him; feared by such as could injure. . . . To satisfy his appetites without rashly staking his character was the wise youth's problem for life. He had no intimates save Gibbon and Horace, and the society of these fine aristocrats of literature helped him to accept humanity as it had been—and was: a supreme ironic procession, with laughter of the gods in the background. Why not laughter of mortals also? Adrian had his laugh in his comfortable corner. He possessed peculiar attributes of a heathen god. He was a disposer of men; he was polished, luxurious, and happy—at their cost. He lived in eminent self-content, as one lying on soft cloud, lapped in sunshine. Nor Jove, nor Apollo, cast eye upon the maids of earth with cooler power of selection, or pursued them in the covert with more sacred impunity. And he enjoyed his reputation for virtue as something additional. . . . Placed on Crusoe's island, his first cry would have been for clean linen: his next for the bill-of-fare; and then, for that Grand Panorama of the Mistress of the World falling to wreck under the barbarians, which had been the spur and the seal of his mind.

In these urbane terms, it has been conveyed to us that Adrian is a parasite, a mischievous meddler, and a habitual seducer of girls. Yet who can doubt that the portrait of a shameless hedonist is drawn with sympathy or perhaps envy? Indeed, it was derived directly from one of Meredith's intimate friends. In Adrian's cynical wisdom, then, Meredith offers us not sophistry so much as another way of looking at the truth.

When we consider Meredith's employment of implication at specific points within the total structure of a book, it is most notably manifested in the omitting of complete scenes that most novelists would regard as essential. His method is to prepare for the scene so that his readers expect it to occur; and then, after skipping it, he reveals bit by bit the essentials of what happened. Even in a relatively straightforward novel, *Rhoda Fleming*, which includes a minimum of implications because it deals with less sophisticated people, there is more than one instance of the device. A crucial development in the story is when Edward Blancove, the profligate young squire, is waylaid and attacked by Robert Armstrong, and then Armstrong in his turn is beaten by Blancove's men; but these dark deeds come to the reader only gradually through broken hints.

This particular example may be explained by saying that Meredith is not interested in scenes of physical violence; but a different explanation is needed in *The Egoist* when two important interviews are left out. In Chapter 13, believing that his fiancée, Clara Middleton, is jealous of his former friendship with Laetitia Dale, Sir Willoughby Patterne decides to arrange a marriage between Laetitia and his cousin Vernon Whitford, and he asks Clara to help with the intrigue. She, meanwhile, is desperately eager to escape from her engagement to Sir Willoughby. At the end of the chapter he gives her explicit instructions:

> "And you will go in, and talk to Vernon of the lady in question. Use your best persuasion in our joint names. You have my warrant for saying that money is no consideration; house and income are assured. You can hardly have taken me seriously when I requested you to undertake Vernon before. I was quite in earnest then as now. I prepare Miss Dale. . . ." Vernon was at the window and stood aside for her to enter. Sir Willoughby used a gentle insistence with her. She bent her head as if she were stepping into a cave. . . .

All of chapter 14 is occupied with Sir Willoughby's conversation with Miss Dale, and the chapter ends: "Apparently, considering the duration of the conference between his Clara and Vernon, his cousin required strong persuasion to accept the present." The reader assumes that the following chapter will give the parallel interview. But chapter 15 opens with "Neither Clara nor Vernon appeared at the mid-day table," and in the course of a page the following clues can be gleaned:

> Miss Isabel quitted the room. She came back, saying, "They decline to lunch." "Then we may rise," remarked Sir Willoughby. "She was weeping," Miss Isabel murmured to him. "Girlish enough," he said. . . . Sir Willoughby walked up and down the lawn, taking a glance at the West-room as he swung round on the turn of his leg. Growing impatient, he looked in at the window and found the room vacant. . . . Near the dinner hour the ladies were informed by Miss Middleton's maid that her mistress was lying down on her bed, too unwell with headache to be present. Young Crossjay brought a message from Vernon (delayed by birds' eggs in the delivery), to say that he was off over the hills, and thought of dining with Dr. Corney.

From these hints the reader is left to infer how much the long conversation contributed to the mutual love that was developing half unconsciously between Clara and Vernon.

This omission is entirely tacit; an even more audacious one, at the final climax of the story, is openly acknowledged. In the depth of his humiliation, Sir Willoughby beseeches Laetitia Dale to marry him, even though he had alienated her early devotion by his callous selfishness. At the opening of chapter 49, reverting to the symbol of the Imps of Comedy which has recurred throughout the novel, Meredith asserts that the scene would be too ludicrously painful to appear in a story of high comedy:

> We cannot be abettors of the tribes of imps whose revelry is in the frailties of our poor human constitution. They have their place and their service, and so long as we continue to be what we are now, they will hang on to us, restlessly plucking at the garments which cover our nakedness, nor ever ceasing to twitch them and strain at them until they have fairly stripped us for one of their horrible Walpurgis nights: when the laughter heard is of a character to render laughter frightful to the ears of men throughout the remainder of their days. But if in these festival hours under the beams of Hecate they are uncontrollable by the Comic Muse, she will not flatter them with her presence during the course of their insane and impious hilarities, whereof a description would out-Brocken Brockens and make Graymalkin and Paddock too intimately our familiars.

After this characteristic passage of mock subservience to aesthetic decorum, duly adorned with allusions to *Faust* and *Macbeth*, Meredith gives a bald summary of an episode that lasted for many hours and decided the fate of two major characters in the story.

Being thus capable of flouting normal expectations of complete narration, Meredith naturally taxed his readers' attention often by omitting lesser aids to comprehension—introductory, transitional, and explanatory passages that most novelists regard as the dull but necessary scaffolding of a story. In real life we have to puzzle out the relationship of events for ourselves without neat blueprints, and Meredith felt that we should be prepared to read a novel in the same way, though with the trust that a relationship is there to be found, or the author would not have included what he does include.

It must be pointed out, however, that one of the major novels is needlessly difficult in many modern editions. When Meredith revised *Richard Feverel* in 1878, in order to establish a new copyright, he was probably right in believing that some of its immature extravagances ought to be eliminated; but in an impatient fury he ripped out whole chapters almost at random, with the most perfunctory readjustments. In condensing the first four chapters into one, he discarded much that is vitally needed for full understanding of the story as a whole. To take a small but relevant example: at several points there are allusions to "the Great Shaddock Dogma." Even if the reader knows that the shaddock is a variety of oriental citrus fruit, the phrase is thoroughly obscure. In the original opening chapters, however, it is introduced as a typical jest of Adrian Harley's, referring to the forbidden fruit in the Garden of Eden and applied to Sir Austin's obsession that sex is evil and is responsible for all human calamities. Thus the grotesque phrase, along with another one, "The Apple Disease," takes its place in the pattern of allusions to Adam, and the Serpent, and the Fall of Man, which maintains the central theme throughout.

Sometimes Meredith's omission of relevant material is not as capricious as it appears. In *The Adventures of Harry Richmond* we are apt to be exasperated by uncertainty as to what Richmond Roy's great "cause" actually is. Only through carefully

guarded innuendo does Meredith convey that he is a claimant
to the British throne. In mid-Victorian days an overt suggestion, even in fiction, that the Queen might not be the legitimate
monarch would have been stigmatized as intolerable bad taste,
if not arrant treason. But the necessary vagueness in indicating
the nature of the Richmond claim contributes to the story's
power, for *Harry Richmond* is one of Meredith's best studies
of the relativity of truth. It is his only novel written from the
first-person point of view, and as young Harry grows up we
try to piece together the true facts about his father from the
tantalizing glimpses he obtains. Even at the end we cannot feel
sure whether Richmond Roy is indeed, as he claims, the off-
spring of a secret royal marriage, or the bastard of a prince's
mistress, or an upstart whose exalted parentage is wholly
fictitious. If the last alternative is accepted, we remain in
doubt as to whether Roy is a clever impostor or is genuinely
deluded by his own evidence. Yet all these doubts, instead of
weakening the effect of the story, render it more persuasively
lifelike.

We may turn now to the smaller currency of Meredith's implicative technique—metaphors, personifications, recurrent
symbols of many sorts. His poetic habit of mind made him
lavish with figures of speech; but readers are not accustomed
to find such profusion and expansion and intervolution of
metaphor in prose, and are likely to become lost in the effort
of distinguishing between the metaphor and the literal fact
that it is intended to illuminate. Meredith sometimes com-
mented wryly on his own addiction to figurative adornment, as
in this passage from *Diana of the Crossways*:

> The residence of Sir Lukin Dunstane was on the hills, where a day
> of Italian sky . . . gives distantly a tower to view, and a murky web,
> not without colour: the ever-flying banner of the metropolis, the smoke
> of the city's chimneys, if you prefer plain language. At a first inspec-
> tion of the house, Lady Dunstane did not like it, and it was advertised
> to be let, and the auctioneer proclaimed it in his dialect. Her taste was
> delicate; . . . twice she read the stalking advertisement of the attrac-
> tions of Copsley, and hearing Diana call it 'the plush of speech,' she
> shuddered; she decided that a place where her husband's family had
> lived ought not to stand forth meretriciously spangled and daubed,
> like a show booth at a fair, for a bait. . . . She withdrew the trumpeting
> placard. Retract we likewise 'banner of the metropolis.' That plush of

195

speech haunts all efforts to swell and illuminate citizen prose to a
princely poetic. Yet Lady Dunstane herself could name the bank of
smoke, when looking North-eastward from her summer-house, the flag
of London; and she was a person of the critical mind, well able to distinguish between the simple metaphor and the superobese.

In such a passage Meredith is merely displaying his fascina-
tion with the mystery of words; but elsewhere we find him
incorporating the elusiveness of metaphors into the context of
the story. In *The Egoist* Mrs. Mountstewart Jenkinson is a typical *persona* of Meredith, with her famous talent for cryptic
phrases, and two of them give rise to protracted discussion.
When she sums up the charms of Sir Willoughby in the remark,
"You see he has a leg," several pages are devoted to a record
of the different interpretations that the phrase receives from
Sir Willoughby's relations, friends, and enemies, and through
this we acquire our basic impression of his difficult personality. Later, Mrs. Mountstewart's epithet for Clara, "a dainty
rogue in porcelain," is similarly dissected, with attention to
every conceivable connotation. In these apparently playful
passages Meredith is concerned with a thoroughly serious subject, the multiple shades of significance that can be conveyed
only through metaphor, never by literal assertion.

His addiction to metaphor extends to the use of nicknames
for characters which almost usurp the real names. In *Richard
Feverel*, the butler is automatically "Heavy Benson," Adrian is
"The Wise Youth," Richard is "The Magnetic Youth" or "The
Hope of Raynham." An old aunt of Sir Austin's never achieves
an identity of her own, being termed invariably "The Eighteenth Century." When, in the same chapters, we encounter the
phrase "Mrs. Malediction," we may assume that she is another
aged relative; but we shall be wrong. She is simply a personi-
fication of the family curse that periodically drives the Feverels
to disaster.

The close scrutiny of individual metaphors is related to the
use of recurrent symbols, which is one of Meredith's main devices. The description of Clara as a "rogue in porcelain"
connects itself with the ominous shattering of the Chinese vase
that Colonel de Craye brought as a wedding gift for Clara and
Willoughby; and the whole image of breakable porcelain seems
to have traditional associations with the loss of virginity.

196

In the same novel the double-blossom wild cherry tree comes to be symbolic of natural, spontaneous love; and both here and in several later novels the Alps serve as a powerful symbol of freedom from conventional restrictions.

A particular sort of metaphor, to which Meredith was especially prone, is literary and historical allusion. Even more than ordinary metaphor, it depends upon the reader's ability to participate. If the allusion is not recognized, communication ceases. Often these are merely incidental references, but sometimes they penetrate deeply into the basic themes of the novels. At first sight the sixth chapter of *Richard Feverel* probably seems to be a digressive exercise in broad comedy, being a dialogue between two illiterate rustics, a plowman and a tinker. It might be regarded as merely a further display of the author's virtuosity—his competence to shift from refined speech and manners into the crudest demotic. The clue to the chapter's relevance and its serious theme is provided by its title, "The Magian Conflict." If the reader recognizes the allusion to Manichaeism, he can then accept it as symbolizing the ethical dilemma that suddenly confronts the immature boy.

In the disparity between learned allusions and realistic situations there is likely to be a dimension of irony. In the present instance it is triangular. Richard's adoption of a hero's pose is equally absurd whether viewed in contrast with the cosmic philosophy of Zoroaster or with the alehouse maunderings of the tinker. At the same time, cosmic philosophy becomes ludicrous when reduced to the identities of plowman and tinker, and alternatively the bumpkins are ludicrously inflated into intellectuals.

Sometimes the ironic contrast fails to justify itself. In the original version of *Richard Feverel*, Sir Austin's fury with the nursemaid who comes upon him in a moment of emotional surrender is explained by a mythological allusion:

> Dian was not more chastely jealous of her bath than Sir Austin of the moment when his knightly chainmail was removed, and his heart stood bare. Poor Polly-Actaeon was summoned to the Baronet's study next morning, and was shortly afterwards deported from the Abbey by his man, . . . her cheeks in a deluge, and a seal on her mouth.

The reader's imagination boggles at equating an English bar-

197

onet (who is simultaneously depicted as a feudal knight) with a Greek divinity, and a female one at that. Bewildered by the grotesqueness of the image and the memory of Diana's ruthless vengeance, the reader is apt to think of "poor Polly-Actaeon" as inordinately punished for no fault of her own. Nearly twenty years afterwards, it transpires that the operative phrase was "a seal on her mouth": she was liberally pensioned for the rest of her life. One is still left, however, to speculate as to whether some obscure purpose or merely authorial forgetfulness caused the change of her name in the interval from "Polly" to "Elizabeth."

Usually, no doubt, the presence of capital letters at the beginnings of unfamiliar words suffices to warn the reader of a reference to literature or history. Less identifiable is another kind of allusion that Meredith sometimes employed: parody. In the first chapter of *The Egoist*, his parody of Carlyle should be readily recognized, since Meredith provides a clue by attributing it to "the notable humourist;" yet many critics, even such a sapient one as Priestley, have cited the passage as a horrible example of Meredith's stylistic excesses, instead of seeing it as an impudent burlesque.

Later in the same novel, parody is used as a method for revealing inner states of mind. Sir Willoughby is mentally rehearsing the future scene of magnanimous forgiveness that will follow Clara's expected contrition:

> Supposing her still youngish, there might be captivating passages between them; as thus, in a style not unfamiliar,—
>
> "And was it my fault, my poor girl? Am I to blame, that you have passed a lonely unloved youth?"
>
> "No, Willoughby; the irreparable error was mine, the blame is mine, mine only. I live to repent it. I do not seek, for I have not deserved, your pardon. Had I it, I should need my own self-esteem to presume to clasp it to a bosom ever unworthy of you."
>
> "I may have been impatient. Clara: we are human!"
>
> "Never be it mine to accuse one on whom I laid so heavy a weight of forbearance!". . .
>
> "Must I recognize the bitter truth that we two, once nearly one! so nearly one! are eternally separated?"
>
> "I have envisaged it. My friend—may I call you friend: you have been my friend, my best friend! Oh, that eyes had been mine to know the friend I had!—Willoughby, in the darkness of night, and during days that were as night to my soul, I have seen the inexorable finger pointing my solitary way through the wilderness from a Paradise forfeited

by my most wilful, my wanton, sin. We have met. It is more than I have
merited. We part. In mercy let it be forever. Oh, terrible word! Coined
by the passions of our youth, it comes to us for our sole riches when we
are bankrupt of earthly treasures, and is the passport given by Abnega-
tion unto Woe that prays to quit this probationary sphere. Willoughby,
we part. It is better so."

"Clara! one—one only—one last—one holy kiss!"

"If these poor lips, that once were sweet to you. . . ."

The kiss, to continue the language of the imaginative composition of
his time, favourite readings of which had inspired Sir Willoughby with
a colloquy so pathetic, was imprinted.

Not only Willoughby's ineffable conceit, but also his shoddy
literary taste, is exactly captured by the fact that he thinks in
the hackneyed formulas of the popular sentimental novel. At
the same time Meredith suggests his contempt for such novels
by the contrast with his own elusive style.

Parody, of course, is an exceptional device for revealing the
complexion of a character's mind. More often Meredith re-
sorted to something not unlike what is nowadays known as the
stream of consciousness, sometimes by reproducing actual reverie, as in the first chapter of *One of Our Conquerors*, at other
times by echoing the inconsequentialities of spoken discourse.
A remarkable example occurs in *The Egoist* when Clara, after
breakfast one morning, first openly asks Willoughby to release
her from their engagement. Half stunned by the shock to his
pride, he knows that he must not stand mute, and yet he cannot collect his wits enough to answer her request, and so he
talks at random:

He squeezed both her hands, threw the door wide open, and said,
with countless blinkings:

"In the laboratory we are uninterrupted. I was at a loss to guess
where that most unpleasant effect on the senses came from. They are
always 'guessing' through the nose. I mean, the remainder of breakfast
here. Perhaps I satirized them too smartly—if you know the letters.
When they are not 'calculating.' More offensive than débris of a midnight banquet! An American tour is instructive, though not so romantic.
Not so romantic as Italy, I mean. Let us escape."

Desperately playing for time, Willoughby has seized on a
flimsy pretext—the unappetizing remains of the meal—for insisting that they adjourn from the dining room to his laboratory.
But interspersed among this are fragments of another chain of
association, only to be understood by recalling an early epi-

sode in the book. After he had been jilted by Constantia Durham, Willoughby escaped from gossip and raillery by making a leisurely tour of the world, during which he wrote satirical letters to his family, expressing particular scorn for the uncouth manners of the Americans. Apparently it is merely his chance use of the word "guess" that leads him to think of the American locutions "I guess" and "I calculate," but the association actually betrays the immediate reversion of his mind to the disaster of his previous broken engagement, and the urgency for protecting his prestige by preventing a recurrence. The further association with Italy refers to his plans for their honeymoon there.

It is in techniques of this sort that Meredith was clearly a forerunner of the twentieth-century novel. From the outset of his career, as we have seen, he was confident that "an audience will come to whom it will be given to see the elementary machinery at work; who, as it were, from some slight hint of the straws, will feel the winds of March when they do not blow." Eventually his expectation was fulfilled and his work received its full meed of praise. For approximately a generation, from 1880 to 1910, he was lauded as the greatest living novelist and exerted an immense influence on younger writers. Then an eclipse set in, and has continued until the present day.

I would be the first to acknowledge the defects in Meredith's novels—extravagance, ostentation, digressiveness, lack of proportion. But, though he often exasperates me, I find him to be, on the whole, the most vital, original, and consistently interesting English novelist of the past hundred years. He was the first to see clearly that a novel can be a work of literary art, meriting all the care for style and all the depth of suggestion that have always been expected of poetry. Necessarily, this meant that the best novels can be appreciated only by people with active minds and artistic sensitivity. Meredith's habit of making the first chapter of each novel more difficult to comprehend than anything that followed sprang from a sort of honesty that obliged him to discourage the wrong kind of reader. Oscar Wilde, a representative of the young authors who fell under Meredith's influence, called him "the one incomparable novelist we have now in England. . . . To him belongs philosophy in fiction. His people not merely live, they live in thought. One can see them from myriad points of view. They are suggestive. There is soul in them and around them. They are interpretative and symbolic. And he who made them, those wonderful quick-moving figures, made them for his own pleasure and has never asked the public what they wanted."

Forty years later than Wilde, J. B. Priestley said much the same thing: "He created for himself a new kind of novel, and thereby enlarged the scope of fiction. What he did was to make the art more mobile, more fluid. He bent and twisted the form to suit his own purposes. . . . So far as English fiction is concerned, there can be no doubt that the modern novel began with the publication of *Richard Feverel*."

EXPERIENCES OF THOMAS HARDY

BERNARD J. PARIS

I have had many experiences of Thomas Hardy. Like all great writers, Hardy is complex and multifaceted. Like most readers, I have tended to see only a few things at a time clearly. On each reading of his works, new things have captured my attention, while others have receded into the background. In addition, during the more than twenty years that I have been reading Hardy, I have changed much; I have adopted a number of different perspectives. This has resulted in a wide range of insights, judgments, and responses.

I was first attracted to Hardy by his philosophy, which seemed, much of it, to be true. His beliefs and attitudes reinforced my own; and this is what I was looking for in an author. When I began to read him with the rigor I had learned in graduate school, I became disenchanted with Hardy, both as an artist and as a thinker. His philosophy seemed to be full of contradictions, and his novels seemed crude and incoherent. It took me some time to see that they are, nonetheless, moving stories, and to question the propriety of reading novels in the same way that we read lyric poems. Since I have begun looking at fiction from a psychological perspective, I have come to see that novelists suffer from inner conflicts, like the rest of us. The power of their rhetoric often derives from their need to justify their favorite defensive strategies. Their great genius in the observation and portrayal of human experience does not necessarily make them wise or whole men. Still, they have much to offer. They may have great mimetic gifts, as does Hardy; and they let us know what it is like to be inside of other minds—their own and those of their characters.

I.

I responded to Hardy most powerfully when I was in my early twenties. He seemed, in many ways, a kindred spirit. I saw fiction as an instrument of moral discovery; and I was particularly excited by writers like Hardy, Conrad, and George Eliot, who were exploring the meaning of life in a universe without God. I could not take Hardy's idealistic speculations seriously (nor did he insist that I do so), but I was very much attracted by his agnosticism, his humanism, and his disenchanted vision of man's fate.

Hardy was a militant agnostic, an iconoclast, who both relished this role and smarted under the rejection that it entailed. I, too, liked to tell harsh truths; and I tended to feel outraged or injured when people became upset with me for doing so. Poems like "In Tenebris II" and "Lausanne, In Gibbon's Old Garden" re-enforced both my self-righteousness and my self-pity. I, too felt that "if way to the better there be, it exacts a full look at the worst." Gibbon's words seemed like a perfect battle-cry:

> "Still rule those minds on earth
> At whom sage Milton's wormwood words were hurled:
> '*Truth like a bastard comes into the world*
> *Never without ill-fame to him who gives her birth*'?"

I liked *Tess* and *Jude* for their abrasiveness, and I enjoyed the discomfiture of Hardy's contemporaries. At the same time, I empathized with his suffering at the hands of his critics and read with delight his explanation of his decision to abandon fiction for poetry:

> To cry out in a passionate poem that (for instance) the Supreme Mover or Movers, the Prime Force or Forces, must be either limited in power, unknowing, or cruel—which is obvious enough, and has been for centuries—will cause them merely a shake of the head; but to put it in argumentative prose will make them sneer, or foam, and set all the literary contortionists jumping upon me, a harmless agnostic, as if I

were a clamorous atheist, which in their crass illiteracy they seem to
think is the same thing. (F. E. Hardy, *Life*, II, 58)

Hardy bitterly assailed religious and social orthodoxies; but he
did so, he felt, in the name of truth and love. I had a vested interest
in not registering his pleasure in aggression and in not seeing
through his protestations of innocence.

Hardy seems to have believed in a First Cause; the issue for
him was not God's existence, but his nature. He was preoccupied with the problem of evil and fascinated by the refusal
of human beings to draw the obvious conclusions from the
injustice of their lot. Men have been much kinder to God than
he has been to them: ". . . even while they sit down and weep
by the waters of Babylon, [they] invent excuses for the oppression which prompts their tears" (*Return of the Native*, VI, i).
Hardy felt that man is mocked by Fate. The greatest irony is
for man to exalt the forces which destroy him, to blame himself, to exonerate God. Hardy's procedure is to argue from
effects to causes: given the absurdity of the world, what can
God be like? In his poems he conjures up a fascinating array of
possibilities, many of which have the effect of arraigning or
mocking the First Cause. His "sober opinion" is "that the said
Cause is neither moral nor immoral, but *un*moral: " 'loveless
and hateless . . . which neither good nor evil knows' " (*Life*,
II, 216-217). Hardy's arraignments of God, his protests on
behalf of man, sounded in my ears a note of metaphysical re-
volt. They gave man a dignity, I felt, far greater than he could
ever derive from cringing before a beneficent God whose ways
must be deemed just not because they are right in the eyes of
man, but because they are His. Hardy refused to relinquish the
human perspective; he made man the measure of all things.

Man, in Hardy's universe, is both great and small. He is the
plaything of Fate but the judge of Creation. Man, not God, is
the hope of the universe; he is pitifully weak, but he alone has
conscious purpose and values. Hardy's evolutionary meliorism
is based on the existence of man. Since a conscious being has
evolved out of blind force, there is a possibility that force will
be brought under the control of consciousness, which will then
inform more and more of the creation. There is a side of Hardy

205

which sees man from the cosmic perspective. He dwells upon man's alienated state, the absence of a responding consciousness out there in the cosmos, the insignificance of our feelings and doings when seen against the backdrop of infinite time, space, and matter. More powerful, however, is the phenomenological perspective. To each of us, the universe depends for its existence upon our consciousness; it comes into being at our birth and perishes at our death. While we exist, we invest all things with value, depending on the pleasure or pain which they bring us; and these values are real and indisputable. The indifference of the universe in no way alters the fact that our experience is immensely important to us. When seen from his own point of view, each man is a God, the center of a universe.

The cosmic and the phenomenological perspectives combine to produce one of the most powerful qualities of Hardy's fiction, his near universal empathy and compassion. When we see man from inside and outside at once, he emerges as an innocent, passionate, sensitive creature who is doomed to pain and frustration. Fate is oppressive; but Hardy, as narrator, is usually sympathetic. He is the understanding father, the compassionate mother, the appreciative lover for whom we all long. He is on the side of wish, of desire, of happiness—in short, of the pleasure principle. When he is compelled by grim reality to thwart or destroy his characters, we feel that it hurts him almost as much as it hurts them. If he were making the rules, he would give us what we want; he would fashion all things fair.

It is because he sees most of his characters from their own perspective that there are so few villains in Hardy's works. He sees Fate and society from the individual's point of view and finds them to be flawed, pernicious, cruel; but he tends to excuse or to empathize with his characters, even when they cause a good deal of mischief. As members of the mass called society, we often afflict our neighbors; but as individuals we are victims of internal and external forces which are beyond our control. We can choose neither our natures nor our circumstances. If our temperaments or our interests put us into conflict with our fellows, we are victims of an imperfect order in which wish and reality are forever at war. Sometimes, in order to generate sympathy for a protagonist, Hardy presents other characters as ill-intentioned or culpably limited (Alec, Angel). But very often he presents conflicts from the perspective of each of the participants; we sympathize with all and find it difficult to blame any. In the Clym, Mrs. Yeobright, Eustacia triangle, for instance, we understand why each character acts as he does, and all are pitiable. Such characters as Troy, Wildeve, Mrs. Charmond, Fitzpiers, Henchard, Lucetta, Angel Clare, and Arabella are not, in the final analysis, excluded from our sympathies. The phenomenological perspective is very appealing. We feel that Hardy is on our side, that he sees how we suffer. We are all innocent victims.

The painfulness of Hardy's work arises from the combination of his sympathetic treatment of individuals with his dark view of the human condition. From the point of view of desire, the world is out of joint. The chief source of man's misery is his possession of consciousness in a world which is governed by blind force. We have evolved too far; we are out of harmony with the instinctual drives within ourselves and with the external order. Most of man's desires are unrealizable; he is doomed at birth to a life of meaningless misery. His hopes, his dreams, even his reasonable expectations, are mocked by reality. He is the prey of time and chance, of disease, age, death, and all the other natural calamities. He turns for relief to his fellow humans, but he finds little solace there. The love relationship is usually unhappy as a result of disillusionment, mismating, and inconstancy. Not only nature, but society as well is ill-adapted to our natures; we are galled by laws, customs, and conventions which make life harder than it has to be. As the well-intentioned Phillotson is made to exclaim: " 'Cruelty is the law pervading all nature and society; and we can't get out of it if we would!' " (*Jude*, V, viii).

Hardy's grimness profoundly disturbed many of his contemporaries. It has affected me in different ways at different times. In my early twenties, I savored it. Like Clym Yeobright, I had "reached the stage in a young man's existence when the grimness of the general human situation first becomes clear" (III, iii). We do not know what brought Clym to this stage, just as we do not know what produced the young Hardy's disillusionment. His intellectual history does not seem to offer a sufficient explanation, and his personal history is obscure. Whatever the cause, as an artist Hardy seems to have been arrested at an advanced stage of youthful disenchantment. A great many of his novels and poems, from all phases of his career, are written from this perspective. He dwells over and over again upon his discovery that time, chance, and change mock our dreams with their bitter ironies. This has great resonance for readers who are themselves undergoing a loss of innocence.

In my own unhappiness, I found Hardy's disenchanted vision consolatory. It assured me that I was discovering the truth about life and that my problems were man's fate rather than something peculiar to myself. They were less humiliating that way. It reinforced my self-pity, justified my anger, and confirmed my innocence. As Sue says, " 'things in general' " are to blame, " 'because they are so horrid and cruel!' " (*Jude*, IV, iii). It glamorized my misery and disillusionment. In *The Return of the Native*, and elsewhere, Hardy raises our suffering to the level of poetry and gives the dark view a kind of grandeur.

II

The Hardy novel which has most interested me over the years is *Tess of the d'Urbervilles*. I have written on this novel on four different occasions (including the present one), and I have responded to it each time in a different way. In the preceding pages I have attempted to reconstruct my initial response to Hardy. I shall describe my subsequent experiences of Hardy by tracing my relationship to this novel, which I regard as his greatest work of fiction. This will require some recapitulation of views which I have expressed in print [" 'A Confusion of Many Standards' ": Conflicting Value Systems in *Tess of the d'Urbervilles, Nineteenth Century Fiction*, XXIV (1969), 57-79]; but most of what follows will be new.

As an undergraduate I wrote an enthusiastic paper on "The Rhetoric of *Tess of the d'Urbervilles*" (1951) in which I analyzed the means by which Hardy controls both our emotional and our ethical response to his heroine. I was completely caught up in the author's point of view. I saw Tess exactly as he wanted me to. I agreed that she was pure. My sympathy was intense.

I wrote on *Tess* again in 1964. By this time, I had come to demand a high degree of integration in both philosophical and aesthetic systems, and I had written a book on a much more sophisticated and coherent novelist—George Eliot. After teaching *Tess of the d'Urbervilles* many times, I had become convinced that it just doesn't make sense. In attempting to establish Tess's purity or innocence, Hardy employs ethical norms which are incompatible with each other. As a result of this "confusion of many standards" (J. S. Mill's phrase), his arguments often contradict each other and can in no way be unified into a coherent moral vision.

Tess is pure because she never meant to do wrong. Since we live in an ironical world, in which events rarely turn out as we intend them to, we should not be held responsible for our acts and their consequences, but only for our moral dispositions. Even if we accept the argument that people should be judged by their intentions rather than by their acts and recognize that Tess intended the opposite of what she did, it does not follow that Tess is pure. For Tess to be pure, her intentions would have to be pure, and to establish the purity of her intentions we need some standard apart from the intentions themselves. Hardy makes us *feel* that Tess means well, but he does not actually defend her intentions in terms of an ethical norm.

In direct conflict with the argument from intention is Hardy's contention that Tess is pure because there is nothing wrong with what she has done. Hardy's argument seems to be that we cannot judge an act's goodness or badness by its conformity or lack of conformity to the ethical standards of society; for society's conventions and laws are merely arbitrary, man-made, and do not, therefore, carry their sanction in themselves. The true standard of values is the natural order of things; acts are good if they are in harmony with nature, bad if they are not. Conventions which are "out of harmony with the actual world" are harmful and must be reformed. The argument for Tess's purity from the goodness of her intentions implies that her

209

sexual relations with Alec were bad. The argument from nature as norm presents her acts as good—or, at least, innocent—and her intentions as—what? Hardy was apparently unaware of the fact that Tess's intentions would be seen not as good but merely as conventional if judged in terms of their conformity to nature. They were just as misguided as the conventions from which they were derived.

The use of nature as a moral norm carries with it several important implications. If nature is a moral norm, then the cosmic order of things must be an ethical as well as physical process. In an astonishing display of compartmentalization, Hardy uses nature as a moral norm and at the same time regards nature as amoral. If *Tess* is an attack on society and convention, it is equally an attack on the cosmic process. We live on a blighted star. Nature's ways and man's yearnings are quite disparate. There is no justice in the cosmic order.

Hardy is no more successful in attacking conventional values than he is in defending Tess's purity. He criticizes institutions and attitudes of society without having a clear value system of his own as a basis of evaluation. He makes us feel antipathetic toward conventions just as successfully as he makes us feel sympathetic toward Tess, but he does not show us why we should reject the conventions and what we should put in their place. When he shifts his emphasis from the arraignment of the cosmic order to the arraignment of society, Hardy seems to be driven back to nature for a norm by which to judge the human order, not realizing that an amoral nature can provide him with no moral norm. Hardy feels that many things are wrong in society, but he does not know how philosophically to ground his social criticism. Because his cosmos is amoral and consciousness is man's only source of justice and hope, it would be more logical for Hardy to adopt the position of Mill and Huxley that man has in society a moral order which combats the amoral cosmic process and creates a home for the human spirit. And sometimes he does. But there are many conventions that he dislikes, and since he does not know how to distinguish between good and bad conventions, he seems often to reject the social order altogether.

What Hardy could have used was something like the greatest

happiness principle of the Utilitarians which enabled them throughout the nineteenth century to attack social abuses while retaining a high regard for society as a humanizing, meliorating agency. The whole point of Mill's "Nature" is that human well-being and not conformity to nature should be our standard of value. This value system is adumbrated in *Tess* in the form of Angel Clare's recognition of the importance of each man to himself and of the right which we all have to be treated as a Thou by our fellows (XXV). This could very well have provided an ethical center for the novel. Both intentions and conventions could have been judged by their tendency to have either a favorable or unfavorable influence upon human well-being. Because Angel recognizes the participation of others in his own nature and condition, his standard of value is not simply his own happiness, but the well-being of all involved. After his marriage, of course, Angel violates his own values; but they provide a norm by which he himself can be judged.

There *is* a standard of values in *Tess*, then, which is applicable to the problems that Hardy raised and which could have provided a consistent moral norm. But it does not constitute the real thematic core of the novel. The novel has no real thematic core. We simply cannot integrate its conflicting value systems.

I concluded the original version of " 'A Confusion of Many Standards' " with some scathing remarks. Critics defend Hardy against attacks such as mine, I observed, by reminding us that Hardy insisted again and again that he is not a systematic thinker, that his works present a series of "impressions" or "seemings" rather than convictions or arguments. But Hardy himself, in the Preface to *Jude the Obscure*, described his novels as "an endeavor *to give shape and coherence*" [my italics] to his "seemings, or personal impressions"; and in this endeavor, in *Tess* at least, he has clearly failed. Hardy was wise to turn to the writing of brief lyrics in which his fleeting and discordant fancies and speculations could be crystallized one by one, without loss of shape and coherence.

As might be expected, I had trouble getting this essay accepted for publication. Readers to whom journals send such manuscripts are likely to have formed an identification with the author under discussion, or at least to like him very much. I have in my files a sheaf of reader's reports which contain everything from biting attacks on me to elaborate defenses of Hardy. Being enamoured of my own ideas, I dismissed most of my critics as wrong-headed or imperceptive. Within a year or two, however, I came to the conclusion that I *had* been too hard on Hardy.

Several things contributed to this change of heart. My readings in literary theory and my psychological approach to fiction (which I began to develop in 1964) led me to question the emphasis I had been placing on organic unity. I realized that I had been explicating novels with the techniques which I had learned in Earl Wasserman's courses in Romantic poetry and that I had been judging them by the standards of success which are most appropriate to the shorter forms of literature. I had been demonstrating in course after course that the great Victorian novels are artistic failures; they tended to disintegrate under the kind of close reading to which I subjected them. Frye's *Anatomy of Criticism* and Auerbach's *Mimesis* helped me to see that realistic fiction by its very nature attempts to combine incompatible elements. The detailed portrayal of social and psychological reality works against form (which derives from mythic patterns) and theme (the realistic novelist always sees more than he can understand). If we go to novels looking for unified aesthetic systems, we are usually going to be disappointed. The absence of organic unity is a flaw, to be sure; but novels have other values; and it is a mistake to reject them as failures because they cannot compete with shorter forms on the criterion of integration.

These theoretical considerations were reinforced by a rereading of the novel. Having written out my thematic analysis, I was free to respond to other things. I found that *Tess of the d'Urbervilles* is a very moving story which is mainly about the experience of its heroine and is only peripherally concerned with the thematic issues to which I had exclusively addressed myself.

I deleted the offending paragraph and wrote a new concluding section which gained the essay immediate acceptance. I called attention there to some of the novel's strengths. *Tess of the d'Urbervilles* is, I contended, more than anything else, the story of a sensitive, lovable, and well-meaning girl whose fate is horribly cruel and unfair: "Inside this exterior . . . there was the record of a pulsing life which had learnt too well, for its years, of the dust and ashes of things, of the cruelty of lust and the fragility of love" (XLII). Tess's story is moving because, despite her helplessness, Tess has a stature that makes her suffering profoundly touching. Tess has dignity because she is loved by the author, because he enters wholeheartedly into her experience of the world, because her feelings have for him, and are made to have for us, an intense reality. Hardy is Tess's advocate: his primary concern is not to revise the old morality in a systematic way, but to win sympathy and acceptance for his heroine. The structure of rationalizations which he erects for Tess's defense is as full of inner contradictions as such structures usually are.

Hardy's identification with Tess is, I concluded, the source of both great strengths and glaring weaknesses. It is responsible for the novel's impressive dramatic, rhetorical, and emotional power, and for its brilliant rendering of Tess's sense of the world. It is also responsible for the novel's failure as social criticism. Hardy is too wrapped up in the phenomenological perspective to be a social thinker. He cannot analyze problems or suggest solutions; he can only cry out in pain and protest. His closeness to Tess enables him to portray her character with absolute authority, but it prevents him from understanding her very well. His analysis of her motives is quite superficial, and often wrong; and his judgments are set askew by an identification which leads him to glorify unhealthy attitudes and self-destructive solutions.

As the last few sentences suggest, I had already begun to formulate the psychological analysis of Tess which I shall offer here. This analysis was suggested to me by a student who, having had several courses with me, expressed surprise that I was not using Horneyan psychology in the study of this novel. I explained, patiently, that I use the psychological approach only where it is appropriate and that Tess is not the sort of fully developed character who should be analyzed in motiva-

213

tional terms. As soon as our conversation ended, I began to reread the novel; and within an hour I was dumbfounded at my own lack of perception. I soon realized that Tess is one of the great characters in literature and that Hardy has far more psychological perception and mimetic skill than he is ever given credit for.

III

There are, at present, two main schools of thought concerning characterization. Marvin Mudrick calls them the "purists" and the "realists." Characters in literature, the purists argue, are different from real people. They do not belong to the real world in which people can be understood as the products of their social and psychological histories; they belong to a fictional world in which everything they are and do is part of the author's design, part of a teleological structure whose logic is determined by formal and thematic considerations. The realists hold that character creation can be an end in itself, that some characters are so fully realized as to have a life of their own, and that such characters can—and, indeed, should—be understood as though they were real people. The Purist discussions of such characters are highly reductive; they neglect a vast amount of detail which has little formal or thematic significance, but which is there for the sake of the mimetic portrait, because the author needs it in order to represent a human being.

I am a realist. The purists are right about characters which have predominantly aesthetic or illustrative functions; but their arguments do not apply to the highly individualized, richly developed characters who are the protagonists of so many nineteenth-century novels. I have developed a rationale for discussing such characters as though they were real people in *A Psychological Approach to Fiction: Studies in Thackeray, Stendhal, George Eliot, Dostoevsky, and Conrad* (Indiana University Press, 1974); and I must refer the reader to that work for a full treatment of the theoretical issues. I was not led to the realist position, however, by theoretical considerations. I discovered that certain characters are representations

214

of people as a result of my ability to analyze them in motivational terms, with the help of Horneyan psychology.

When I first encountered Horney, in 1959, I was deeply impressed by her correlation of certain value systems with certain neurotic defenses. It explained to me why I had identified so completely with George Eliot while I was writing my dissertation on her and why I was no longer so enthusiastic about her beliefs. With the completion of my dissertation, which had given me trouble, I shifted from a self-effacing defense system which closely paralleled George Eliot's, to an expansive orientation which did not find living for others to be an appealing philosophy. Over the next several years Horney helped me to understand many things about myself, but it did not occur to me to use her theories in the study of literature. In 1964, however, I had a flash of insight the implications of which I am still working out. I saw that the thematic inconsistencies of *Vanity Fair* make sense when we see them as manifestations of an inner conflict between self-effacing and expansive attitudes. It was not long before I realized that the leading characters of this novel are also intelligible in psychological terms. I have since discovered that Horneyan theory has an amazing congruity with the representation of psychological phenomena in a great many novels, including some of Hardy's. Most of the great nineteenth-century novelists saw and portrayed far more than they could understand or interpret adequately. We now have at our disposal conceptual systems which enable us to analyze what these authors were able to represent, and we are beginning to do justice to the greatness of their mimetic achievement.

In *The Mayor of Casterbridge*, Hardy's rhetoric reinforces the notion that character is fate. Circumstances play their role in Henchard's downfall, but his chief enemy is himself. In *Tess*, as we have seen, we have an innocent and noble heroine who is hounded by adverse circumstances to an early death. Tess is "a pure woman," a "poor wounded name," whom "the President of the Immortals" destroys for his "sport." In *The Mayor*, Hardy's rhetoric focuses our attention upon Henchard's character and invites us to study it. The rhetoric of *Tess* focuses our attention not upon Tess's character, but upon

Hardy's celebration and defense of it and upon the external causes of her destruction. Tess is at least as complex and interesting a character as Henchard, but it is easy to read the novel and to be deeply affected by it without seeing Tess very clearly at all. When we do see her clearly we perceive that she, like Henchard, makes a large contribution to her own downfall. When we are under the spell of the rhetoric, we fail to see Tess as a mimetic portrait; when we understand her character, we find that it does not sustain the rhetoric. Psychological analysis shows Tess's story to be vastly different from the one that Hardy thinks he is telling and that we respond to with such intensity.

Before I discuss Tess's character, I must first present a very brief outline of Horney's theory. A full account of Horney and of related Third Force psychologists can be found in Chapter II of *A Psychological Approach to Fiction.*

In an atmosphere of warmth, security, and esteem, says Horney, a child "will develop . . . the unique alive forces of his real self: the clarity and depth of his own feelings, thoughts, wishes, interests . . . . : the special capacities or gifts he may have; the faculty to express himself, and to relate himself to others with his spontaneous feelings. All this will in time enable him to find his set of values and his aims in life" (*Neurosis and Human Growth*, p. 17). Under unfavorable conditions, when the people around him are prevented by their own neurotic needs from relating to him with love and respect, the child develops a feeling of being weak, helpless, isolated, unworthy. The "basic anxiety" which is thus generated makes the child fearful of spontaneity; and, forsaking his real self, he develops neurotic strategies for coping with his environment. These strategies are of three kinds: the individual can become self-effacing or compliant and move toward people; he can become aggressive or expansive and move against people; or he can become detached or resigned and move away from people. Each of these solutions produces its own set of values and character traits.

The person in whom self-effacing trends are dominant tries to gain attention and approval by being humble, self-sacrificing, undemanding, dutiful. He values goodness and

216

love above all else and tends to glorify suffering. He has powerful taboos against all that is presumptuous, selfish, and aggressive, believes in turning the other cheek, and counts on his
virtue being rewarded. The predominantly expansive person tries
to be strong, efficient, and exploitative. He is ambitious, craves
recognition, abhors helplessness, and is ashamed of defeat
or suffering. He believes that might makes right and that the
world is a jungle in which each man is out for himself. The
basically detached person worships freedom, peace, and self-
sufficiency. He handles a threatening world by renouncing his
desires and by shutting others out of his inner life. He may have
strong need for superiority, but he realizes his ambition in
imagination rather than through actual accomplishments.

In the course of neurotic development, the individual will
come to make all three of these defensive moves compulsively;
and, since they involve incompatible character structures and
value systems, he will be torn by inner conflicts. In order to
gain some sense of wholeness, he will emphasize one move
more than the others; but the suppressed trends will continue
to exist and may emerge powerfully when the predominant
solution fails.

While interpersonal difficulties are creating the movements
toward, against, and away from people, and the basic conflict
between them, concomitant intra-psychic problems are producing their own self-defeating strategies. The destructive
attitude of others, his alienation from his real self, and his
self-hatred make the individual feel terribly weak and worthless. To compensate for this he creates an idealized image of
himself and embarks upon a search for glory. He takes an intense pride in his idealized self, and on the basis of its attributes
he makes neurotic claims upon others. His claims make him
extremely vulnerable, for their frustration threatens to confront
him with his despised self, with the sense of nothingness from
which he is fleeing. The defense of his pride requires him to
impose stringent demands and taboos upon himself, resulting
in what Horney calls the tyranny of the should. The function
of the shoulds is "to make oneself over into one's idealized
self" (*NHG*, 68). The shoulds are a defense against self-loathing, but, like other neurotic defenses, they tend to aggravate

217

the condition they are employed to cure. Not only do they increase self-alienation, but they also intensify self-hate, for they are impossible to live up to. The penalty for failure is the most severe feeling of worthlessness and self-contempt. This is why the shoulds have such a tyrannical power.

In our very first glimpses of Tess we see two characteristics which combine to determine much of her behavior and to create many of her difficulties. These are her pride and her sense of responsibility for her family. John Durbeyfield, apprized of his noble lineage by Parson Tringham, rides home in a carriage, singing " 'I've-got-a-grit-family-vault-at-Kingsbere —and knighted-forefathers-in-lead-coffins-there!' " When her companions titter, a "slow heat" rises in Tess "at the sense that her father [is] making himself foolish in their eyes." She tells her mother later that she " 'felt inclined to sink into the ground with shame!' " (III). The same sensitivity leads Tess to reject the idea of hiring a young man to take their hives to market when her father is too drunk to go.

Though he refers to Tess's pride repeatedly in the novel and brilliantly depicts its dynamics, Hardy does not dwell upon its sources; and we must put together a variety of clues to get some idea of its origins. Tess's excellence in school, her superiority to her parents, and her "deputy-maternal" role as eldest child undoubtedly contribute to it. It may be partly a defense against the humiliations to which the childishness of her parents often exposes her. Perhaps she has imbibed some of it from her father, who is " 'so Proud on account of his Respectability' " (XXXI). The intensity with which the whole family responds to the revelation of its descent from the d'Urbervilles suggests that the news fulfills a powerful craving for superiority. Joan immediately hopes for a grand match for Tess. But this is nothing new: "the light-minded woman had been discovering good matches for her daughter almost from the year of her birth" (VI). However much she discounts her mother's "matrimonial hopes for her," her long exposure to them cannot help but generate longings and fantasies in Tess and a sense that her sexual destiny is to be a special one.

Tess returns home early from the dance because "her father's

odd appearance and manner" make her "anxious," and she
wonders what has "become of him." When she enters the
Durbeyfield cottage, she finds her mother "hanging over the
Monday washing-tub, which had now, as always, lingered on
to the end of the week." Tess feels "a chill self-reproach that
she had not returned sooner, to help her mother in these
domesticities, instead of indulging herself out-of-doors." She
experiences "a dreadful sting of remorse" that "out of that tub
had come . . . the very white frock . . . which she had so carelessly greened about the skirt. . . . " Tess's "chill self-reproach"
and "dreadful . . . remorse" are the products of her own
shoulds; her mother "seldom upbraided her . . . at any time"
(III). Her parents do not upbraid her partly because they are
themselves so irresponsible. Their lack of concern adds to
rather than lightens her burden; the less her mother worries
about the wash, the more Tess is oppressed by it. There is little
need to exert much pressure on so dutiful a child.

Tess's anxiety about her father and her feeling of guilt toward
her mother are both aspects of her compulsive feeling of
responsibility for her family. Tess does not receive the parental
care which would give her a feeling of security and the freedom
to grow in accordance with her nature. Instead she must from
an early age assume responsibility for the care of the younger
children and for the welfare of the family as a whole. She must
be a parent not only to the children but to her mother and father
as well. From the beginning of the novel to the end, she has an
overwhelming feeling that the family's fortunes are in her
hands, that it is she who must be their Providence. Her own
needs, wishes, feelings, and aspirations must be sacrificed to
the common good. Joy, spontaneity, self-actualization are out
of the question.

Throughout the first phase of her relationship with Alec
d'Urberville, from the decision to go to Tantridge to the decision to break with Alec even though she is pregnant, Tess is
torn between the demands of her pride and her compulsion to
sacrifice herself for her family. "Tess's pride," Hardy tells us,
makes "the part of poor relation one of particular distaste to
her" (V). She is extremely reluctant, moreover, to pursue a
gentleman suitor and to expose herself to his scorn. Balanced

219

against her pride is, of course, her compliance. As Joan observes, " 'she's tractable at bottom' " (IV). Tess has reacted to the burdens placed upon her by her family not by rebelling against them, nor by detaching herself from them, but by accepting them fully and feeling them as powerful internal demands which she must satisfy if she is not to hate herself. Joan senses this and is confident of her ability to manipulate her daughter by playing upon her self-effacing trends.

Tess's tractability is greatly increased by the death of Prince, for which she feels totally responsible. This violation of her role as the family's mainstay fills Tess with "self-reproach" (IV), lowers her "self-esteem" (IV), and makes her "more deferential than she might otherwise have been to the maternal wish" (V). She has many misgivings about taking the job in Tantridge (Alec's intentions are, after all, fairly clear), but she gives in to the pressure exerted by her mother and the younger children. Her consent means that she must give up her goal of becoming a teacher: "She had hoped to be a teacher at the school, but the fates seemed to decide otherwise" (VI). The fact that she makes this sacrifice so readily and that it is dwelt upon so little indicates the feebleness of Tess's wishes for herself and the strength of her self-effacing tendencies.

It is evident that, despite her own protestations and her author's to the contrary, Tess knows why she is going to Tantridge. She cannot admit it to herself, but her main object in going is to fulfill the family's (and her own) long-standing dream of being elevated by a grand alliance. When Tess seems reluctant, the children wail, " 'Tess won't go-o-o and be made a la-a-dy of!' " As Joan explains to John, it is not her "d'Urberville blood," but her "face," that is, her sexual allure, which is her "trump card" (VII). That is why Joan dresses her up in her Sunday apparel. Tess has misgivings about this; but she defends herself against them and at the same time rationalizes her acceptance of something she half wants by deferring to her mother's superior wisdom: "Mrs. Durbeyfield was only too delighted at this tractability" (VII). Tess later blames her mother for "dressing her up so prettily" (VIII), but the fact is that she prepares this excuse for herself by her dutiful self-abandonment.

Tess is, indeed, tractable. Without owning it to herself, and with much inner conflict, she attempts to carry out her family's commission. She is supposed to captivate Alec. She does. She is supposed to sleep with him, if necessary. She does. Joan's idea is that " 'if he don't marry her afore he will after' " (VII). Tess stays around after the seduction in hopes that Alec will play *his* part. It is only when she perceives that he has no thoughts of marriage that she recoils from him, outraged, and seeks to restore her pride by breaking with him even though she is pregnant.

When she returns home a fallen woman, Tess claims that she "was a child" when she went to Tantridge and blames her mother for not telling her " 'there was danger in men-folk' " (XII). Her behavior toward Alec during the first three months of her stay clearly indicates, however, that she is aware of his intentions and is afraid of him. Alec's attentions put Tess under a terrible strain. She must elude him without offending him. Her inner conflict is manifested clearly when, while they are riding in the Chase, Alec asks if he may treat her "as a lover": "She drew a quick pettish breath of objection, writhing uneasily on her seat, looked far ahead, and murmured, 'I don't know—I wish—how can I say yes or no when—' " (XI). Tess cannot say yes when it means disgrace; she cannot say no when it means disconcerting the whole scheme for rehabilitating her family. What she wishes, perhaps, is that Alec would ask her to marry him, even though she does not love him.

Hardy presents Tess's fall as the result of a concatenation of circumstances over which she has little control. She is the innocent victim of Alec's treachery, of the moral looseness of Tantridge, and of cosmic indifference. Tess's pride and her compulsion to sacrifice herself for her family are no less important causes of her fate, however. Car Darch takes offense at Tess's laughter partly because she is jealous of Alec's attentions to Tess, but partly also because of Tess's haughty demeanor. Car feels, rightly, that Tess is laughing at her from a height, and her pride is offended. When Car wants to fight, Tess is outraged: " 'Indeed, then, I shall not fight!' said the latter majestically; and if I had known you was of that sort, I wouldn't have so let myself down as to come with such a whorage as this

is!' " This arrogant speech brings down "a torrent of vitupera-
tion" upon Tess. Tess is "indignant and ashamed." She is
ashamed, presumably, because she has exposed herself to this
contamination, this outrage upon her dignity. Not only does
she feel sullied by these vulgar proceedings, but her claims to
superiority are being thrown in her face: " 'I'm as good as two
of such!' "

Tess is "edging back to rush off alone" when Alec appears
and urges her to jump up behind him: " 'we'll get shot of the
screaming cats in a jiffy.' " Tess is "almost ready to faint, so
vivid [is] her sense of the crisis." She is torn between her fear
of Alec and her desire for a vindictive triumph which will restore her pride. As they ride off toward the Chase, Tess
clings to Alec, "still panting in her triumph, yet in other respects dubious" (XI).

Tess is too exhausted by the exertions of the day and the
turbulent emotions of shame, indignation, fear, conflict, and
triumph which she has experienced to observe that Alec is taking her into the Chase or to make a spirited resistance to his
new stratagem. Her resistance is further weakened by the
inner conflict which is activated by his generosity to her family:

> "Bye the bye, Tess, your father has a new cob to-day. Somebody gave
> it to him."
> "Somebody? You!"
> D'Urberville nodded.
> "O how very good of you that is!" she exclaimed, with a painful sense
> of the awkwardness of having to thank him just then.
> "And the children have some toys."
> "I didn't know—you ever sent them anything!" she murmured, much
> moved. "I almost wish you had not—yes, I almost wish it."
> "Why, dear?"
> "It—hampers me so."
> "Tessy—don't you love me ever so little now?"
> "I'm grateful," she reluctantly admitted. "But I fear I do not—" The
> sudden vision of his passion for herself as a factor in this result so dis-
> tressed her that, beginning with one slow tear, and then following with
> another, she wept outright. (XI)

Like her mother, Alec knows how to make Tess tractable.

Tess weeps because she knows that Alec's kindness to her
family is part of his pursuit of her, that her submission is the
price of his bounty, and that she cannot, for her family's sake,

turn him away. Instead of remaining alert and resisting Alec's advances, as she has done up till now, Tess "passively" sits down in the leaves he has heaped, falls into a reverie when he leaves, and is asleep when he returns. She is tired, to be sure, but her passivity and drowsiness are more symptoms of psychological than of physical fatigue. She can neither resist nor submit; nor can she contend any longer with her inner conflicts. By going to sleep she escapes her conflicting emotions, eliminates the need of choosing a course of behavior, and puts herself in the hands of fate. If anything happens, she is not to blame.

Both Tess and her author account for Tess's remaining with Alec for several weeks after the seduction in a very vague way. Tess tells Alec, " 'My eyes were dazed by you for a little, and that was all' " (XII). Hardy explains that Tess, "temporarily blinded by his ardent manners, had been stirred to confused surrender awhile." Both Tess and Hardy need to deny the fact that Tess stayed on because she hoped that Alec would marry her. That, after all, was the only possible solution to her inner conflict. Tess tells Alec that she didn't " 'understand [his] meaning till it was too late' " and that she made up her mind to leave as soon as she saw what she " 'ought to have seen sooner.' " It was not his sexual designs that Tess did not understand and failed to see soon enough, but his determination to treat her like another one of his lower-class mistresses. When her mother reproaches her for not getting Alec to marry her, Tess thinks to herself: "Get Alec d'Urberville in the mind to marry her! He marry *her*! On matrimony he had never once said a word." Tess thinks, now, that she might not have snatched "at social salvation" even if he had asked her, but she is full of injured pride and needs to reaffirm her dignity in this way.

When Tess realizes that Alec has no intention of marrying her, she can no longer sacrifice her pride to her family's needs. The injury is too great. Her strongest need is to reassert her pride by showing Alec that she is not one of his playthings. She needs desperately to prove that she does not belong to the "whorage" of Car Darch and that ilk. When her mother says that "any woman" but Tess would have gotten the man to marry her "after that," Tess replies proudly, " 'Perhaps any woman would except me.' " Tess's pride dictates not only that she must leave Alec and tell him repeatedly that she does not love him and tell herself that she would not have married him even if he had asked, but also that she must accept no assistance from him, even though she is poor and pregnant and he is guilty, wealthy, and eager to help.

Tess is angry with Alec and angry with her mother; but she is most angry, of course, with herself. She " 'detests,' 'loathes,' and 'hates' " herself for her weakness. She has these feelings, we are told, because she does not love Alec; and the fact that she was ready to sell herself undoubtedly contributes to her self-contempt. But the chief reason for her self-loathing is neither her lack of affection for Alec nor the "moral hobgoblins" of religion and convention (XIII); it is, rather, the seemingly irrevocable damage she has done to her idealized image. With her idealized self shattered, her despised self rises to the fore. Hardy is quite right in feeling that Tess is too hard on herself; her self-hate *is* excessive. The loss of her self-respect and of her honored position in the family and the community plunges Tess into despair. Instead of being the family's savior, she is its shame. Tess wishes for death, obscurity, obliteration: "Her depression was terrible . . . she could have hidden herself in a tomb."

Tess defends herself by withdrawal: " . . . her sole idea seemed to be to shun mankind." She retreats into her bedroom; she subjects herself to "long domicilary imprisonments" (XIX). Tess regains some measure of courage and serenity by detaching herself subjectively as well. She sees herself from a cosmic perspective. Whatever the consequences of the past, "time would close over them; they would all in a few years be as if they had never been, and she herself grassed down and forgotten." She soothes herself by reflecting that the world's opinion of her is not terribly important, that she is only "a passing thought" to others, that "alone in a desert island" she would not have been in despair "at what had happened to her." Thus fortified, she determines to get what pleasure she can from the present moment and is able to bear "herself with dignity" and to look "people calmly in the face at times, even when holding the baby in her arms" (XIV).

The death of Sorrow eliminates some of the consequences of Tess's fall. The reawakening of her youthful energies and of her desire for enjoyment leads her to dream of a fresh start. She resolves that there will "be no more d'Urberville air-castles in the dreams and deeds of her new life"; she will "be the dairy maid Tess, and nothing more" (XV). But "one of the interests" of Talbothays "to her was the accidental virtue of its lying near her forefathers' country," and she has a vague hope that some "good thing might come of her being in her ancestral land." Hardy speaks of her period of withdrawal as "silent reconstructive years" (XVI) and suggests that she is still undergoing a process of favorable growth and "transmutation"; but Tess at Talbothays is essentially the same person that she has been all along. She is sadder and wiser—that is, she is more fearful and resigned—but it is clear that her resignation and her realism are giving way before the upsurge of youthful hope. Maybe the past can be annihilated. Maybe the loss of virginity is reversible (XV). Maybe her d'Urberville ancestry will still bring her glory.

Tess falls so passionately in love with Angel Clare because through him she can satisfy her pride and fulfill her dream of glory. Angel is a gentleman, an "admirable and poetic man," whose learning at first seems to place him far above her. When Tess discovers "the distance between her own modest mental standpoint and the unmeasurable, Andean altitude of his, she [becomes] quite dejected, disheartened from all further effort on her own part whatever" (XIX). Tess has always been the smartest person around; her early dream, like Angel's, was to be a teacher of men. Angel's intellectual superiority crushes her pride and makes her feel like "a nothing."

Angel's love is so precious to Tess because it lifts her out of the ordinary world and transports her to the "Andean altitude" which he occupies. Once he loves her, she can transfer her pride to him and participate in his superiority. It becomes an immense satisfaction rather than a humiliation to feel that his "soul [is] the soul of a saint, his intellect that of a seer" (XXXI). She worships him idolatrously (XXXIII); he is "godlike in her eyes" (XXIX); she looks at him "as if she [sees] something

immortal before her" (XXXI). Her worship of Angel is a form
of self-exaltation; the more she idolizes him the greater the
glory which she acquires by possessing him. The passion of the
other girls intensifies Tess's desire. His preference for her confirms her superiority (XXIII); she has "won [him] from all
other women" (XXXI). When she and Angel are together, she
is no longer "any woman," "one of a long row only"; she
dwells in a world of poetry and is herself a mythical being—an
Artemis, a Demeter, an Eve (XX). Angel sees her as she longs
to be seen, as she sees herself in her most exalted moments.
He confirms her idealized image of herself. Nothing is more
intoxicating, more irresistible than this.

Her love of Angel throws Tess into terrible conflict; her
thirst for glory clashes with both her resignation and her self-
effacing shoulds. Though she comes to Talbothays full of
youthful energy and a "zest for life" (XVI), Tess has taken a
firm resolution never to marry. Only by resigning herself to
"a future of austere isolation" (XXVIII) can she escape her
past, preserve her honor, and protect herself against renewed
self-contempt. When Angel begins to court her, she tries to repress her feelings and to stay aloof, but to no avail. When he
proposes, she refuses "with pain that [is] like the bitterness of
dissolution" (XXVII). Tess feels that to marry him under false
pretences is a "wrong" which "may kill him when he knows"
(XXVIII); she is " 'sure' " that she " 'ought not to do it.' "
What Angel offers her is so precious, however, and, once her
resignation is broken down, so essential to her existence, that
she simply cannot obey her conscience in this matter, particularly after her letter miscarries. Her "one desire" is "to make
herself his, to call him her lord, her own—then, if necessary, to
die" (XXXIII).

On the day of the wedding Tess is a "celestial person" who
moves "about in a mental cloud of many-coloured idealities"
and feels "glorified by an irradiation not her own." But when
the sound of the church bells dies away reality reappears and
her guilt rises to the fore. By the time they reach home she is
"contrite and spiritless." When she learns that Retty has attempted suicide and that Marian has been found drunk, she
feels that she must confess: "It was wicked of her to take all

without paying. She would pay to the uttermost farthing; she would tell, there and then" (XXXIV).

Tess "tells" and then passively accepts Angel's punitiveness because only by suffering can she satisfy her self-effacing shoulds and relieve her self-hate. She cannot effectively challenge his rejection of her because she shares it herself: " 'I feel I am so utterly worthless!' " (XXXVI). Tess acquiesces in Angel's treatment of her not only because she feels worthless and guilty and needs to suffer, but also because her submission enables her to retain possession of him and to preserve him as a source of glory. The loss of Angel's adoration is a staggering blow; but as long as Tess can feel that Angel is hers she has not lost everything. Her chief means of possessing him, now, is through slavish submission; as long as he treats her as his, then she feels him to be hers. " 'I shan't do anything,' " she tells him,

"unless you order me to; and if you go away from me I shall not follow 'ee; and if you never speak to me any more I shall not ask why, unless you tell me I may."

"And if I do order you to do anything?"

"I will obey you like your wretched slave, even if it is to lie down and die.' " (XXXV)

Tess is, indeed, prepared to die if by so doing she can establish herself finally as Angel's possession.

The possession of Angel has value for Tess only if he is an exalted being. This is why, after a few attempts at self-defense, Tess takes "everything as her deserts, and hardly [opens] her mouth" (XXXVI). Hardy celebrates her behavior: " 'quick tempered as she naturally was, nothing that he could say made her unseemly; she sought not her own; was not provoked; thought no evil of his treatment of her. She might just now have been Apostolic Charity herself returned to a self-seeking modern world." Tess's motives for accepting all blame, repressing her resentment, and abandoning her just claims are, I think, more self-seeking than charitable. Having transferred her pride to Angel, she must protect her image of him as a glorious creature. In order to do this, she accepts total responsibility not only for her own faults, but for his behavior. The worse he behaves, the more culpable she is. Tess can live with

227

almost any amount of self-condemnation as long as Angel remains God-like and remains hers.

Tess's behavior from the time of Angel's departure to her second capitulation to Alec d'Urberville is dictated largely by the motives which we have so far examined. Hardy's rhetoric presents Tess as once again the victim of forces and circumstances beyond her control, but psychological analysis shows that in this phase of her existence, as in the earlier ones, Tess's fate is to a significant degree the product of her character.

Tess withdraws from her family in order to protect her pride. She sends them twenty pounds to re-thatch the house, but she cannot let them know that she is "a deserted wife, dependent, now that she had relieved their necessities, on her own hands for a living." After "the *eclat* of a marriage which was to nullify the collapse of the first attempt," this "would be too much indeed" (XLI).

"The same delicacy, pride, false shame, whatever it may be called" (LIII) prevents her from turning to Angel's parents for help, once she has exhausted her resources. When her discovery of Angel's proposal to Retty drives her finally to seek out the Clares, she is deterred from carrying out her intention by a series of circumstances which exacerbate her sense of worthlessness and fear of humiliation. When they are reunited at the end, Tess tells Angel that because of her family's desperate plight she was "obliged to go back" to Alec (LVII); but this is not true. She could have applied to the Clares. This thought occurs to her shortly before her capitulation:

> "I shall not come—I have plenty of money!" she cried.
> "Where?"
> "At my father-in-law's, if I ask for it."
> "*If* you ask for it. But you won't, Tess; I know you; you'll never ask for it—you'll starve first!" (LI)

Her pride system is such that it is easier for Tess to become Alec's mistress than to expose herself to the judgment and scrutiny of Angel's parents.

Another source of Tess's trouble is her passivity. If she had written to Angel soon and often, he might have returned in time. Her passivity is, in part, a continuation of the slavish submission which she displays on her honeymoon. Hers is a "silence of docility"; it means that "she [asserts] no rights, [admits] his judgment to be in every respect the true one, and [bends] her head dumbly thereto" (XLIX). Tess's passivity stems also from her self-abandonment and self-pity. She wanders about randomly, "obliterating her identity," and cutting herself off from family and friends (XLI). She thinks of Angel in a "warm clime" while she sleeps in the fields, cold and unprotected: " 'Was there another such a wretched being as she in the world?' " Tess finds a kind of romance in the sorriness of her plight and the magnitude of her despair. This gives her a vested interest in preserving or intensifying her misery. If she is the most wretched person in the world, she is not an ordinary person, one of a long row only. Her wretchedness, moreover, is a proof of her love and nobility, especially since she does not blame Angel for it and remains loyally devoted.

Despite her sufferings as an abandoned wife, Tess continues to repress her resentment and to glorify her husband. The meaning of her life still lies in being possessed by Angel and in participating, thereby, in his glory. If he would come to her she would be "well content" to "die in [his] arms" if only he had forgiven her. If he cannot forgive her and allow her to live with him as his wife, she will be "content, ay, glad, to live with [him] as his servant . . . so that [she] could be near [him], and get glimpses of [him], and think of [him] as [hers]" (XLVIII). The protection of her pride in Angel requires not only that Tess refuse to blame him for her plight, but also that she defend him against the criticism of others. She won't seek a position at Talbothays because "her return might bring reproach upon her idolized husband" (XLI). She warns Alec d'Urberville not to "speak against" her husband (XLVI), and when Alec calls him a "mule," Tess "passionately" strikes him with her glove, hard enough to draw blood (XLVII). This is a foreshadowing of the murder, which is precipitated by an insult to Angel. He " 'called you by a foul name,' " she explains to Angel, " 'and then I did it' " (LVII).

When Tess writes her denunciatory letter to Angel it is a clear sign, for the reader who has understood her thus far, that she had abandoned hope of realizing her pride through him and

229

is going to capitulate to Alec. Having despaired of getting Angel back, she can allow her repressed resentment to emerge: " 'O why have you treated me so monstrously, Angel! I do not deserve it . . . I can never, never forgive you!' " (LI). Her accusations excuse her in advance for what she is going to do.

Alec gains power over Tess chiefly through his repeated offers of assistance to her family. Tess's second capitulation is in many ways a repetition of the first. Her family is again in dire straits; Tess again feels responsible; and Alec again plays very cleverly upon her compulsion to sacrifice herself for the younger children. But more than this is going on. Alec also seems to exercise a strong personal influence over Tess. On every occasion that she encounters him after Angel's departure, Tess experiences terror, dread, and anxiety. Alec is a domineering, manipulative, masterful man; and Tess, despite her strong determination to resist him, has an impulse toward submission in his presence.

Alec and Tess have a kind of master-slave relationship such as often develops between expansive and self-effacing partners. " 'Remember my lady,' " warns Alec, after Tess has struck him, " 'I was your master once! I will be your master again' " (XLVII). Tess's resistance, the fact that she has never loved him or yielded readily to his will, makes her all the more attractive and strengthens Alec's determination to conquer; for Alec does not want love, or even sex, so much as triumph. Tess, though unwilling, and torn by inner conflicts, finds Alec difficult to withstand. In his presence, she feels herself to be weak, dependent, paralyzed, made for a victim. He satisfies a need she has for punishment and masochistic self-immolation. After she strikes him, she sinks down before him in submission:

> "Now, punish me!" she said, turning up her eyes to him with the hopeless defiance of the sparrow's gaze before its captor twists its neck. "Whip me, crush me; you need not mind those people under the rick! I shall not cry out." (XLVII)

Why not?

Tess has never had a strong, protective father; it is she who has had to perform the parental role. She has sought to care for her family, however, not through self-assertion and the pursuit of mastery, but through self-sacrifice and submission. Her goal has been to find a powerful male who would take care of her and her family. She has been conditioned by her family and her culture to see submission to a protector as the appropriate way to fulfill her security needs. Her first attempt to gain a protector misfires; Alec offers assistance, but on terms which are unacceptable to her pride. She looks to Angel for protection also, and he promises it; but she once more finds herself alone and unaided. Her pride prevents her from applying to the Clares. With the reappearance of Alec, who is soon promising once again to relieve her wants, to lift her out of subjection, and to care for her family, Tess is tempted to transfer her submission from Angel to him. She desperately wants to remain loyal to Angel; but Alec's expansiveness triggers her self-effacing responses and makes her terrified of giving way. The fact that Alec has possessed her sexually, whereas Angel has not, increases her sense of being in his power. The only way she can hold on to Angel is by feeling herself to be his; but Angel's silence makes her despair of having him on any terms. Alec's continued pressure and the worsening fortunes of her family finally overcome her resistance. As Alec's mistress she fulfills her duty to her family, but at a terrible price.

Angel's return throws Tess into "unspeakable despair," as she realizes that he would have been hers if she had waited. She hates Alec for having persuaded her that Angel would never return and for having caused her, once again, to lose him. When Alec taunts her and insults Angel, Tess plunges a knife into his heart. Her motives are vengeance, defense of her pride, and, most important, perhaps, a hope of regaining Angel. By her act she not only removes Alec as an obstacle, but she also proves to Angel how much she loves him: " 'It came to me as a shining light that I should get you back that way. I could not bear the loss of you any longer—you don't know how entirely I was unable to bear your not loving me! Say you do now, dear, dear husband; say you do, now I have killed him!' " (LVII). Tess has laid down her life for Angel, as Izz said she would (XL).

Tess has no desire to live. She wants to make "herself his, to call [Angel] her lord, her own," and then to die. She feels

guilt for her crime—" 'How wickedly mad I was!' " (LVIII)—
and wants to be punished. Most important, she wants to die in
her recaptured Eden, with Angel loving her and thinking well
of her. Tess wants to die in her dream, in full possession of her
glory. To live means to suffer conflict and change, to be exposed to failure and self-hate. Thus, when she is apprehended
at Stonehenge, she is at peace: " 'It is as it should be. . . . Angel,
I am almost glad—yes, glad! This happiness could not have
lasted. It was too much. I have had enough; and now I shall
not live for you to despise me!' " (LIX).

The trouble with the ending, aesthetically, is not that it is too
grim, but that it is too happy. Not only does Tess die at the perfect moment, with her dream come true, but her wishes seem
to control the action in other respects as well. She wants Angel
to marry 'Liza-Lu, and the final scene indicates that he will.
Tess wants this marriage because through it she will (1) retain possession of Angel—" 'if she were to become yours it
would almost seem as if death had not divided us' " (LVIII)—
and (2) bequeath to her family the gentlemanly protector
which it has been her duty to provide. Once he leaves for Brazil,
Angel stops being a mimetic character; his change of heart and
his cherishing of Tess at the end are necessary for the fulfillment of the novel's thematic and aesthetic patterns, but they
are essentially unmotivated. Though they do not belong to
Hardy's mimetic portrait, they are not out of harmony with it,
and Angel retains some semblance of being a real person. In
the final scene, however, he is nothing but a puppet, a figment
of Tess's dream which the author has made come true.

Our psychological analysis of Tess leads us to several addi-
tional conclusions about the novel as a whole. The implied
author's intense sympathy for Tess seems to be a product of
his identification with and admiration of her self-effacing
character structure. It is this sympathy which controls the
novel's rhetoric throughout and which accounts for the dream-
like quality of the ending. It also produces a great mimetic
portrait which, when properly understood, works against,
rather than sustains, the novel's aesthetic and thematic patterns.

We should note, however, that there is a very important way in which the novel's rhetoric and its mimetic portrait of Tess reinforce each other. Both generate an empathic involvement with Tess, an entry into her experience of the world, which makes us feel her human weight and dignity, despite her weaknesses. We may feel that Hardy praises her too much, but we can join with him in loving her, just as we love anyone whose inner life has been made real for us.

IV

The psychological approach illuminates Hardy's fiction in a number of ways. It helps us to understand his artistic personality, to appreciate his growth as a mimetic artist, and to distinguish between his representation and his interpretation of life. I have not space to develop these points with the thoroughness which they demand; but I shall try to suggest, in closing, my current thinking.

Hardy's artistic personality (that is, the personality which we infer from all of his novels) displays all of the Horneyan trends. Hardy is aggressive toward social and cosmic forces which limit the individual. He arraigns God, he attacks widely held conventions and beliefs, he bewails the vulnerability and helplessness of man. He is sympathetic toward restless, passionate, discontented, dreamy people like Eustacia and Mrs. Charmond; some of their outbursts sound remarkably like his own. At the same time, characters who reflect his own rebellious, iconoclastic, unconventional side are always crushed. Sometimes he portrays them as victims, and sometimes he indicates that they are getting their just deserts. The one novel in which he sees character as fate is about an aggressive hero. In any event, expansiveness does not work. Social ambition, the pursuit of sexual conquest, and the attempt to master fate always cause trouble. In Hardy's universe, passionate aspiration of any sort invites disaster; his romantics are either chastened or destroyed, and sometimes both.

Self-effacement ought to work; but, since there is no just God in the Heavens, it usually does not. Hardy is usually blind to the unhealthiness of self-effacing behavior (his attitude toward Sue when she becomes guilt-ridden is an exception). He tends to glorify his compliant characters as good, loving, unselfish, dutiful, saint-like, as he does with Tess. In a just universe, such qualities would be rewarded. The destruction of such noble people justifies bitter remarks about the President of the Immortals. When self-effacing characters succeed (as does Diggory Venn), Hardy feels that he is being unrealistic, that he is violating his austere artistic code. His universe is one in which expansive people are struck down and self-effacing people, as a rule, are victimized by their fellow-men and by fate. There are more exceptions to this in the earlier than in the later novels. As he becomes confident of his status and his powers, his vision becomes darker and his art more austere.

The most favored strategy in Hardy's novels is resignation. The philosophy which he attributes to Elizabeth Jane at the end of *The Mayor of Casterbridge* is Hardy's advice on how to be. Resignation is often combined with self-effacement, as it is in Elizabeth Jane, Gabriel Oak, Diggory Venn, Giles Winterbourne, and Marty South. The last two lead frustrated lives; but they are glorified by Hardy's rhetoric more, perhaps, than any other characters. Resigned people may not achieve happiness; but they, at least, avoid being made into fools. They do not expect much (and hence cannot be terribly disappointed); and they bear their suffering with stoical dignity.

Resignation appears to be the dominant trend in Hardy's artistic personality. Hardy seems to be a man who has been traumatized by disappointment and who is determined never to be so deeply hurt again. His novels are pervaded by a basic distrust of life. One defense against a world that is always mocking or deceiving us is to be constantly on guard; by dwelling on the worst that fate can do we at least protect ourselves against her ironies. Another defense is to reduce our aspirations, to discipline our feelings, to regard whatever happiness may come our way as but a passing episode in a general spectacle of pain. By telling over and over again the stories of passionate, aspiring, or good and trusting people who are mocked by fate, Hardy at once gives expression to his subordinate trends and envisions their consequences. The destinies of his characters justify his resignation: there, but for his bitter wisdom, goes he.

When we approach his characters as representations of people, we can see that Hardy matured remarkably as a mimetic artist. Many of his earlier characters have a few well-defined psychological traits, but we are not given detailed and coherent pictures of their motivational systems, and it is difficult to relate their attitudes and behavior to a sophisticated conception of their psyches. Even the most memorable of them—Bathsheba, Gabriel Oak, Clym, Eustacia, Mrs. Yeobright—seem to be fragmentary and superficial creations when compared with a character like Tess. *The Mayor of Casterbridge*, *Tess of the d'Urbervilles*, and *Jude the Obscure*, however, contain great mimetic portraits. Henchard, Elizabeth Jane, Jude, and Sue are highly individualized characters who can be understood in the same way that we have understood Tess.

As Hardy's characters become more complex, his thematic treatment of them becomes less compelling. He seems particularly blind to the contribution which their neuroses make to their unhappy lives. He can see through solutions which he rejects, such as Henchard's expansiveness or Sue's religious mania; but for the most part, even while he is portraying their psychological problems in great detail, he continues to blame his characters' misery almost wholly upon nature, fate, society, and things in general. The less fully developed his characters are, the easier it is to accept Hardy's view of them and their fate. If we understand his mimetic characters psychologically, however, we cannot help being sceptical of his interpretations and resistant to his rhetoric. We have seen how this works in *Tess. Jude the Obscure* is an even more striking example. Jude is far more the victim of his neurosis (and of the bleak childhood which produces it) than he is of the social and cosmic injustices upon which Hardy loves to dwell.

Like a great many authors (and people), Hardy tends to confuse existential, historical, and psychological problems. As I have indicated, this was one of the early sources of his appeal for me. It is tempting to romanticize our sufferings by seeing the world as out of joint. However grim the resulting world view, it is more palatable to pity ourselves as the victims of external forces than to take responsibility, in part at least, for our own difficulties. This kind of externalization may protect our pride and ward off self-hate; but it is ultimately self-

235

defeating. We cannot begin to work at our problems until we have owned them. We have little to gain from Hardy in the way of conscious insight. He rationalizes, denies, projects, and in a variety of other ways avoids being aware of what he sees. His pride in facing reality is not justified.

The mark of a great realist is that he somehow transcends his defensive needs and accurately portrays a reality which he cannot afford to understand. His rhetoric, his interpretation of life, even, sometimes, his structuring of the action may be a reflection of his conflicts or a justification of his predominant solution with its accompanying value system and world view. But insofar as he is capable of portraying reality, in some of its aspects at least, mimetically, we have a triumph of healthy perception. Hardy tells us that his characters are victims of society and fate; but he shows us, through his careful depiction of their inner lives, the way in which their compulsiveness combines with circumstances to destroy them. He tends to glorify certain defensive strategies, but he shows us their destructiveness to the personality.

I am not suggesting that we simply ignore or analyze away Hardy's own perspective. We should regard it, rather, as a source of insight into his phenomenology. However confused or defensive his responses may be, Hardy is a sensitive and gifted man who is struggling, like the rest of us, to make sense of reality. It is a rich and powerful experience to enter into his perspective, to see life through the medium of his temperament. Fiction helps us to know what it is like to be other people and to have their experience of the world.

Criticism, in its way, does a similar thing. All criticism is, in some measure, autobiographical. We tend to be fascinated by authors whose preoccupations are somehow reflective of our own, who confirm or challenge our sense of the world, or who articulate attitudes, values, or solutions toward which, or away from which, we happen to be moving. We may write as though we have no personal stake in the interpretations we are expounding, but analysis will usually reveal a vested interest of some sort.

I was drawn to Hardy initially because I identified strongly with some of his attitudes and with certain aspects of his vision.

His agnosticism and his insistence on a humanistic perspective still appeal to me. His arraignment of the cosmic and social orders is very forceful; but I see, now, that he has little conscious recognition of psychological problems and that his analysis of the relationship between internal and external factors is distorted by his defensive needs. His resignation is an understandable response to life; I have plenty of it myself. But, in my stronger and better moments, I believe that we can fulfill our natures and get the most out of life only by opening ourselves to experience. I am drawn to Hardy now, in part at least, by my need to criticize him. His defenses have an attraction still about which I am uncomfortable. In arguing with him, I am trying to convince myself. We have a need to repudiate those aspects of ourselves which we are attempting to outgrow, and this often takes the form of seeing through them when we encounter them in others.

Our aesthetic responses are likewise a reflection of ourselves. However much we may try to weigh and balance an author's virtues and defects, we are limited by our own sensibilities. Most of us respond really well to only a few aspects of literature, and it is hard to know when we are over-estimating their importance. I am quite aware that there are important values in Hardy to which I have never responded strongly and to which I have not done justice here. Fortunately, there are other critics who have found these things particularly rewarding and who have a gift for calling them to our attention. This is what critics do for us: they allow us to see works of literature through the medium of their highly developed sensibilities and from their particular perspective. None of them offers more than a partial truth, and none is free from distortion.

Since my perspective has changed, and with it my sensitivity, I have offered several views of Thomas Hardy. Naturally, I think that the last is the best, and I tend to see my former perspectives from my current one. But anyone who has changed much is bound to be humble about his present truths, to recognize that they, like their predecessors, may someday be transformed by new revelations.

237

GEORGE GISSING: HUMANIST IN EXILE

JACOB KORG

The novels and short stories George Gissing wrote between 1880 and 1903 offer a detailed panorama of the social life of late Victorian England, but Gissing himself found no foothold for a permanent commitment in this varied terrain. Wherever he turned he saw only frustration, ignorance and injustice, and his novels are dominated by such themes as urban poverty, the passion for money, the growing vulgarity of taste, the repressiveness of middle-class life and the deficiencies of the basic institutions of society, such as politics, the economic system, education, religion and marriage. Even the efforts of reformers to improve these conditions gave him no encouragement, for he felt that the practical men were grasping and egotistic, and the idealists ineffective. Gissing himself was no reformer, though he made the mistake of taking himself for one when he was young. He came to feel, early in his writing career, that the disorders of civilization he was observing could not be remedied because they were deeply rooted in the nature of things. For refuge from this despair he often turned to the literature of Greece and Rome, for he found in the classics a humanism and sense of tranquillity that were lacking in the modern world. But his best novels confront the injustice of the cosmos as it is manifested in the life of the nineteenth century steadily and courageously, refusing to accept the scientific or religious myths devised to mitigate it. His purpose was not to call for reforms, for he felt that they were futile, but simply to bear witness to truths that he thought others refused to recognize.

239

Gissing often felt that he lived in an inhospitable age, and was a stranger in his own time, but he found many of its characteristic beliefs congenial. He is marked as a nineteenth-century spirit by his materialist conception of truth and his sense of social responsibility. He was, temporarily, both a socialist and a Comtist; he sympathized with the aesthetic idealism of Ruskin and Morris; his ordinary fictional mode was the realism that dominated the contemporary novel; he supported feminism; when the Boer war broke out, he professed pacifism; and he was a rationalist in religious matters. On the other hand, some of the major components of the nineteenth-century state of mind were clearly alien to him. He distrusted science and the scientific method, fearing that they would extinguish valuable human qualities and promote war. He paid little attention to evolution. In an age of widening democracy, he was firmly opposed to entrusting the common people with political power. At a time when most Victorians were congratulating themselves on their country's progress, Gissing saw nothing but cultural decline, and the threat of worse to come.

The opinions Gissing's novels contributed to the Victorian current of ideas were so original that few took them seriously. He rejected many of the common assumptions, such as the natural goodness of man and the greatest happiness principle, and analyzed society according to principles which seem both unenlightened and inconsistent. Frank Swinnerton, one of Gissing's first critics, described him as "a man who preferred his own thoughts to the world he dimly apprehended beyond the circle of his immediate surroundings." His point of view is hardly distinguishable at times from bleak reaction; but it is his own, worked out on the basis of his fastidious tastes, the lessons he learned from the misfortunes of his life, and his love of antiquity. When the right allowances are made, it can be seen that his ideas are, within their limits, liberal and humane. It may seem inconsistent of him to emphasize the evils of poverty, yet refuse to allow the poor the power to help themselves; but the values that he favored were aristocratic ones incompatible both with poverty and democracy. He could present paupers as a criminal class and as helpless victims; he saw that they could play both roles because poverty affected the morality as well as the living conditions of the poor. Unrestrained capitalist expansion and the popular control of industry through socialism are generally thought of as contrary policies; but Gissing regarded both as destructive expressions of egotism and materialism, and considered them equally dangerous to human values. He despised Christianity as a retrograde superstition, but he was opposed to militant atheism, because he realized that religion did much to soften human nature and cultivate its possibilities. Somewhat similarly, he felt that Puritanism, in spite of its repressiveness, must be recognized as a civilizing influence. Victorians normally regarded the spread of literacy and the growing interest in art and music among the common people as good signs; but Gissing pointed out that interests of this kind could coexist with selfishness and inhumanity. There was probably nothing he hated so much as commerce and the social system built upon acquisitiveness and the fear of insecurity; but he also realized that money was the key to the privacy and tranquillity he loved. These views cannot, in the final analysis, be reconciled with each other, but they seem nevertheless to revolve around a distinct center, the conviction that mere existence, even in comfort, without the means of living gracefully and humanely, is not a goal worth struggling for.

The kind of life Gissing regarded as an ideal is best illustrated in *The Private Papers of Henry Ryecroft* (1903), but it is not an ideal many would accept. For Ryecroft, his retired man of letters, who is weary and middle-aged, the atmosphere of peace and seclusion so beautifully conveyed in his calm prose is an enjoyable change from the troubles of his earlier days, but most people would find it pointless and monotonous. His satisfactions, which consist of reading familiar books, ruminating, walking in the country, observing nature, and recalling the past are hardly enough, in themselves, to justify existence. Work, love and a sense of accomplishment are obviously missing; but it is not likely that Gissing would have changed his dream of perfection very much, even if he had written it when he was younger. For him, the best imaginable life was one which offered a refuge from the irremediable woes of society. Ryecroft reflects that at one time he would

241

have felt guilty at living in comfort on an income capable of supporting several poor families. But now he has become convinced that the attempts to correct such injustices only do harm. "More than half a century of existence," he says, "has taught me that most of the wrong and folly which darken earth is due to those who cannot possess their souls in quiet. . . . " And he thinks of his own style of life as a positive, almost a social good. " . . . I believe that the world is better, not worse, for having one more inhabitant who lives as becomes a civilised being. . . . How well would the revenues of a country be expended if, by mere pensioning, one fifth of its population could be induced to live as I do!"

Gissing's perception of the social novelist's proper mission was equally independent. In his *Charles Dickens* (1898) he asserted that "truth, for the artist, is the impression produced on *him*, and . . . to convey this impression with entire sincerity is his sole reason for existing." In his novels, Gissing intended to achieve, not mere objectivity, which he distrusted as a literary counterpart of science, but the personal and self-exposing variant of it which is called honesty. Poverty, his first great theme, was also the key to a theme that was more truly his own, the division between the callous, mercenary civilization of the late nineteenth century, and the sensitive idealist who suffered the misfortune of being born into it. Realism calls for the exclusion of subjective elements, but Gissing's novels often contain at least one character, usually the protagonist, who enacts some part of his own spiritual frustrations. In fact, he came to regard his treatment of these figures as his most important contribution to fiction. "My books," he wrote to his close friend Morley Roberts, some years after he had given up the novel of poverty and turned to other subjects, "deal with people of many social strata. There are the vile working-class, the aspiring and capable working-class, the vile lower-middle, the aspiring and capable lower-middle, and a few representatives of the upper middle class." Far from attributing worth to any particular level of society, Gissing did show, as he claims, that there is a diversity of moral worth within every segment of it. "But what I desire to insist upon is this: that the most characteristic, the most important part of my work is that which deals with a class of young men distinctive of our time—well educated, fairly bred, *but without money*. . . . This side of my work, to me the most important, I have never yet seen recognized."

Even the novels occupied with the masses of the urban poor are centered upon isolated men and women who have somehow managed to preserve their better instincts amid the dark energies of industrial civilization. In these counterparts of himself Gissing found subjects for sympathy and opportunities for authentic social insights. The most significant characters of his slum novels, Arthur Golding of *Workers in the Dawn* (1880), Osmond Waymark, Julian Casti and Ida Starr of *The Unclassed* (1884), and Sidney Kirkwood of *The Nether World* (1889) have the sensitivity and spiritual generosity that is usually associated with people who have lived in comfort. Their existence does not mean that poverty encourages excellent human qualities, but rather that the anomalous arrangements of modern society are capable of producing anomalous results by placing people in environments where they do not belong.

Gissing was not the first to perceive that the individualism encouraged by the social mobility of the nineteenth century had sinister potentialities. In their various ways Charlotte Brontë's governesses, Pip in *Great Expectations* and Becky Sharp in *Vanity Fair* illustrate the dangers confronting those who step out of the social class they have been born into and find that they cannot enter another without forfeiting some aspect of their integrity. Gissing may have had his own case in mind in focusing upon the young man without money, but he was right to believe that this figure represented a characteristic problem of the period. Social groupings were no longer as clear as they had once been, moral and class standards were less firm, and the adventurous individualist who took advantage of this relaxation to follow some new course, or simply to act in accordance with his private convictions, might find himself adrift in the interstices between classes, beset by loneliness, self-suspicion, and the simpler hardships of deprivation and unemployment.

Gissing experienced all this in his own life. The son of a chemist who kept a shop in the town of Wakefield, he was born into the provincial lower middle class. Orphaned by the death of his father when he was thirteen, Gissing found a congenial environment for a time at school, where he was a brilliant student and won many prizes in English and classical literature. He was able to enter Owens College in Manchester by earning the highest grades in the kingdom in the Oxford local examination, thereby winning a three-year scholarship. But after moving into the city to be near the College, he had his first disastrous encounter with the symptoms of urban poverty, an experience that altered the course of his life. There was a tavern near the College frequented by disreputable women. In it Gissing met a seventeen-year-old prostitute named Nell Harrison. He fell in love with her, had relations with her, and tried to persuade her to change her way of life. Up to this time he had been a young man of irreproachable gentility, relentlessly determined to make his way in the world by academic prowess, but his concern with Nell deflected him from his course. He regarded her as a victim of society, and felt that the effort to save her from the streets justified any measures. He missed some of his classes to take her on a holiday to the seashore, and then, finding that he could not support her on his scholarship, began to steal money and other articles from the rooms in the College where the students kept their belongings. He was caught, imprisoned, and through the intercession of friends, sent to America where he traveled for a year, earning his living as well as he could, and going through a variety of experiences. In the fall of 1877, he returned to England, settled in poor lodgings in London with Nell, and set out, at the age of twenty, to become a novelist, in a mood of buoyant cheerfulness which his situation hardly justified. He was without money, friends or reputation, burdened by a record as a criminal and by a wife of questionable morals who was in poor health, an alcoholic, and, as it turned out, impossible for him to control. He had little sympathy for or interest in the poor among whom he lived, but felt no desire to associate with middle-class people who might learn about his past or inquire about his wife. In this way, he cut himself off as thoroughly as possible from all ordinary social relationships.

244

This isolation was not permanent. At various times in later life Gissing had a few good friends, paid visits and joined week-end parties. But he gained a reputation as a recluse, and never lost his distrust of gatherings where his secrets might become known, or where the irregularity of his life might cause embarrassment. As he grew older, he realized that the placid life he aspired to depended on an acceptance of ordinary conventions, and he resented the massive indifference of the institutions he had defied in his youth. "The truth is," wrote his character, Henry Ryecroft, in the reflections which are often accurate records of Gissing's own thoughts, "that I have never learnt to regard myself as a 'member of society.' For me, there have always been two entities—myself and the world, and the normal relation between these two has been hostile. . . . This, of which I once was scornfully proud, seems to me now, if not a calamity, something I would not choose if life were to live again."

Sensing that his experience of alienation was not unique, Gissing dealt with it in his second novel, *The Unclassed*, whose title is an attempt to formulate the theme he had in mind. Its major character, Waymark, is an impecunious schoolmaster with advanced opinions who writes a novel that no one will buy which apparently deals with social conditions but is meant to justify itself as a work of art. He is, of course, a close copy of Gissing himself. Together with his friend, an oppressed chemist's assistant named Casti, he anticipates the character-type which Gissing came to regard as his most important, the man or woman who is not at home in any class or group, who has fallen out of touch with society through pride or weakness, and nourishes personal values and visions that others cannot share.

Society is not entirely responsible for the sufferings of these characters. They are invariably helpless, vulnerable, self-pitying and even self-destructive, often seeming to bring disaster upon themselves. Gissing knew that these were traits of his own, and he once wrote, in a letter to his brother Algernon, that the family shared a "total lack of practical strength" which made their economic survival a miracle. In the choice

245

between people rendered impotent by sensitivity and the harsh world that threatened them, Gissing preferred, as T. S. Eliot did,

> The notion of some infinitely gentle
> Infinitely suffering thing.

When Kingcote, the hero of *Isabel Clarendon* (1886), goes to live with his widowed sister in poverty, his morale is shattered by the squalid lodgings, he cannot face the ugly landlady, and is irritated by the presence of children; but he is not condemned for this lack of spirit. Gissing did not subscribe to the widely held belief that the survival of the fittest was a principle appropriate to human society, that the weak ought to be exterminated simply because they were weak.

In spite of their indecisiveness, Gissing's heroes are both talented and fiercely egotistical. Their efforts to achieve recognition generally take the form of a bitter conflict with established society ending in some shameful action which shatters their self-esteem, discredits them publicly, and even leads to death. It was undoubtedly the Owens College episode that established this pattern for the study of ambitious young people in Gissing's mind. But he felt that his career as a novelist was also a struggle against public opinion. Gissing was not immune to the desire for fame. Writing to his sister about a visit he was planning to make in 1886, after he had published half a dozen novels, he said, "Thank Heaven I can go without the torture of feeling myself *Nobody*. . . . No, I can't endure to be *nobody*. I knew that would have to come to an end." Yet he encountered solid resistance in trying to establish himself. He had to publish his first book at his own expense, after many rejections, and it sold so poorly that he lost everything he had invested in it. The publisher who accepted a second novel, *Mrs. Grundy's Enemies*, subjected it to bowdlerization over Gissing's strong objections, ultimately decided not to publish it at all, and rejected *The Unclassed* because it had a prostitute as one of its characters. *Isabel Clarendon* (1886) was accepted for publication only after it had been revised for two volumes rather than three, and, was so poor a commercial venture that Gissing never received any payment for it. He found the reviews of his books so unreceptive that after a time he stopped reading them. His novels never sold well; he managed to achieve a satisfactory income in later years only by producing many short stories which could be placed quickly. His most popular book, *The Private Papers of Henry Ryecroft*, which brought him a certain fame in the year before his death, was not a novel but a sequence of essays, and Gissing was embittered by the observation made by some critics that it showed him to have the gifts of an essayist rather than a novelist. It is clear that, in dramatizing the resentments of those whose talents are ignored or corrupted by an insensitive society, he was expressing feelings of his own.

He was using his own experiences also in putting characters of this kind within a context of poverty. Gissing spent much of his life in poverty, thought about it deeply, and feared it. He often had reason to reflect on the irony of the fact that the lack of certain bits of paper or metal could deprive him of peace of mind and force him to waste many hours in tutoring, and he refused to acquire the economic sophistication which might make this state of affairs intelligible. He had a morbid and exaggerated fear of ending his days in the workhouse, like his character, the novelist Edwin Reardon of *New Grub Street* (1891): "He knew what poverty means. The chilling of brain and heart, the unnerving of the hands, the slow gathering about one of fear and shame and impotent wrath, the dread feeling of helplessness, of the world's base indifference. Poverty! Poverty!" Gissing himself seems to have spent much time in meditations of this kind, and through them acquired some appreciation of the terrifying power of money dramatized in Balzac's novels, and the fetishistic quality Marx attributed to it. Like Marx, Gissing never lost sight of the sturdy agnostic awareness that the deity to which the unjust economic system was dedicated was man-made. He once recorded in his *Commonplace Book* an anecdote from Knight's *Where Three Empires Meet* in which a Kaffir, seeing an Englishman buying food, makes inquiries and is told that without money a man would starve. "It was the best joke he had ever heard. He then explained this ridiculous system to his companions, and they roared in chorus." Gissing had once confronted the absurdity of economics himself. In the *Ryecroft Papers* he tells of the time when he satisfied his hunger by eating blackberries plucked at the side of the road. This episode acquired a momentous significance as he recalled how he had starved during his London days for want of a few coins to buy food. His days of sympathy with the poor are over, says Ryecroft; but his renewed insight into the injustice of the economic system enables him to appreciate the motives of the reformer who wants to change it.

Because of his conflicting feelings toward the poor, Gissing presented poverty as a complicated phenomenon, involving many paradoxes. His novels contain occasional appalling excursions into the lowest depths where madness and hunger are found; but he is also capable of seeing a Dickensian humor in the eccentricities of plain people, and a certain homely appeal in the simple comforts of the respectable poor. He gives powerful accounts of the helplessness of workingmen in the face of economic crises, and the effects of want upon family life. He is never sentimental about the poor, but a melancholy poetic tone sometimes emerges in his brooding descriptions of the pathetic pleasures and loves of people at the edge of starvation. Ultimately, his attitude toward the poor changed to a startling hostility. When he came to London and set out to share the life of the slums, he expected to find the simple human virtues among his neighbors, but was soon forced to conclude that the pressures of need and narrowness of experience had transformed human nature in them, depriving them of self-control and imagination, and making them capable of unthinking callousness and brutality. He had thought, naïvely, that every poor man would want to be an artist or a scholar if he were given the opportunity, that he would prefer an orderly life and civilized pleasures to what he had. But he soon learned that the culture of poverty had no place for the things he valued. When the heroine of *Demos* (1886) hears a friend idealize the poor, she wants to cry out, "But it is a mistake! They have not these feelings you attribute to them. Such suffering as you picture them enduring comes only to the poetry-fed soul at issue with fate." In these thoughts we hear Gissing's youthful naïveté corrected by the slightly less naïve aesthetic idealism he adopted at a later stage. In reading his vindictive descriptions of idle holidaying crowds, chaotic family scenes, street brawls and the like, one feels that Gissing never forgave the poor for his disillusionment with them.

At the same time, however, he recognized that they were not fully responsible for their tastes and feelings, but were being exploited by a system beyond their control. The sense that the poor are victims of social injustice emerges most powerfully when Gissing confronts violent figures driven mad by drink or deprivation, thieves, or prostitutes. The plight of Nell, his first wife, who appears as Golding's wife, Carrie, in *Workers in the Dawn*, linked social pathology and social injustice firmly in his mind. This connection became even clearer some years later. Gissing had been forced to send Nell to live elsewhere, and she had returned to her life as a prostitute. In 1888 she died in abject poverty, and when he went to see her body, Gissing found eloquent evidence of her suffering in her squalid room. In his next novel, *The Nether World*, he set out to condemn the society which tolerated such things, but his book did not quite follow his intentions. It dramatized the sufferings caused by poverty more effectively than any of his earlier books, but it also showed that all attempts to remedy them, and even his own protest must be futile in a universe that is basically unjust.

After *The Nether World* Gissing turned to other subjects. But he never forgot poverty, or his fear of it, and it often forms a substantial minor interest in his novels of middle-class life. Even *Veranilda* (1904) his historical novel about ancient Rome, which has nothing to do with social problems, has a glimpse of the poor. One of the characters, Decius, encounters a crowd of poor people in the streets of Rome and hears them complaining about the shortage of food. He responds as Gissing did in his later years: "The sight of suffering was painful to him, and the cries of the vulgar offended his ear; he felt indignant that these people should not be fed, as Rome for so many ages had fed her multitude, but above all, he dreaded uproar, confusion, violence." The sense of injustice is there, but it is only a minor part of a reaction which consists mainly of a desire to maintain peace of mind. This is enough to drive the fastidious

249

Decius away from the frequented part of the city altogether: "His hurried pace did not relax until he was lost again amid a wilderness of ruins, where browsing goats and darting lizards were the only life," a flight which corresponds to Gissing's retreat from social problems to his studies, his love of antiquity and the peace of nature.

The educated young man without money whom Gissing described as his special contribution to fiction is an ideal vehicle of social criticism, and meets perfectly the specifications for the mirroring consciousness laid down by Henry James in his Preface to *The Princess Casamassima*. Because he is isolated, the Gissing hero is exposed to suffering and humiliation, and because he is intelligent and unhampered by conventional ideas, he is able to assess his experiences perceptively. In Gissing's early novels of the slums, the life stories of young men and women of this kind are used to reveal the obvious social disorders of poverty, ignorance, drunkenness and demoralization. But these characters really come into their own as vessels of awareness in the novels written after 1889, where they encounter the subtler social dislocations of middle class life: greed, hypocrisy, repression, marital problems, discrimination against women, class barriers, the debasement of literature and the press and the vulgarization of politics, art and literature.

The hero of *Workers in the Dawn*, Arthur Golding, is a prototype who anticipates Gissing's later protagonists. A poor foundling raised in the slums by a learned bookseller, he is divided between political agitation on behalf of the working people among whom he lives, and the gift for art he has developed in the studio of a wealthy painter. As he moves between social classes and hears different theories of social reform, he meets with the barbarity of the poor, the fanaticism of radical zealots, the hypocrisy of religious missionaries, the selfishness and complacency of the wealthy, and the discouragement of well-meaning reformers who are defeated by the conditions they try to change. Two rather abstract philosophies, the doctrine that art promotes reform by cultivating the moral imagination, and Comtism, gain extended hearings; but they are useful mainly as attacks upon the inertia of an indifferent society. Golding himself never resolves the conflicts between his loyalty toward his class and his obligation to his artistic talents, or between his duty to the poor girl he has married and his love for Helen Norman, the sensitive and educated ward of his art teacher. Having learned from Helen that art serves human good better than politics can, Arthur alienates his working-class friends by telling them that his primary commitment must be to his art. The love between him and Helen is destroyed because he realizes that the act of leaving his wife, even though she has deserted him and returned to the streets, would impose an intolerable burden of conscience on him. Helen learns that the conventional religion she despises may be effective in carrying out the philanthropies which interest her. And Arthur's effort to fulfill his responsibilities toward his wife is a failure, for she deserts him again. In this way, the people who have refused to take shelter from the conflicting ideologies of the day by committing themselves blindly to one sect or another are defeated by the discrepancies between their ideals and a reality far more complex than they had suspected.

Most of the outsiders in *The Unclassed* fare better. Gissing is, of course, ignoring plausibility outrageously when he presents such a character as Ida Starr, the cast-off child of a prostitute who has been driven to harsh labor as a child and to prostitution as a young woman, and who works regularly as a laundress, but nevertheless speaks well, writes a decent letter and recognizes a line from "Twelfth-Night" at a moment's notice. Even more implausibly, she behaves like a woman who is not only confident of herself, but sophisticated in a variety of directions. She is enlightened enough to strip for a swim in a lonely place, to serve an unjust prison term without becoming embittered, and to turn to active philanthropy when she comes into a fortune. The fact that it is impossible to accept Ida as a product of her experiences is a fictional weakness, but it is also an indication of the urgency Gissing felt to depict the type he meant her to represent. Waymark also knows something about the suffering of the poor. He learns Ida's story, teaches in a school that exploits both students and masters, and works as a rent collector in a slum neighborhood, but does nothing more about social abuses than make use of them as material for a novel. Social injustices offend the rational sense of these more or less phlegmatic observers, who are cut off from both the rich and the poor by the originality of their manners, morals and opinions, but do not arouse profound emotions in them. Because they are witnesses of the social drama rather than participants, they survive their misfortunes and live to approach a happy ending. But Julian Casti, in the same novel, is a better prefiguring of Gissing's characteristic young man, for though he has educational aspirations, the slums lay a heavy hand on him by forcing him to marry a shrewish wife and imprisoning him in drudgery that eventually kills him.

Demos is a departure from Gissing's usual pattern, for while Richard Mutimer, its protagonist, is bred in poverty, ambitious, and exiled from his class, he is not educated, and is not the hesitant weakling, vulnerable to every moral compunction, who is the center of many of the novels. In fact, Gissing uses him to illustrate the narrowness, mean aggressiveness and unimaginative cruelty of the self-educated. When he comes into a fortune he shows that he has the capacity to organize a great socialist enterprise, and the intelligence to aspire to the manners and standards of the leisure class, but he lacks the love of beauty and the moral sensitivity of those who are genuinely civilized. His ruthlessness and dishonesty, which Gissing insists on presenting as class traits, alienate him from his new associates and even from his wife. Yet because he has abandoned the poor girl he was supposed to marry, lives in comfort, and puts his managerial responsibilities first, he is also cut off from his family and his old socialist mates. He is marooned in a wasteland between social classes, and isolated from the ideology that vitalizes his movement. Gissing carefully constructs this isolation by showing Mutimer rejecting such currents of the time as Marxism, anarchism and William Morris' aesthetic socialism, and choosing an independent course which ends in defeat, in spite of his great personal strength.

Gissing's early novels dramatize the obvious effects of economic competition on slum life, incisively linking cause and effect; in *The Unclassed* for example, the people are persecuted by the rack-renter who means to exploit his property to the full, and the sewing-girls who work in a factory are paid so little that they are forced to go out on the streets at night. But it is a root evil among the rich as well as the poor, and Gissing shows that it can be the cause of that most intolerable injustice, the death of a baby, in either setting. In *The Nether World* a poor mother takes her sick baby to the hospital, but it dies before the doctor can see it, a result, as Gissing makes amply clear, of a conspiracy of economic factors. The father, though trained for a craft, earns little, because cheap mass production has reduced the demand for his skill; acting on the attitudes he has learned from his breeding in the slums, he grows impatient with the growing family he cannot support, frequents the taverns and turns to crime. The young mother knows nothing about housekeeping or caring for her children because she has been reared in poverty by a drunken mother. The death of the baby in *The Whirlpool* (1897) is not caused by want, for its parents are wealthy, but it is the climax of a chain of events originating in money matters. A wealthy capitalist makes a welcome offer of a loan to a businessman as a way of silencing him while he has an affair with his wife. Alma Rolfe, the novel's leading female figure, becomes the cause of the capitalist's death when the jealous husband sees her at his house, mistakes her for his wife, and kills the lover. Disturbed by this and other troubles, Alma bears a sickly little girl who soon dies. The father's first thought is that she is fortunate to be spared the pain of life.

Economic motives usually operate more subtly in middle-class settings, however, attacking the spirit rather than life itself. In *A Life's Morning* (1888), Gissing displays a special interest in the character of Richard Dagworthy, a middle-aged, self-made mill-owner whose ruthlessly acquisitive instincts are accompanied by a certain sensitivity to beauty and refinement. Dagworthy falls in love with the well-educated daughter of one of his employees, and when she refuses him, can find no better way of continuing his suit than threatening to ruin her father unless she agrees to marry him. The adaptation of the methods of the marketplace to the purposes of love has disastrous results.

In his last completed novel, *Will Warburton* (1905), Gissing presents a generous-hearted man of commerce who is compelled by financial reverses to leave his business and become a grocer. He learns that he cannot afford his usual kindly feelings, but must charge even his poorest customers the full price of what he sells, and must do his best to drive a competitor out of business, in spite of the needs of the man's family. He hears the sounds of London as the roar created by the struggle against hunger, mingling the pain of the oppressed with the cries of the oppressors, and wonders whether he will survive, and what his dependent mother and sister will do if he should be unable to continue. "How—he cried within himself—how, in the name of sense and mercy, is mankind content to live on in such a world as this?"

Gissing's serious young people of virtuous aspirations and far-seeing ideals might raise this cry from the slums where they are trapped. Poverty descends on them in a variety of ways. They are encumbered by needy dependents, forced to abandon their talents in order to work at unsatisfactory jobs, exploited by people whom need has degraded, or morally oppressed by a sense of responsibility for the suffering around them. The task of giving slum life authentic novelistic substance involved Gissing in a truly sociological effort. He visited such areas as Whitechapel, Lambeth and Clerkenwell, and accompanied working-class crowds to the Crystal Palace on a Bank Holiday; what he transcribed into his novels served the purpose of awakening his public to the existence of conditions many were still unaware of, and showing how slum life could transform people into criminals, drunkards and prostitutes. For many readers the customs and thoughts of Gissing's slum characters were as foreign as those of African bushmen. In this respect, his novels have something in common with the work of such social investigators as Henry Mayhew, Charles Booth and Beatrice Webb. However, they also use the facts of poverty to project insights available only to imaginative observation. They demonstrate the ominous truth that in the life of poverty, as in other environments, daily experience molds psychological development; that in a commercial civilization the profit motive penetrates every aspect of life, paralyzing generosity and good will, and that the social classes cannot be partitioned off from each other, morally or materially. They express a despairing conviction that society, though established by man, is controlled by economic energies which have nothing to do with human needs or desires.

The subjection of individual human beings to some great, remorseless power which has captured and enslaved them is made perfectly visible in Gissing's numerous descriptions of London and the lives of its people. Gissing, like Dickens, Baudelaire, James Thomson and T. S. Eliot is one of the great prophets of the modern city, and uses the images of city life as an iconography of degradation. He had a perfectly clear vision, unobscured by any notions of progress or the need for productivity, of how the city reduced people to indistinguishable atoms, squeezing everything vital out of them, and pouring these energies into the great, demonic demonstrations of its industries and roaring streets. As he looks about at the streets, houses and pedestrians of a poor neighborhood, faithfully annotating its significant features, Gissing ordinarily reads two messages from them: ugliness and slavery. Darwin saw, in the foliage that had overgrown Indian ruins in America, evidence of the struggle for existence in nature; Gissing saw evidence of a similar struggle in the squalid shops, monotonous walls, strenuous toil and repulsive odors of the slums. "Barracks, in truth," he says in a characteristic description of a slum neighborhood; "housing for the army of industrialism, an army fighting with itself, rank against rank, man against man, that the survivors may have whereon to feed. Pass by in the night, and strain imagination to picture the weltering mass of human weariness, of bestiality, of unmerited dolour, of hopeless hope, of crushed surrender, tumbled together within those forbidding walls."

Like Dickens, Gissing felt that the forces abroad in the city were pestilential, invisibly moving from place to place through the channels of commerce to blight the lives of the people. He conveys this through panoramic descriptions, and also follows his characters into the scenes of their private lives, where his close-ups of boredom, discomfort and irritation recall the imagery of Baudelaire's poems about Paris. In *The Nether World*, the clothes the people wear are puffed up with moisture, infested by the rot of the houses where they live; Clara Hewett, forced to stay in a flat in the slums, is hemmed in by prison-like masonry, haunted by the sinister noises of the streets and neighboring rooms. Gilbert Grail in *Thyrza* (1887) sits until midnight thinking of his hopeless life as a worker in a factory, and of waking at five in the morning to work until seven, when he will be too tired to read the books he loves. In Gissing's novels, urban life is a counterpart of Hardy's nature; both are embodiments of powers indifferent or hostile to human values.

Economic motivations are capable, not only of corrupting individual character, but also of subverting the social order generally. Institutions originally conceived to serve the common interest or to bind the community together are transformed by money pressures into instruments of debasement and exploitation, so that the whole of life is dominated by the standards of competition. *In the Year of Jubilee* (1894) deals in part with the use of a national festival as a promotional medium in accordance with the accepted view that all things are done for profit. It is a surprisingly early perception of the fact that mass production must result in mass psychology. One of its conspicuous minor characters is an advertising man who praises his industry's capacity for manipulating people's opinions as a great civilizing force. "Do you suppose people kept themselves clean before they were reminded at every corner of the benefits of soap?" he asks. Gissing shows how the press, one of his favorite targets, has leveled the ideas of the people, so that they unthinkingly worship common idols. "National Progress, without precedent in the history of mankind!" crows the Philistine Mr. Barmby, thinking of the material advance England has made since the accession of Victoria in terms of the number of cabs and newspapers. Conversations, street scenes, the furnishings of homes, a taste for violence, and attitudes toward marriage and family life reveal the same sort of unthinking banality of mind, the mechanical reactions of a mechanical age. This new herd instinct is symbolized by the great festival of Victoria's first Jubilee, when millions of celebrants filled the streets. There are minor disorders in the scene Gissing describes, but perhaps more sinister is the way in which the people keep order, "carelessly obedient," so that the dominant sound is the "thud, thud of footfalls numberless, and the low, unvarying sound that suggested some huge beast purring to itself in stupid contentment."

256

But Gissing's best treatment of this subject is *New Grub Street,* the novel he devoted to the effects of mass production upon his own profession. Gissing was compelled to write steadily throughout most of his life to earn his living, sometimes selling his novels just in time to avoid destitution. What effect this may have had upon the quality of the novels themselves can only be conjectured, but his insights into the ironies of practicing an art as a profession in a competitive society gave him the material for his finest novel, and his most profound critique of the conception of life as a commercial enterprise. His novelist-hero, having had a modest success with his first efforts, finds that he lacks the motivation to continue writing, and that his family therefore faces poverty. All about him he sees others profiting from quasi-literary activities, and in surveying these miscellaneous writers, Gissing presents a broadly ranging conspectus of the corruption of literature in industrial society. The vast industrial establishment with its educational annexes has produced an army of superficial readers hungry for light reading, especially in periodical form. This condition introduces competitive standards into the literary scene, making popularity and the capacity for rapid production vital considerations; instead of being the product of inspiration and joy, literature is produced by toil and hack work. Instead of producing a shared culture, it becomes a mere commodity which is consumed and forgotten. Gissing shows that literary work, in his day, generates a range of character types that would be typical of any industry; the toiling exploited journeyman, the grinding entrepreneur, the parasite feeding off the hopes of innocent literary aspirants, and the successful cynic who is able to exploit supply and demand for his own advantage. Gissing's hero simply turns his back upon this scene, and leaves writing to do some humble, honest work. But the decision divides him from his wife, undermines his health and eventually leads to his death. In an age of trade, his wife tells him, art must be practiced as a trade. No more final denunciation of the ordinary commercial standards of nineteenth-century life could be imagined.

New Grub Street shows that competition can destroy things of value that should, properly speaking, have no connection with money at all. *Born in Exile* (1892) shows how far this corruption can go. in attacking the fundamental basis of morality. Its protagonist, Godwin Peak, one of the best examples of Gissing's intelligent and ambitious men of humble origin, is too enlightened to want money itself, but has an irresistible yearning for the life-style that depends on it. The meanness of his background and some of his experiences as a brilliant student at his College convince him, as they convinced Gissing, that he is living in a thoroughly unjust society. He feels that he will be able to overcome his debasing competitive impulses, do meaningful work and open his mind to humanizing influences only in an atmosphere of wealth, ease and cultivation. He admires the comfort of conventional life, but has contempt for its morality. He tells his friends that he believes in nothing, that it is possible to be without convictions, that true honesty is unattainable, that life can be guided by what has since been called "situation ethics" rather than by principles. Equipped with this moral nihilism, he courts the daughter of a well-to-do family, not because he loves her, but because he aspires to her social class. Having heard that poor clergymen are sometimes able to marry above their station, he pretends to reject his old agnosticism, and prepares himself to enter the Church. This involves a double crime. He is, of course, deceiving the girl and her family. And since he is a chemist by training and occupation, and accepts the philosophy of science, his professions of religious faith contradict his own convictions. But he has come to believe that in a meaningless world moral abstractions are also meaningless. He tells himself that he will be doing no harm, that genuine good can emerge from falsehood, that the role he is playing brings comfort to the pious, and that happiness is an illusion in any case. Peak's sophistries, which range in scope from the quibbles of Bishop Blougram and Mr. Sludge to the elemental nihilism of Raskolnikov, reflect a collapse of moral values in which egotism, the philosophy of science and economic injustice all play a part. He realizes that he is committing himself to "a life of deliberate baseness," and thinks that he can survive this confrontation with the emptiness of his vision of the world. But he has a moment when he doubts his own identity, and he finds that, in spite of his efforts, he has not made himself a part of the social circle he admires. He is ultimately exposed and dies in disgrace, but this does not mean that his interpretation of his plight has been repudiated, only that the isolation created by economic injustice has been confirmed.

During one of his moments of failing inspiration, Edwin Reardon, the novelist of *New Grub Street*, reads a line or two of the *Odyssey*, reflecting that Homer did not write to earn money or to meet a deadline. This reproach is inherent in all of the criticism Gissing directed against the modern world. He was no builder of Utopian systems. He rejected all the characteristic social remedies of the nineteenth century, but did not show that he had any principles on which a better order of things could be based. The seclusion, love of study, liberty and individuality which are praised in his novels and the Ryecroft papers do not amount to a social system. Yet he did have an unconscious standard of value by which he measured the deficiencies of nineteenth-century civilization. That was the culture of Greece and Rome, as he conceived it.

Gissing was already a devoted classical student when he was a schoolboy in Wakefield, and his attachment to antiquity grew steadily throughout his lifetime. He was a constant reader of Gibbon's *Decline and Fall of the Roman Empire*, had a superb command of many classical texts and steeped himself in the sixth century in preparation for writing his historical novel, *Veranilda*. In spite of this quasi-professional knowledge, however, he always saw antiquity through a haze of romance and personal associations. During the travels in Italy recorded in *By the Ionian Sea* (1901) he felt resentment toward the intrusions of modern towns and factories into lands once sacred to Homer, Apollo, Horace and Virgil. For him, visiting these places was a way of entering a closed world, like Yeats' Byzantium, where the imagination could wander without encountering the painful realities of the present. Describing a steamer trip across the Bay of Naples in *By the Ionian Sea*, a trip he was to include in *Veranilda*, he wrote, "Today seemed an unreality, an idle impertinence; the real was the long-buried past which gave its meaning to all about me, touching the night with infinite pathos. Best of all, one's being became lost to consciousness; the mind knew only the phantasmal forms it shaped and was at peace in visions." The classical world was not only an escape however; it was also the embodiment of the virtues that were missing in modern life. For one thing, it was pre-Christian, and therefore free of one of the illusions of the contemporary world that Gissing found most pathetic and contemptible. Its surviving art and literature were prevailingly aristocratic, exempt from mercenary motives. Among them Gissing had found philosophers who praised wisdom, study and moderation, lyric poets who dwelt on the placid, uncontentious life of the countryside, and tragedians and epic poets who saw man's life as a lofty and significant drama in which he encountered forces beyond his control, and was forced to acknowledge his limited capacities. To Gissing, the most striking defect of modern industrial civilization was its inability to share the heritage of antiquity. His social criticism is unintelligible when it is divorced from his love of classical culture.

His classicism explains, for example, his consistent rejection of contemporary proposals for social reform. The later nineteenth century was, of course, a time of broadening democracy in England, when male suffrage was universal, Parliamentary government was strong, the labor unions were growing, and various socialist movements were building their power. Victorian liberalism was based on the principle of perfectibility, with its implications that the poor could be improved by just treatment, and that the majority of the populace could be educated to govern. Gissing himself had been a radical when he was twenty, but a few years later, when he wrote a novel about socialism, he called it *Demos*, the term used for the common people of the ancient Greek city-states. As we have seen, he knew from his own experience that the life of the London poor did not encourage generous instincts or wise judgment, and for a time this had the effect of making him sympathetic with them. But when he observed them through classical eyes, he adopted a view toward the proletariat found nowhere else in the wide spectrum of contemporary opinion, the contemptuous attitude an aristocrat of Periclean Athens might have had toward the mob which threatened his traditional power. In Aristophanes' comedy *The Knights*, Demos is personified as a deaf and credulous old man who is victimized by unscrupulous servants fighting for his favor, a situation that the playwright meant to reflect the contemporary political situation. In titling his novel as he did, Gissing was opposing the prevailing liberalism of his time with an attitude toward the poor borrowed from antiquity, and characterizing them as unstable, ignorant, easily led and unworthy of political responsibility. The novel itself articulates this case vividly, showing the socialist leader giving in to temptations, and the masses responding to manipulation by rival factions until they ultimately turn against him and kill him.

Because he loved learning, Gissing might have been expected to agree with the view that education was the key to the solution of social problems. Ever since Robert Owen's time Victorian liberals had felt that the improvement of the individual through education was a sure way of improving society. "Let us reform our schools," said Ruskin, in a magisterial formulation of this principle, "and we shall find little reform needed in our prisons." But Gissing thought that mass education would tend to debase learning rather than to uplift the people. In *Thyrza* (1887) he presents a thoughtful young reformer who tries to make a difference in the lives of workingmen by giving them lectures in English literature; the class is a failure with most of the men because their interests are limited to practical matters. Gissing perceived the painful contradiction inherent in mass education: that it promoted freedom at the expense of allowing the tastes and opinions of the mediocre to prevail. In *On Liberty* J. S. Mill had blamed education for the conformity which was already conspicuous among Englishmen: "Comparatively speaking, they now read the same things, listen to the same things, see the same things, go to the same places, have their hopes and fears directed to the same objects, have the same rights and liberties, and the same means of asserting them. . . . And the assimilation is still proceeding. . . . Every extension of education promotes it, because education brings people under common influences, and gives them access to the general stock of facts and sentiments." Gissing might have taken this passage as his text for such works as *New Grub Street* and *In the Year of Jubilee*, which were written about thirty years after *On Liberty*, and showed the advancement of the process Mill described. He objected to all

261

forms of expression that depended on popularity, including newspapers, periodicals and even plays. He felt, with the example of classical literature in mind, that genuine culture is accessible only to an aristocracy that enjoys the leisure and tranquillity for it. As he shows through *Thyrza*, and through the example of Jessica Morgan in *The Whirlpool*, who is always preparing for examinations, mere study in the absence of conditions conducive to true liberality of mind is futile. Besides, he saw that the spread of literacy made the production of literature for profit rather than for artistic motives inevitable.

When he expressed his love of antiquity by writing *Veranilda*, the fulfillment of a desire, he wrote to a friend, that he had nursed for ten years, he approached his subject, not as a social critic or a lover of high culture, but as an antiquarian and a novelist concerned with the diffusion of feelings through the fabric of daily life and custom. *Veranilda* is essentially a tale of love and intrigue whose people are, in the main, unlettered and indifferent to social justice. It is not set in a period of high civilization, but in sixth-century Rome, a time when the attenuated pagan tradition had been joined by the strong flow of Christianity, and when Rome was overrun alternately by Byzantine and Gothic armies. It manifests a feeling for the laminations of history, as one culture overlayers another, and for the details of daily life that exhibit this effect. Thus, pagan deities and saints are invoked in the same conversation, a small pagan temple is used for the worship of the Virgin, and a daughter of one of the first noble Roman families to have embraced Christianity marries a Goth. One aspect of the historical complex is reflected by an allusion to Virgil's Fourth Eclogue, which Christian exegetes interpreted as a prediction of Christ. The spirit of the time, monopolized by war and religion, is more or less indifferent to the grandeur of former ages; ruins are an ordinary part of the landscape, and once noble houses are dilapidated or altogether abandoned.

Veranilda is something of a puzzle, not only because Gissing's social awareness is replaced in it by a historical one, but also because, after going back to the general period when the cultural values he advocated really existed, he dropped his didactic stance and depended on atmosphere and action for his effects, with only the mildest of moral overtones. The most spiritual part of the story takes place at the famous Abbey of Monte Cassino, and is presided over by the figure of St. Benedict, an emphasis which is, of course, surprising. It seems as if Gissing was willing in *Veranilda*, to allow the remote world in which he spent a good part of his imaginative life to speak for itself, in the conviction that it could say nothing wrong. Even Christian sentiments, if they are approached as elements of the culture of antiquity, can be relied upon to awaken the reader to the superiority of past times; and the same is true of the kidnapings, extortions and murder which are parts of the story. In the presence of antiquity, Gissing's critical sense was disarmed and became passive; it was charmed into idleness by his feeling that all was part of a great historical cycle of indisputable value. The attitude toward modern times reflected in his novels is exactly the reverse; there even goodness and generosity are cursed because of the intrinsic evil of the industrial age.

Thus, the most significant effects of Gissing's humanism are found, not in *Veranilda*, but in his criticism of the modern consciousness that knew nothing of Greece and Rome. He thought of his novels as an effort to remedy this by bringing the classical sensibility to bear on modern life. While he was writing *Thyrza*, a story set in the slum district of Lambeth, he wrote to his sister: "With me it is a constant aim to bring the present and the past near to each other, to remove the distance which seems to separate Hellas from Lambeth. It can be done, by grasping firmly enough the meanings of human nature." What Gissing saw in the contemporary world that corresponded to Hellas was the spectacle of noble human beings striving against powers far stronger than they. The social and economic forces released by industrial civilization are in his world what the fates were to the Greeks; his victims, however, are not the robust heroes found in the ancient epics and tragedies, but men whose virtues are particularly vulnerable to the world in which they find themselves. It is a part of Gissing's classical inheritance that he does not consider human beings to be the mere instrumentalities of social forces, but creatures capable of intense sufferings and high aspirations. Even his novels on social themes devote a major part of their action to private issues, especially those of love and courtship, in which human nature displays itself without disguise. For these also, misfortune is the usual outcome. There is a dark pagan feeling, in every aspect of Gissing's novels, that the universe is in the possession of powers who tolerate man only at their pleasure.

Gissing's absorption with social problems should not be allowed to obscure the fact that his most crucial encounter with the consciousness of his time took place within the framework of fictional technique. In his use of the novel form, Gissing carried on a significant dialogue with the Victorian spirit. Because he wrote an excellent critical book on Dickens (some of whose ideas were used by Edmund Wilson in his 1941 essay, "The Two Scrooges,") he is sometimes regarded as a Dickensian novelist, and it is not surprising that his conception of the novel should have much in common with that of Dickens. *Workers in the Dawn* and other early novels aspire, as *Dombey and Son* and *Bleak House* do, to be far-reaching spectacles that expose the condition of humanity in a complex age. They present cross-sections of a stratified society, employing the counterpoints of multiple plots and contrasting social levels to achieve something like a definitive rendering, usually with special emphasis on the poor and humble. As in Dickens, and in certain works of Disraeli, Mrs. Gaskell and Charlotte Brontë, the social conscience becomes a fictional method at times, guiding the selection and organization of the material. After a few unsuccessful early attempts, Gissing did not try to imitate Dickens' humor, symbolism or melodrama. He was tolerant of Dickens' tendency to sacrifice authenticity for the sake of entertaining or promoting a moral view but he preferred another motive in his own work: fidelity to his perception of actuality.

The model he took as a beginning novelist was therefore not Dickens, but George Eliot. In adopting the neutral realism and the exhaustive treatment of character and incident which she established as the prevailing fictional mode of the latter part of the century, he was also accepting certain related attitudes. These include the belief that the vital truths are those which can

264

be learned by observation and verified by empirical means and materialist standards. They also imply that events are determined through links of cause and effect which can be uncovered by the thorough analysis of social custom and psychology. George Eliot's realism claims a knowledge only of actual experience, not of absolute truth, reflecting the agnosticism which Gissing shared with her. It does not preclude the expression of the author's individuality through autobiographical elements, direct commentary and unconscious bias in the choice of materials. It cannot do without physical "reality;" but its strongest emphasis is on the rendering of its characters' reactions to reality rather than on reality itself.

In his early novels especially, Gissing undertook to imitate George Eliot's full exploitation of the resources of fiction, the vigorous and extended development of description, dialogue, character-analysis, biographical background and atmosphere that is responsible for making her novels seem cumbersome to many modern readers. This was a mode suited to the depiction of a stable social scene, with established standards and habits of life. The conflicts that arise when the accepted ideas about morality and behavior are violated gain force from the solidity with which the social milieu has been evoked. *Isabel Clarendon* uses this technique, for most of its action takes place in comfortable, settled surroundings. Before the first episodes of the plot come into view, the reader must accompany Kingcote through some encounters with a dancing bear, a stolen purse, a magic spring, the legend attached to it, and a congenial clergyman. These, like other subsidiary elements in the novel, provide a periphery for which the main characters and events form a center, and weight them with meanings they would not have if they were isolated. But when Kingcote is forced to move to poor London lodgings, the sense of an organized social life disappears, and the technique of accurate description is diverted to the purposes of critical realism, as the details speak for themselves.

> He left the candle guttering at the foot of the stairs, and entered a room of which the door stood open immediately on his left hand. There was a low fire in the grate; the candle outside helped him to discern a sofa which stood before the window, and on this he sank. A hissing

> sound came from below stairs, and the house was full of the odour of frying fish. . . . The room was very small; the couch, a round table, a cupboard with ornamental top, and four chairs, scarcely left space to walk about. On the table was a green cloth, much stained; the hair of the sofa was in places worn through, and bits of the stuffing showed themselves.

The patient accumulation of well-observed detail that served George Eliot as a demonstration of the essential coherence and continuity of daily life has become a muted outcry against intolerable conditions that is all the more effective because it is factual and understated.

The influence of George Eliot is also visible in Gissing's integrated and elaborate plots. He gave much thought to structure, and the results are apparent in the careful disposition of his episodes, the linkage of subordinate plots to the main action, and the steady forward movement of incident found in all but his earliest novels. Developments are carefully prepared in advance, and unfold themselves with few coincidences. The better novels have comparatively little decisive action. This economy promotes the air of realism, conserves the dependence of action upon character, and gives the story the slow, steady rhythm of everyday life. In George Eliot these qualities reflect the reliable causality of the universe, the intelligibility of the social structure, and the conviction that events are generally explicable in terms of the conditions that lead to them; they form, when taken together, a context within which the morality of the choices made by the characters can be judged.

No such assurances are to be found in Gissing's plots, whose determinism has an entirely different implication, a fatalistic one. Within them the weakness of the characters and the sinister energy of some external factor usually combine to bring about a catastrophe. *Denzil Quarrier* (1892) is the story of an essentially virtuous couple who live as man and wife, but cannot be legally united because of the woman's earlier abortive marriage. Because Quarrier wants to run for Parliament, they make a pretense of being married in France. A disaffected friend of Quarrier's, who envies him both his wife and his candidacy, accidentally meets the first husband and sends him into the town to insure Quarrier's defeat by exposing the wife's bigamy. The husband is too late to influence the voting, but he drives the wife to suicide. Quarrier's intention of deceiving the public, his wife's weakness, the friend's dislike of him, the chance that puts the first husband in his way and the rigidity of marriage customs all lead, in a parallel course, toward the final disaster. Quarrier's observation, after it is all over, that he now sees the need for social law, is really an ironic way of underlining the point that under the given circumstances what happened was inevitable.

Gissing characteristically embodies his fatalism in some specific determinant found in the social context. Thus, in *New Grub Street*, the husband whose earning powers are failing and the wife who has high expectations of him provide material for the plot; but it is the cruelly demanding competitive struggle that motivates them to argument, separation, poverty, illness and death. In *The Odd Women*, the force that brings about the failure of most of the characters is clearly identified as the social inferiority of women. A shopgirl marries an elderly man she does not love in order to escape the hardships of her work, and finds that her husband, who subscribes to the traditional view of the family, thinks she must be absolutely obedient, and tyrannizes her. The social element combines with a weakness of character as the young wife takes a lover, is discovered, is driven out of her home, and dies in childbirth, a dénouement that is felt to be inherent in the original situation, and in the practice of discrimination against women which produced it.

Gissing resisted the more powerful strains of realism that were migrating to England from the Continent in the 1880's because he did not share the convictions they embodied. He did not have Zola's faith in scientific method, and did not accept his theory that it could be transposed to fiction. Although he cultivated an artistic detachment, he did not maintain the austere, quasi-religious attitude toward his art which is at the root of Flaubert's merciless and dispassionate readings of life. As a self-confessed aristocrat, he did not approve of the self-effacing, egalitarian sort of realism that limits itself to flat observation and forbids interpretation. There is an implication in the naturalist method that personal expression is illegitimate, that the author is no more than a substitute for the camera or the tape recorder. When realistic doctrines and the interests of the imagination conflicted in this way, Gissing knew where he stood. He had no illusions about the value or the possibility of objectivity in fiction, but wanted his works to be strongly marked by his own character, to be things which no one else could have written. His realism was not meant to eliminate the author's feelings, but to free them; it was a way of throwing off conventional limitations, an enfranchisement of the imagination, the result of something like a revelatory encounter between the facts of social life and the special perceptiveness of a unique sensibility. In this respect he had more in common with the French realists of an earlier generation, such as Balzac and Flaubert, than with the naturalists of his own, such as Zola and George Moore. Some of the sordid scenes in Gissing's early novels may have a superficial resemblance to Zola's work; but examination will show that the revulsion or indignation they evoke result from the application of George Eliot's scrupulous, intimate methods of genre description to material taken from slum life rather than from an imitation of Zola.

As his first novels show, Gissing was not born with the gift of psychological analysis; but he soon acquired an impressive ability to depict both the bewilderments of serious minds and the subtle, decisive movements of thought which lead to fundamental changes of opinion and spiritual rebirth. His first major success along these lines appears in *Demos*, where a well-intentioned woman of good breeding marries a plebeian socialist leader and adopts his views, only to discover that she has mistaken her own convictions, and that her temperament makes it impossible for her to share his beliefs. The foregrounds of most of Gissing's novels are occupied, in this way, by minds contending with questions of moral principle, social behavior, or emotion, and their major interest is likely to be the modulation of these thoughts under the pressures of gathering knowledge and experience. He was, of course, participating in one of the major modes of Victorian fiction, and might have been influenced by the doctrines of Henry James, who said, in defense of character-analysis, "What a man thinks and what he feels are the history and character of what he does," and denied that a distinction could be made between novels of incident and novels of character by asking, "What is character but the determination of incident? What is incident but the illustration of character?"

His actual model, however, was, again, George Eliot. Like her, he took as his central characters people who go beyond merely reacting to their daily problems, and feel the need to formulate and act upon some coherent theory of life. This similarity may owe something to the fact that Gissing and George Eliot had both been Comtian enthusiasts, remained agnostics, and felt that a commitment to some intellectual view was the fullest expression of moral responsibility. In George Eliot's novels the ideas of the characters are never given much authority; she is less interested in their validity than in their effects upon the people's lives. The ideas that are emphasized are those belonging to the general view of life expressed through the novel as a whole. Gissing, on the other hand, takes more seriously than George Eliot the possibility that people might try to lead their lives according to principle, and makes the novel a test of both the character and his commitment. The beliefs for which his people struggle are significant contemporary creeds; *Workers in the Dawn* deals with Comtism and the question of art or politics; *Demos* with socialism; *Thyrza* with education; *The Odd Women* with militant feminism; these are all treated substantively, not merely as facets of character, and the outcome of the novel amounts to a judgment about them as well as about the people who are concerned with them.

About 1892, Gissing began to employ a new, direct narrative style side by side with his usual more expansive one. Because of social and economic developments, some of them described in *New Grub Street* and *In the Year of Jubilee*, novels began to appear in one volume instead of three, and a strong periodical market for short stories developed. Gissing had written short stories before, but had had only a limited success with them; he now felt called upon to write for a public that demanded a more economical, dramatic and accessible style, and the results include the one-volume novel, *Denzil Quarrier*, such novelettes as *Eve's Ransom* (1895) and *The Paying Guest*

(1895), and numerous short stories. These involved much less thoroughness in character analysis and the establishment of atmosphere, and strong emphasis on a striking character or an interesting situation. They called upon his ingenuity rather than his most profound convictions, but they nevertheless exhibit his characteristic irony or pathos in a somewhat intensified form. A good number of them show that Gissing had a gift for humor that appears only rarely in his longer works. He did not give up writing long, solid novels, but augmented his income by turning out short stories and brief character sketches for periodical publication while working on his books.

In this, as in more fundamental ways, Gissing was adapting practices he had inherited from the earlier Victorian period to the requirements of changing times. Before he came on the scene, such novelists of social opinion as Dickens, Disraeli and Mrs. Gaskell had been able to voice effective protest through sensational or sentimental accounts of poverty and social injustice. But Meredith and George Eliot perceived that the novelist's responsibility to his art and to the moral sense it was capable of articulating called for a more faithful rendering of external reality and a degree of detachment from contemporary attitudes. Gissing tried, at different times, to emulate both of these approaches to fiction, and profited from both. He proposed to express his convictions about the state of society through the mature novel of character and environment which George Eliot and Meredith had brought into existence. He shows his protagonists confronting moral issues without idealizing them; he displays the enormity of social evils without artificial dramatics; and he puts the suffering and waste caused by poverty before the reader without sentimentalizing the poor. In his best novels, he succeeds in making formal and moral aims fully available to each other, managing his convictions so that they employ, instead of exploiting, the resources of fiction. When he is at the top of his form, Gissing achieves a remarkable integration of these elements. Each figure, action, motive and detail of setting is sound, plausible and convincingly presented, and is at the same time a telling exposure of some social condition or aspect of character. It is as true of Gissing as it is of any novelist to say that for him the practice of his craft was in itself a criticism of life.

Lying on his deathbed after much suffering in his final illness, Gissing murmured "Patience, patience." Though he was an agnostic, he was talking to a clergyman, and though his listener was English, he spoke in French, the language of the place where he was dying, Ispoure, a remote village in the foothills of the Pyrenees. When his friend, H. G. Wells, came to see him the next day, Gissing begged to be taken back to England; but he was fated to die where he was. The small incongruities of his last hours are perhaps appropriate reflections of Gissing's impression of the universe in which he found himself. Even in novels that take social injustice as their themes, he devoted much attention to private problems like frustration in love, self-deception, loneliness and conflicts which originate in the inadequacies of human nature, not in society. By emphasizing this dimension of life, where evils have no clear remedies, Gissing was undermining the Utopian assumption of the late nineteenth century that all problems would disappear if a rational social order could be established.

Early in his career he had discovered a crucial secret: "Lay to our souls what flattering unction we may," he wrote, "we shall not escape from the eternal truth that the world is synonymous with evil. . . . Man becomes conscious that to represent himself as tempted by evil is a reversal of the truth; evil is the essence of his being. . . . Our existence is something which should not be; the vehement desire of its continuance is a sin." Gissing never published these statements. They occur in "The Hope of Pessimism," an essay written in 1882 in which he repudiated Comtism and with it all possibility of social reform. The essay expresses the hostility Gissing felt in the frame of the universe, and the ugly egotism of man, and looks forward to a final victory in which humanity will purge the earth of its presence by refusing to perpetuate itself. His inverted version of Tennyson's "One far-off divine event/ To which the whole creation moves" is the extinction of human consciousness.

This pessimism is at the core of Gissing's novels, but his

social criticism is not his fullest expression of it. Early in his career, when he thought social abuses might be remedied, he adopted protest as a weapon against them. But when he came to feel that they were no more than contemporary forms of the inherent evil of the human estate, the indignation, compassion, and even the despair of his early novels became inadequate. Side by side with them appears a quiet, inconspicuous narrative style, utterly characteristic of Gissing, whose implications embody the ironic hope he drew from pessimism. Here, for example, is his description of a room in the slums and the woman who lives in it, from *The Nether World*:

> . . . a room which was not disorderly or unclean, but presented the chill discomfort of poverty. The principal, almost the only, articles of furniture were a large bed, a washhandstand, a kitchen table, and two or three chairs, of which the cane seats were bulged and torn. A few meaningless pictures hung here and there, and on the mantel-piece, which sloped forward somewhat, stood some paltry ornaments, secured in their places by a piece of string stretched in front of them. . . . . . Mrs. Hewett sat on the bed, and bent forward in an attitude of physical weakness. Her age was twenty-seven, but she looked several years older. At nineteen she had married; her husband, John Hewett, having two children by a previous union. Her face could never have been very attractive, but it was good-natured, and wore its pleasantest aspect as she smiled. . . . You would have classed her at once with those feeble-willed, weak-minded, yet kindly-disposed women, who are only too ready to meet affliction halfway, and who, if circumstances be calamitous, are more harmful than an enemy to those they hold dear. She was rather wrapped up than dressed, and her hair, thin and pale-coloured, was tied in a ragged knot. She wore slippers, the upper parts of which still adhered to the soles only by a miracle. It looked very much as if the same relation subsisted between her frame and the life that informed it, for there was no blood in her cheeks, no lustre in her eye. The baby at her bosom moaned in the act of sucking; one knew not how the poor woman could supply sustenance to another being.

This neutral, merciless tone of detachment, barely regretful, barely ironic, presents what is being observed, squalid, unjust, sinister, or otherwise, and leaves the reader to the hazard of his own conclusions about it. The piece of string that keeps the ornaments from falling off the sloping mantel says more than pages of indignant protest could. The joke about Mrs. Hewett's life and her body as a parallel to the soles of her slippers is a cruelty born of anguish. It reflects, not the suffering of the character in her particular misfortunes, but the deeper pain of the author, who is aware of the universal condition she embodies, but is forbidden, by the rules of his art, to cry out.

When he writes in this mode, which begins to appear sporadically as early as *The Unclassed*, and becomes dominant with *The Emancipated*, Gissing creates the impression that the novel form suits him, not because he is interested in the annotation of mundane details, or in ordinary people coping with ordinary problems, but because it is both a defense against an ultimate despair and a means of observing those who persist in the folly of hopefulness. It is like "Patience, patience" in French, a borrowed sentiment spoken in a borrowed idiom, just enough to suggest intolerable truths not fit for open expression.